A Practical, Scientifically Grounded Approach to Values-Flow

What if the life you want is not waiting on the [illegible] out available to you right now, exactly as you are? V[illegible] combines Acceptance and Commitment Therapy, Dialectical Behaviour Therapy, and Flow Theory into a practical, scientifically grounded approach to living the life well lived, despite the ups and downs that life inevitably brings. It integrates values-based action, mindfulness, and emotional regulation to empower readers to experience meaningful engagement and thriving in life within ordinary everyday contexts.

Each chapter introduces actionable "Flow Nudges" and measurable practices, making it easy to apply these concepts in everyday life. A four-step loop (Attend, Reflect, Inform, and Act) explains how to overcome self-doubt, accept difficult emotions, and choose challenges that matter. From managing work stress to finding joy in parenting or study to simply enjoying life more, this book provides science-based strategies to cultivate resilience, achieve optimal performance, and live life well.

This is a vital resource for both individuals looking to enhance their personal growth and those who help others thrive. With its accessible language, cultural sensitivity, and progressive skill-building, this book offers a roadmap to living a life of vitality, connection, and purpose.

Cedomir (Ced) Ignjatovic is a Clinical Psychologist and Director of Embrace the Moment Psychology & Wellbeing Coaching in Sydney. His clinical work and his research on flow, values, and sustainable engagement feed each other: what he learns in the therapy room shapes the questions he studies, and what he finds in the data shapes how he practises. He completed his PhD at the University of Melbourne's Centre for Wellbeing Science, and lives in Sydney with his family. You can find out more about Dr Ignjatovic's work at https://embracepsychology.com/

Peggy Kern is a Professor at the University of Melbourne, Australia. Her research is collaborative in nature and draws on a variety of methodologies to examine questions around who thrives in life and why, including understanding and measuring healthy functioning, identifying individual and social factors impacting life trajectories, and systems-informed approaches to wellbeing. You can find out more about Professor Kern's work at www.peggykern.org

A Practical, Scientifically Grounded Approach to Values-Flow

Helping Everyday People Thrive, Optimally Perform, and Vitally Engage in Life

Cedomir Ignjatovic and Peggy Kern

Routledge
Taylor & Francis Group
LONDON AND NEW YORK

First published 2027
by Routledge
4 Park Square, Milton Park, Abingdon, Oxon OX14 4RN

and by Routledge
605 Third Avenue, New York, NY 10158

Routledge is an imprint of the Taylor & Francis Group, an informa business

British Library Cataloguing-in-Publication Data
A catalogue record for this book is available from the British Library

ISBN: 978-1-041-29770-3 (hbk)
ISBN: 978-1-041-29769-7 (pbk)
ISBN: 978-1-003-77117-3 (ebk)

DOI: 10.4324/9781003771173

Typeset in Galliard
by SPi Technologies India Pvt Ltd (Straive)

We dedicate this book to those who have journeyed with us through the highs and lows of life, including family members, friends, clients, students, and colleagues. Thank you for believing in us when we didn't believe in ourselves, guiding us through the choppy waters of life and supporting us in our journey towards the life well lived.

Contents

Illustrations

Figures

Tables

Acknowledgements

From Ced

I want to thank Professor Peggy Kern for her support, and for elevating me to systems-level thinking. Peggy took on a clinician with too many questions and not enough framing, and she gave both the patience and the scaffolding to turn that into something coherent. A lot of what is good in this book started in a conversation with her. Before Peggy, there was Professor Lindsay Oades. Lindsay was an early and formative influence on my work, and the one who showed me that a clinical psychologist could focus on the wellbeing of patients and not only the illbeing. He taught me that the two belong in the same room. I also owe him a specific debt. He was the one who introduced me to Peggy at the University of Melbourne, and that introduction became the crucial years of my PhD journey and much of what followed.

I want to thank my clinical supervisor, Tania Alexander, who taught me ACT and DBT side by side, and showed me how they could be harmonised rather than held apart. It felt only dialectical, in the end, to refuse to be undialectical about the two of them. I also want to thank the first responders, the workers' compensation clients, the teachers, and the families who let me into their lives over many years. This book is an attempt to give back a small part of what you gave me.

To Vedrana, my wife, who has been the grounding and loving force underneath all of this. The book has a steady voice because the home we have built together is steady. Whatever is good and patient in these pages came from you first. And to my daughters (Vienna and Arianna). My greatest hope is that somewhere in this book you find a small, useful thing when you need it. A sentence that helps, a practice that holds, a framing that makes a difficult day a little easier. If even one line reaches you at the right moment, the years of writing will have been worth it.

To my brother, Vojislav, who has been there through every turn of this long and winding journey. You have borne witness to more of it than anyone else, and you have never looked away. I could not have walked it without you beside me.

From Peggy

I want to thank my PhD supervisor, Professor Howard S. Friedman, for taking me on as a graduate student, teaching me how to write for different audiences and be a rigorous, methodical researcher. He has been my advisor, mentor, collaborator, and friend, as I've navigated the highs and lows of academia. I thank my various colleagues who have collaborated with me over the past two decades, opening my mind to different ways of thinking and working, and always pushing me to do my best work to meaningfully contribute to research and practice.

I am grateful for my work with Dr Cedomir Ignjatovic, whose energy, willingness, and openness keep me motivated and engaged. Our work together has helped me integrate my own personal experiences with mental illness with clinical perspectives on the very therapies that I was being taught. I have loved exploring innovative ideas together.

I am deeply grateful for my family, who have encouraged and supported me throughout my life and career. They have stayed by my side through both my successes in my personal and professional life and my struggles with serious mental illness. They have stuck by my side, always encouraging me, loving me, believing in me, and inspiring me to hold on to hope even on the darkest days.

From Both of Us

We are both deeply grateful to Professor Antonella Delle Fave, whose work on optimal experience and psychological selection shaped our thinking long before we met her, and whose friendship and generosity have shaped it since. We also thank Charles Swenson, who gave us a few hours of his time and a window into how flow was always quietly sitting inside DBT. Those conversations reached a part of the book we could not have reached without him.

Finally, we are grateful to you, the reader. Thank you for your interest in living life well and your openness to explore the ideas we provide within these pages. We hope that you enjoy and benefit from reading this book as much as we enjoyed and benefitted from writing it. We wish you the very best on your journey to the life well lived.

Foreword

One of the major difficulties people find when they read or talk about clinical psychology is understanding the differences between the many intervention approaches currently available to clients and practitioners. This broad range of approaches actually derives from the progressive development of a small number of established clinical models that gradually branched off, based on the accumulation of empirical evidence highlighting areas of potential treatment improvement, the spreading of lifestyles and behaviours impacting on the mental health of specific population sectors, or the identification of symptoms that require more effective treatment strategies.

This diversification process is largely similar to what happens in the field of biomedicine: new technological tools reveal previously undetectable pathologies, previously known diseases get redefined, and new medicaments and treatments are gradually added to the available set of therapeutic strategies. Despite these analogies, the diversity of clinical approaches in psychology is often perceived as confusing, lacking a unifying conceptual framework, and based on weak empirical evidence. These critical claims are often related to people's need to more clearly understand what should take place during a clinical consultation, and how and why their life and experience could improve through it. While information on organic diseases and biomedicine is daily disseminated across media by authoritative scholars, accurate and detailed discussions around subjective experience, psychological symptoms, and treatment options are often limited and not always intelligible.

The first merit of this book is to counterbalance this vagueness by conveying to non-experts a clear description of two intervention approaches that are increasingly adopted to address psychological problems: Acceptance and Commitment Therapy (ACT) and Dialectical Behavior Therapy (DBT). In addition, the authors highlight convergences and differences between the two approaches; furthermore, they engage in detecting potential for their fruitful integration and reciprocal strengthening to the benefit of individuals' mental health and wellbeing.

The second and more practical merit of this book lies in its novelty: adopting a radically original perspective, it provides a step-by-step pathway towards personal growth, development, and fulfilment, by combining ACT and DBT strategies with the promotion of Flow experience through a value-based meaning-making process. Flow—also labelled as optimal experience—is a positive state of complete absorption and engagement in a subjectively relevant and complex task that promotes wellbeing and supports the person's development of competence in the long run. While Flow structure and connections with wellbeing have been widely established, its role in the context of clinical interventions is quite underexplored. One of the core messages of this book, particularly relevant for clinical practitioners, is to see the potential of interpreting therapeutic processes through the lens of wellbeing promotion, by identifying and supporting flow experiences in their clients' daily lives.

Last but not least, this book provides readers with practical tools to develop awareness of their daily psychological functioning and to identify directions and strategies for attaining higher wellbeing. These tools are solidly based on the concepts and processes adopted in ACT and DBT, as well as on the well-established role of Flow as a crucial component of the individual development pathway. Importantly, while guiding readers across this journey, the authors emphasise the intrinsically dynamic structure of human daily experiences and personal growth trajectories, acknowledging the natural fluctuations between positive and negative states, good and bad days or periods, and successes and failures, thus offering a realistic view of the constant interplay between the human aspiration to growth and wellbeing, and the obstacles, challenges, and constraints that force us all to exploit our amazing flexibility and potential for effective adjustment to real life. Readers could sometimes feel overwhelmed by the detailed description of the theoretical frameworks guiding ACT, DBT, and Flow practice in the first chapters of the book. However, this initial exercise of perseverance and enduring attention will allow them to discover in the following chapters how these principles can be effectively embedded in their daily life, nourishing and orienting their own pathway towards self-development and self-actualisation.

~ *Antonella Delle Fave*
University of Milano, Italy

Preface

Why do some people thrive in life whereas others struggle? This is a question we've been asking for the past two decades.

For years we kept noticing the same gap. Ced worked in the consulting room, trying to help exhausted first responders, teachers barely holding on, and workers whose lives had been flattened by stress and injury. Peggy worked in research labs and classrooms, studying what allows people to thrive despite the ups and downs that life brings, even as her own mental health suffered. Why does living well feel so far away for so many people, including people whose lives look perfectly fine from the outside?

Most of the advice we read treated a good life as a reward that waits on the other side of symptom reduction. Fix the anxiety. Clear the depression. Resolve the trauma. Then, at some point, you get to start actually living. That sequence made sense for a long time. It also left a lot of people waiting.

This book is our attempt to stop waiting.

It draws on three bodies of work we have spent our careers inside. Acceptance and Commitment Therapy insists that values-based action can happen right now, even when your head is loud. Dialectical Behaviour Therapy provides concrete skills for the moments when emotion threatens to tear everything apart. Flow Theory reminds us that absorbed, meaningful engagement is part of what humans are built for.

You might wonder whether these three traditions belong together. At times they argue with each other. ACT and DBT hold different positions on whether emotion can be changed directly. Flow Theory comes from a different intellectual lineage altogether. We have not tried to iron those tensions out. The argument is part of the honesty.

What you will find in these pages is a practical approach, built on decades of science and tested in the rooms where people live. Each chapter offers small, usable practices called Flow Nudges. You do not need to read the book in order. And you do not need to attempt every practice. You need only a willingness to try.

We wrote this for anyone who has ever sensed there might be more to life than getting through the week, including therapists, coaches, teachers, parents, managers, and the everyday adventurers making their way through ordinary days. The skills are the same whether you are helping yourself or helping someone else.

You are already on the journey, right now, as you read this. You do not need to feel ready. You do not need to wait until the conditions are perfect, because they rarely are. Wherever you are at with your own mental health journey, this book has something to offer. We hope it travels well with you.

~ *Cedomir and Peggy*

Part 1

Introduction and Theoretical Foundations

1 Introduction

Chapter Overview

This chapter introduces the book, including the structure and key focal areas. We begin with a description of the House of Functioning, which is a visual metaphor for describing how well you are living life, including the basement of despair, the lower floor of quiet desperation, the upper floor of thriving, and the attic where flow and transcendent experiences occur. It's helpful to locate yourself in the House and understand that wherever you are is the perfect place to begin your journey. We introduce the three core pieces that we draw on within the Values-Flow framework: Acceptance and Commitment Therapy (**ACT**), Dialectical Behaviour Therapy (**DBT**), and **Flow Theory**. Together, these contribute to the Values-Flow framework, which aims to create meaningful, values-aligned engagement with life, leading to a life well lived.

Introduction

In a world increasingly shaped by global upheaval, natural disasters, digital noise, and endless to-do lists, it's easy to lose sight of what it means to live fully and vibrantly. Traditional mental health approaches revolve around symptom reduction, slaying the dragons of anxiety, stress, and depression so that we can "get back to normal" when life goes awry. Yet many of us yearn for something more. There's a part within us, even if it's a small, forgotten voice, that longs for a life that's not just free of misery but one packed with meaning and personal growth. **We long to thrive despite the everyday challenges that life throws at us**.

This book is an invitation to move beyond mere survival to fully embrace a life well lived. It blends insights from **ACT**, **DBT**, and **Flow Theory** to provide a values-guided pathway in which discomfort is acknowledged and skilfully navigated. Importantly, **thriving in life** emerges not from eliminating struggle but from engaging with what matters to you.

The House of Functioning

Marsha Linehan created DBT in the late 1980s. She was both a therapist and an individual with lived experience of mental illness, which deepened her

DOI: 10.4324/9781003771173-2

understanding of what it means to feel invalidated by the very systems designed to help. She believed that traditional Cognitive Behavioural Therapy approaches to mental health were insufficient for various mental disorders. She originally focused on Borderline Personality Disorder, but the approach has since been successfully applied to various mental disorders. Importantly, whether or not you have experienced mental illness, we believe that DBT skills are useful for your mental health journey.

The story goes that when a patient once asked Marsha how to conceptualise their progress through treatment, she grabbed a marker and sketched a house on the whiteboard. That simple drawing became one of DBT's most enduring metaphors: the House of Treatment. We have revised this image to represent different levels of functioning (see Figure 1.1). The House of Functioning is our adaptation of Linehan's House of Treatment, used in this book as a reader-facing metaphor rather than as a formal DBT stage model.

Take a moment to look at this House. It's a map of human functioning and human possibility. Right now, you are living somewhere in this House.

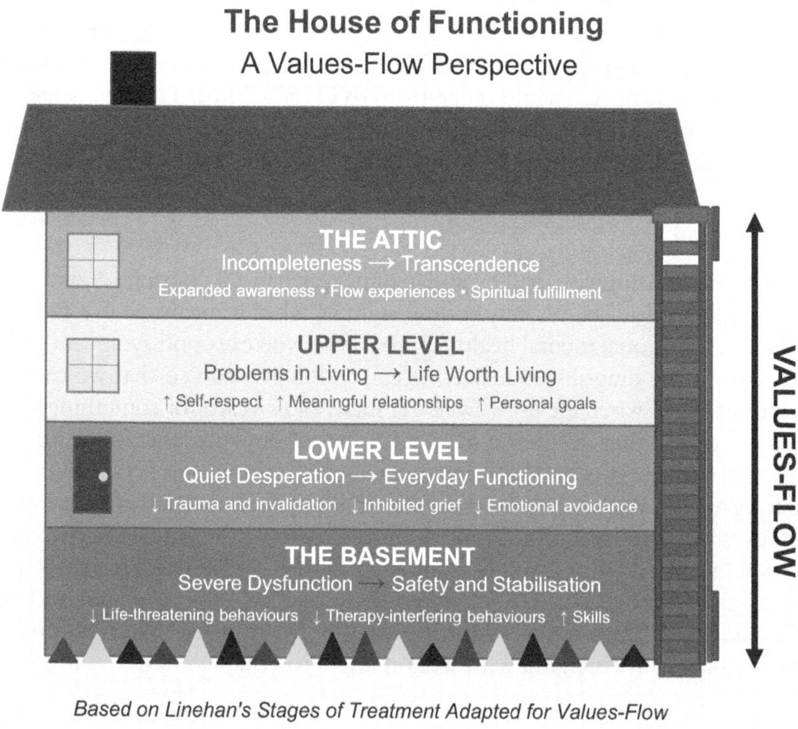

Figure 1.1 The House of Functioning.

(Adapted from Linehan's House of Treatment.)

The **basement** represents *crisis.* In the basement, you're not just struggling to live, but it feels like you are *burning in hell.* The flames of unbearable emotional pain lick at everything you try to do. You might feel like you are wandering in the dark, overwhelmed by floods of emotion that make ordinary functioning impossible. You might be unmotivated to do anything; every action is overwhelmingly effortful. In some cases, the darkness of suicidal thoughts makes it impossible to see any way forward. Or you might not want to die, but you also don't want to live. You might engage in various forms of self-harm, including substance abuse, disordered eating, non-suicidal self-injury, or other life-threatening behaviours.

If you've ever experienced severe mental illness, you know what it feels like to be in the basement. Or if you've watched someone you know struggle, you can imagine what it's like.

When you're in the basement, *stabilisation* and *building safety* are the only goals that matter, and those goals often matter more for the therapist than for you. Doctors and therapists aim to reduce life-threatening behaviours, decrease actions that interfere with therapy, and provide skills that keep you alive. Medication, intensive therapy, and hospitalisation are often important parts of treatment, aiming to calm the emotional storm long enough so that you can actually engage with life-sustaining skills.

The **ground floor** represents *surviving life.* You're not experiencing severe distress, but you also aren't experiencing wellbeing. You might have less severe levels of depression or anxiety. You're getting by in life but not thriving. You might experience emotional pain that you don't know how to manage, or you might have troublesome social relationships. The goal is to deal with the struggles of everyday life, and learn how to recognise and regulate emotions, build tolerable relationships with other people, and develop the skills that create a stable foundation for living. For some, this floor also involves beginning to address the quieter forms of suffering, such as unresolved grief or a persistent sense of emptiness, that keep life feeling hollow even when acute crisis has passed. Here you learn the basic skills of distress tolerance, emotion regulation, and interpersonal effectiveness that create a foundation for living. Medication might again be used to help you stay calm or function at what could be considered a normal level. This floor is the focus of much of psychological treatment, in which therapists and counsellors work with a client to improve their life and return to "normal" functioning.

The **upper floor** represents *a life worth living.* You don't struggle with mental illness—you might have a mental illness, but symptoms are well managed and do not interfere with your everyday life. You are motivated to not only avoid pain, but also to pursue feelings of contentment. On this floor, you are creating *a thriving life*—the normal fluctuations of a life lived well rather than one that is merely endured. Happiness levels may go up and down as you experience the highs and lows of life, but you manage the waves as they come. You might work with a counsellor or coach to develop a greater degree of self-respect, have meaningful relationships with other people, and set and achieve personal goals. You also contribute to the wellbeing of those around you. The wellbeing sciences have spent the past several decades describing what the upper floor looks like and providing strategies to reach the upper floor.

And then there's the **attic**, which represents *transcendence*. Charles Swenson, one of Linehan's closest collaborators, recalls that Marsha rarely spoke about the attic, except late at night, often after a glass of wine, when conversation turned philosophical. In those moments, she would describe something beyond crisis stabilisation and trauma processing: a life that's full of spirituality, flow, meaning, joy, endurance, and freedom. Not just a life worth living, but *a life genuinely lived*. Crucially, Linehan's vision of the attic was not about the elimination of all suffering. It included what she called a sense of incompleteness, which is the recognition that even a rich, meaningful life contains an existential gap, and that genuine freedom involves holding that incompleteness with equanimity rather than trying to fill it. This connects to something flow researchers have long observed: that the deepest experiences of engagement often arise not despite difficulty but through it, when a person meets a meaningful challenge with full presence and adequate skill.

Linehan believed that the attic exists and that it matters, but the work of her and countless others has necessarily focused on pulling people out of burning basements and building a stable ground floor. Positive psychology and related sciences help people live on the upper floor. A few scholars, such as Mihaly Csikszentmihalyi, Abraham Maslow, and Scott Barry Kaufman, have focused on the attic.

Together, there is a deep well of knowledge of how to live well in life. This book is an attempt to help you live on the upper floor of the House of Functioning, with regular visits to the attic. But here is something important. Flow, the absorbed engagement that characterises the attic at its best, is not confined to the attic. Flow can and does occur at every floor of the House. A person on the ground floor who becomes genuinely absorbed in a meaningful conversation is likely to be experiencing flow. A person in the basement who finds a moment of real engagement with a coping skill is touching the edges of flow. The attic represents the deepest, most sustained, and most self-chosen experiences of flow, but the capacity for absorbed engagement is available wherever you are.

Where Are You in the House?

Before we go any further, take a moment to locate yourself in the house.

Are you in the **basement**? Is life feeling like a burning building right now, with crisis after crisis, emotions so intense that they threaten to consume everything? Are you engaging in behaviours that put your life or physical and mental health at serious risk? If so, this book has something for you, but you may also need more intensive support. The skills we describe can be used at any floor of the house. A burning basement needs firefighters, not just furniture. But even in the basement, the question of what makes life worth living is not premature. Indeed, values clarification can be one of the most powerful interventions in a crisis, precisely because it provides a reason for you to keep going.

Are you on the **ground floor**? Life is manageable, but it doesn't feel particularly meaningful. You're surviving, not thriving. This is where most people live, and it's a perfectly reasonable place to be. But if you're reading this book, some part of you suspects there might be more than just getting by, more than living the status quo. The skills we describe here not only will help you survive life, but also teach you how to thrive.

Are you on the **upper floor**? You are thriving in life, with a sense of contentment, despite the ups and downs of life. Relationships, career, and daily functioning are generally in place. You have more positive than negative emotions. Still, you feel like there could be something more.

Or maybe you've already visited the **attic**, experiencing moments of flow, deep meaning, and optimal engagement with life. You long for more of these experiences. The attic feels like a place you visit by accident rather than a room you regularly inhabit.

Importantly, the House of Functioning is not a linear journey. You don't start in the basement and climb up to the attic, successfully ticking off the "live life well" goal. New crises emerge. Old patterns resurface. You might spend Tuesday morning in the attic and Tuesday afternoon on the lower floor. That's not failure—that's life.

You also might be in different places in the House in different areas of life, including your physical health, mental wellbeing, social relationships, sense of mastery and accomplishment, spirituality, and cognitive functioning. For instance, you might be on the upper floor in terms of achievement, being extremely successful at work, but on the lower floor in terms of your personal relationships with others.

There's no one right place to be in the House. Where you are today might be different from where you were last week or where you'll be tomorrow. Your location might differ across domains of your life. Knowing your current location helps you know what you need. Wherever you are right now is exactly the right place to begin.

You Don't Have to Wait

Importantly, the upper floors aren't just for those who have climbed every stair. The "life well lived" conversation begins as soon as you realise that there is more to life than mere survival. If you are working with a therapist or coach, you can find contentment, a sense of meaning and purpose in life, and optimal engagement from day one, even while you work on foundational concerns. If you are on your own personal journey, we encourage you to start thinking now about what it would mean to live well.

Sociologist Corey Keyes provides an important perspective that is relevant to this conversation. Most scholars and practitioners think about wellbeing along a single continuum, ranging from severe mental illness to completely flourishing in life. Keyes introduced the **dual continua model**, in which illbeing and wellbeing are not opposite ends of one spectrum; they are two separate dimensions that can and do coexist.

You can be struggling with depression *while* experiencing moments of meaningful engagement in daily tasks. You can be managing anxiety *while* having deep and genuine relationships. You can be on the ground floor of the house, trying to survive life, but still catch glimpses of what the attic has to offer. Indeed, flow experiences can be the very reason that you get up each day, engage in therapy or coaching sessions, and start to apply the skills we describe in this book. The attic offers the hope that life has more to offer, and any struggle is worthwhile.

From an ACT perspective, this is a crucial point. One of the most common traps people fall into is the belief that they need to feel better before they can live better. ACT calls this the **control agenda**. ACT suggests the opposite: committed action in the direction of values can happen right now, with whatever you are feeling, from whatever floor of the house you currently stand on.

The Jazz of Living Well

Linehan had another favourite metaphor: jazz. She loved the idea that even though you might have the skills to live well, using those skills is more like a jazz musician than a classical performer. You never do the same thing twice. You're constantly improvising, responding to what's happening right now, creating something that didn't exist a moment ago.

One of the things that Linehan often spoke about in terms of the jazz of living well is what she called "speed, movement, and *flow*." That last word wasn't incidental. Flow wasn't just something that might happen to individuals as a happy byproduct of treatment. It was central to her vision of how therapy itself should work, and how life itself could be lived.

Swenson, reflecting on years of working alongside Linehan, put it simply: "Marsha thought flow was critical to doing good therapy, and critical to people leading better lives."

Jazz requires not only technical skill, but also presence, responsiveness, willingness to take risks, and the ability to stay engaged even when you don't know exactly where the music is going. That's not a bad description of a life well lived.

What This Book Offers

This book takes the spirit of improvisational engagement and makes it explicit. We blend insights from ACT, DBT, and Flow Theory, not by smoothing over their differences, but by holding their creative tensions.

ACT and DBT, while both "third wave" therapies with roots in behavioural science, hold genuinely different positions on key questions. Can internal experiences be directly changed? Should we pursue positive emotional states? How structured should our interventions be? Rather than pretending these tensions don't exist, we explore them in the chapters to come.

ACT teaches us to change our *relationship* to difficult thoughts and feelings rather than trying to eliminate them. DBT teaches us that some emotions *can* be changed through skilful action when those emotions don't fit the facts of a situation. The perspectives and skills arising from *both* ACT and DBT can be useful, *depending upon the situation*. The skill lies in knowing which approach fits which moment.

Flow Theory adds a third perspective: what absorbed, meaningful engagement feels and looks like in everyday life. Mihaly Csikszentmihalyi (pronounced "Me-high Cheek-sent-me-high"), the Hungarian-American psychologist who pioneered flow research, together with Fausto Massimini, Antonella Delle Fave, and their group at the University of Milan, who from 1983 onwards led the most extensive cross-cultural programme of flow research, found that people across vastly different cultures and activities, from surgeons to Navajo shepherds, from Italian farmers to Korean teenagers, described a remarkably similar experience. When challenge meets skill in an activity that carries personal meaning, something shifts. Time slows down or speeds up. Self-consciousness recedes. Action and awareness merge. They often said it felt like being carried by a current, which is why Csikszentmihalyi named it flow, describing what absorbed, meaningful engagement *feels* like.

ACT, DBT, and Flow Theory are like a three-legged stool, which together support the life well lived. In this book, we draw on all three, introducing you to the skills and perspectives that each offer, identifying when each is useful, and exploring how to navigate the inevitable challenges that life brings to help you live well.

At the core of our approach is **Values-Flow**: a framework for navigating life's ups and downs with both the acceptance that ACT cultivates and the skilful action that DBT provides, oriented towards the engaged, meaningful living that Flow Theory illuminates.

Importantly, flow itself is not the goal. Flow is something that sometimes emerges when you are genuinely absorbed in a meaningful challenge, but the willingness to keep showing up, whether or not flow arrives, is equally central to the life well lived. We suggest that **the goal is to live well, through values-aligned engagement in life**. The life well lived occurs on the upper floor, with regular visits to the attic. The strategies in this book help you understand and adopt thoughts, emotions, and behaviours to help you pursue the life well lived.

A Map for the Journey

This book is written for everyday adventurers, as well as the psychologists, coaches, educators, managers, and parents/carers who work with them. You'll learn how to:

- Use ACT- and DBT-informed strategies to address emotional reactivity, avoidance, and unhelpful thinking.

- Integrate "Values-Flow nudges"—small, strategic actions that can help you experience Values-Flow in daily tasks.
- Adjust to challenges so that life's demands feel neither trivial nor crushing, but genuinely growth-promoting.
- Thrive in life, regardless of what life brings your way.
- Embed these practices in the cultural and social contexts in which you reside, helping you to not only transform your own life, but also contribute to the communities and systems around you.

An important note: what thriving looks like, what values are prioritised, and what activities produce flow are all shaped by culture, context, and life circumstances. Flow research spans dozens of countries and a wide range of socioeconomic conditions, and one of its most consistent findings is that while the experience of flow is remarkably similar across cultures, the pathways to it are diverse. A framework for the life well lived must honour that diversity. Throughout this book, we encourage you to interpret these concepts through the lens of your own cultural background, community, and life situation, rather than assuming that one version of the good life fits everyone.

Throughout this book, you'll see references to the House of Functioning. Think of each chapter as bringing another piece of furniture into the upper floor and attic, including the chair of acceptance, the table of values clarification, and the lamp of mindful awareness that illuminates the whole space.

Whatever floor you're currently standing on, this book offers something useful:

If you are in the **basement**, the distress tolerance skills will help you survive the day without making things worse, while the values discussion reminds you why surviving matters, why it's worth climbing out of the flames. But remember, if you are in the basement, it will be helpful to be supported in your journey by a mental health professional. Even here, moments of meaningful engagement are possible and important.

If you are on the **ground floor**, the mindfulness, distress tolerance, emotion regulation, and interpersonal effectiveness skills create a foundation for values-based living, while glimpses of flow remind you what you're building towards: not only surviving life, but actually thriving.

If you are on the **upper floor**, values clarification and committed action turn an adequate life into a meaningful one. Interpersonal effectiveness skills will help you have valuable relationships with other people while maintaining a sense of self-respect.

If you have already visited the **attic**, the skills in this book will help you deepen your understanding of flow and transcendental experiences and help you cultivate such experiences more frequently.

We offer a **practice-based** approach. If you've ever attended a guitar lesson, you know you can't master chords without strumming. The same is true here: you'll need to participate in the "music" of mindfulness, acceptance, and constructive action to experience the benefits they provide. We invite you to engage in guided exercises throughout the following chapters. We encourage you to experiment, play, and reflect upon the different exercises that we offer. Some will land well, others will not. The important thing is that you give them a go.

Sound Bite Summary

To bring each chapter together, we end with Sound Bite Summaries. These help bring together the key ideas from the chapter. Key points from this chapter:

1 The **House of Functioning** provides a map for understanding where you are and where you're going—from the burning basement of crisis through to the lower floor of survival, to the upper floor of thriving, and into the attic of optimal experiences.
2 You don't have to wait until you've climbed every stair. **Glimpses of the attic are possible from any floor**.
3 This book provides **actionable skills** to take you from the basement or ground floor to the upper floors of the house, while populating your house with valuable furniture.
4 **Flow**, the experience of absorbed and meaningful engagement, is not confined to the attic. It can occur at every floor of the house, and the skills in this book help create the conditions for it.
5 Three traditions inform this book. **ACT** provides the stance of psychological flexibility and values-guided living. **DBT** provides the concrete skills to regulate emotions and navigate relationships. **Flow Theory** illuminates what engaged living feels and looks like. Together, they form the **Values-Flow** framework.

Final Word

We live in a time where many people feel disconnected and overwhelmed. But those same people also hold an immense capacity for resilience, purpose, and creative action. **Values-Flow** is your map to unlock that potential for yourself and for those you guide. The skills we cover are the stairs. The upper floors are waiting for you, ready to be furnished with meaning, purpose, and the kind of engaged living that makes the whole House worth inhabiting.

Let's step forward together, mindful, daring, and ready for the everyday adventures that make life truly worth living.

2 Theoretical Foundations

Chapter Overview

This chapter introduces thriving in life as a meaningful goal, which arises from living well despite the challenges that arise in everyday life. We introduce a garden as a metaphor for thinking about the life well lived. We describe Acceptance and Commitment Therapy (**ACT**), Dialectical Behaviour Therapy (**DBT**), and **Flow Theory**, which together create the foundation for Values-Flow. We consider points of convergence and areas of tension amongst these three therapies and theories. The Values-Flow framework provides a synthesis for understanding when to apply each one to lead to meaningful, values-based engagement with life.

Ice Cream or Wine?

Picture this: It's 9 p.m. You've survived another busy day. You've made it through work, the bills are paid, and the kids are in bed. Still, your mind spins, reviewing what's on the agenda for tomorrow. Work meetings, grocery shopping, coordinating your kids' schedules, cleaning the house...the list is endless.

You crave relief. So, you open the freezer and pull out a tub of ice cream. One bowl, then two, and for a few minutes, you enjoy delicious bliss. Or perhaps you crack open a bottle of wine. One glass becomes three, and worries melt away as the alcohol relaxes your brain.

There is nothing wrong with temporary pleasures in moderation. Indeed, incorporating positive activities that add a blast of heartfelt joy into the day can help us survive the daily stresses of life with some semblance of sanity.

But temporary pleasures are gone before you know it. Worries about the future and regrets about the past return with a vengeance.

In terms of the House of Functioning, ice cream and wine are ground-floor strategies. They help you get through the moment. They have their place. But they don't build anything. They don't furnish any rooms. They don't help you climb the stairs. They just keep you from falling through the floor. Sometimes, that's enough. But if you're reading this book, you suspect there might be more.

DOI: 10.4324/9781003771173-3

Why does "feeling better" so often feel so *temporary*? We're wired to try to escape pain and discomfort. Modern society has created many feel-good solutions to help us escape pain and discomfort. But these solutions only offer short-term relief and can often cause longer-term problems.

The good news is that there are solutions that are more long-lasting. In this book, we focus on one such solution: **Values-Flow**, a framework for living that *not only* feels good *but also* can help you build **a more purposeful, energised life**. A life lived on the upper floor of the House, with regular visits to the attic.

Reducing Symptoms ≠ Building a Good Life

Imagine a world where all the bad in the world has been addressed. Psychotherapy has been so effective that depression, anxiety, and other mental disorders no longer exist. There's no more poverty or war. Would this be a utopia?

Unfortunately, it would not. The absence of mental illness is not the same as the presence of wellbeing. The lack of poverty does not ensure that money is used to promote societal goodness. The lack of war does not mean that the tensions that lead to war are gone. The lack of physical illness does not ensure fitness. *The lack of badness is not the same as the presence of goodness!*

In House terms: escaping the burning basement doesn't automatically furnish the upper floors. You can put out every fire and still have an empty house.

Certainly, addressing problems is important, and the psychological sciences have made a lot of progress in reducing symptoms, as well as finding and rooting out core causes. But addressing the problems in the world is only half the story. It is also important to build a life that includes the presence of good relationships with others, physical and mental fitness, a sense of meaning and purpose, and deep engagement with life.

An Ultimate Goal: The Life Well Lived

Our goal in this book is to help you experience the good life. But is that even possible when there are so many problems in our lives? Isn't simply surviving life good enough? The science of positive psychology has demonstrated that there is more to life than just surviving. The good life can and does exist. The challenge is finding that life.

There's a lot of talk about happiness, wellbeing, flourishing, and other positively valued states of being. In this book, we use the term **thriving** to capture **living life well alongside the challenges that arise in everyday life**.

Rather than a temporary feeling that occurs when something positive happens in your life, we focus on the contentedness that arises from a life well lived, even when there are challenges within that life. That is, you don't have to get rid of all the bad feelings and negative experiences of life to thrive. Thriving is an attitude that can be purposely cultivated through riding the waves of life. It arises from accepting thoughts, emotions, and behaviours and living purposefully. Through this, you can feel content with your life, even if there are negative events occurring in or around you.

Thriving, in our framework, means living on the upper floor of the House. Not because you've eliminated all problems, but because you've built the skills that make that floor habitable. And occasionally, when conditions are right and you're fully engaged with what matters, you get to spend time in the attic.

One way that we like to think about thriving is to use the metaphor of a garden.

First, gardens can look very different from one another and yet still be thriving. A cactus garden and rose garden are very different from one another, but both contain their own forms of beauty. The rose garden thrives when it gets lots of water, some sunshine, and other nutrients. The cactus garden thrives with very limited amounts of water and lots of sunshine. Similarly, thriving looks different for different people and is cultivated in different ways. One person thrives when they have lots of interactions with other people and are busily engaged in lots of activities. Another person needs a lot of alone time and limited activities. What makes you feel good? These are keys to what thriving in life might look like for you.

Second, gardens need care to thrive. Neglected gardens wither and die. In the same way, we need to engage in self-care to maintain a sense of thriving in life. Self-care is often thought of as pampering yourself, such as going to a spa, getting a massage, or some other self-indulgence. These certainly can be part of your self-care routine. But even more important are the day-to-day things that you do to take care of yourself, such as eating a healthy diet, getting adequate sleep, moving your body, having positive interactions with other people, and engaging in meaningful activities.

Third, thriving does not simply occur in good times. During spring and summertime, gardens flourish with an outpouring of greenery and flowers. But during the wintertime, a garden can still be thriving. Even as it looks rather decrepit on the surface, below the ground, seeds are germinating and growing. It's the growth that happens during the hard times of the year that results in the most vivid gardens come springtime. Likewise, thriving can occur even when life is challenging. Sure, we might not *feel* happy, but we can still have good social relationships, engage in meaningful activities, and be attuned to life. This is what thriving is all about: functioning well *despite* hardship.

Fourth, gardens consist of multiple plants that influence one another. It would not be a thriving garden if one flower flourished because it took all the nutrients from the surrounding flowers. Similarly, thriving does not happen on your own. Your sense of wellbeing is influenced by those around you, and you influence the wellbeing of others. If you experience wellbeing at the expense of those around you, then you might be flourishing, but you are not thriving.

Finally, gardens exist within a community. A community that cares and contributes to the garden helps it thrive, whereas a community that neglects the garden kills it. Likewise, our lives are influenced by our background, the culture that we live in, and the time of history that we are in. The more that the socio-cultural community that we live in creates opportunities for thriving to occur, and when we are living in attunement to that community, a greater sense of thriving is more likely to occur.

But how do we thrive in life? This is where Values-Flow comes in.

The Pathway Towards Thriving: Values-Flow

In this book, we draw from ACT, DBT, and Flow Theory. Each is useful on its own. ACT and DBT are popular therapies that treat a range of psychiatric conditions, and there are numerous books and articles describing the value of and ways to promote flow. But we argue that it's when you combine the three that the magic really happens. Their combination is what we call **Values-Flow**. By putting these together, you get a practical roadmap for cultivating meaningful engagement in life, even in the face of everyday stress.

ACT, DBT, and Flow Theory each bring something essential to Values-Flow. But we want to be honest from the start: these aren't three puzzle pieces that slot together seamlessly. They hold genuinely different positions on some important questions. Part of the richness of Values-Flow comes from working with these creative tensions rather than pretending they don't exist. Let's take a look at what each of these are and what they have to offer.

Acceptance and Commitment Therapy

ACT was developed by psychologist Steven C. Hayes, with the aim of reducing suffering and building a fulfilling life. It does this not by fighting uncomfortable experiences, but by helping you learn to accept difficult experiences and commit to action guided by personal values.

At the heart of ACT is a single overarching capacity called **psychological flexibility**, the ability to bend to the circumstances that you experience without being broken by them. Imagine two types of trees. One tree is near a creek, protected from the wind, and gets adequate sunshine. It looks like the perfect tree. Another tree is exposed to the elements, pelted by rain, wind, and sun, and has limited access to water. It is gnarled and weathered. A big storm comes along. Which tree survives? The first tree snaps when exposed to the wicked wind. The second tree can weather the storm, bending flexibly to the elements. It's not the lack of difficulty that creates resilience. It's being exposed to challenges over time in a manageable way. This is the heart of psychological flexibility.

Psychological flexibility is enabled through six interconnected facets. Each facet illuminates a different aspect of the same underlying process. Together they describe what it looks like to be open to experience, present in the moment, and guided by what matters.

- **Contact with the Present Moment**: Instead of allowing our thoughts to be consumed by worries about the past or the future, ACT encourages us to be in the present moment and notice what's happening right now. This is the central idea of mindfulness and meditation.

- **Defusion**: When we are experiencing distress, our thoughts and emotions become fused to the experience that we are facing. ACT allows us to create space between thoughts and experiences by seeing our thoughts as words or pictures, rather than as absolute truths controlling us. For instance, a common defusion technique is to become an active observer, saying, "I'm noticing the thought that I can't do this" rather than "I can't do this." This bit of separation provides space for changing our relationship to the present moment.
- **Acceptance**: Fighting our thoughts, emotions, and experiences in life often creates tension and distress. ACT encourages us to allow feelings to be present, without letting them dictate our lives.
- **Values**: ACT suggests that values are central to the life well lived. Values are freely chosen directions that give life meaning, such as connection to others, good physical and mental health, spirituality, or contribution, amongst many others. ACT encourages us to clarify what truly matters, and then to live in such a way that we honour our values rather than live in discord with them.
- **Committed Action**: ACT suggests that discomfort arises from being blown about by the wind, adjusting our actions to try to make others happy, rather than living our own truth. ACT encourages us to engage in and remain committed to activities and behaviours that align with our values, even when difficult thoughts and feelings show up along the way.
- **Observing Self**: The Observing Self (sometimes called "Self-as-Context") is the part of us that notices all our experiences without being wedded to any particular experience. It's the "me" that has been present throughout our lives. It's an awareness that watched us as a child, as a teenager, and as an adult. The Observing Self doesn't evaluate or judge; it simply witnesses. When we tap into the Observing Self, it creates space from which we can respond to life rather than react to it. When we're fused with thoughts ("I am a failure"), stepping into the Observing Self may remind us that we are the one noticing that thought, rather than us being the thought itself.
- **How does this help you cultivate Values-Flow?** If you're locked in battle with anxious thoughts or self-criticism, it's hard to get "in the zone." ACT skills let you unhook from mental clutter so that your full attention is free to dive into tasks that matter to you. Further, the emphasis on values and committed action is central to the definition of Values-Flow.

One of ACT's most important contributions deserves special emphasis, which is the identification of what it calls the **control agenda**. Most of us operate under the assumption that we need to feel better before we can live better. We tend to believe that once anxiety passes, once confidence arrives, once we feel happy, or once we feel ready, then we will take action towards what matters. ACT suggests the opposite. Committed action in the direction of values can happen right now, with whatever feelings are present. The feelings do not need to be fixed first; they can come along for the ride. This insight is central to Values-Flow because it means that the path to engaged living does not require waiting for ideal internal and external conditions. It requires willingness to move towards what matters while carrying whatever internal weather happens to be present.

It is also worth noting here that values work is not easy. To touch what you most yearn for in life is to become vulnerable, because caring about something means accepting that you might not get it, that others might not approve, or that you might lose what you love. Many people develop protective strategies against this vulnerability, such as saying "I don't know" when asked what matters, staying relentlessly busy to avoid reflection, or insisting that nothing can change. These strategies are understandable, but they are also the primary barriers to both values-based engagement and flow. The skills described in the remainder of this book are designed to help you navigate that vulnerability with courage, compassion, and practical skill.

Dialectical Behaviour Therapy

DBT weaves together acceptance and change strategies. It offers concrete skills to handle big feelings, navigate relationships, and build a life worth living.

At the heart of DBT is the concept of **dialectics**: two seemingly incompatible things that can and do coexist. The main dialectic in DBT is acceptance and change. You might think that you are either accepting things or working to change them. DBT suggests that it's only through acceptance that you can make effective change. Another dialectic that we described in Chapter 1 is that mental illness and wellbeing can coexist.

DBT includes four core modules:

- **Mindfulness**: Observing the present moment, letting thoughts and emotions come and go without latching on to them. This aligns with the contact with the present moment in ACT. We'll talk more about mindfulness in Chapter 5.
- **Distress Tolerance**: Actionable skills that allow you to survive emotional crises without making them worse. It provides skills to successfully navigate distressing experiences that occur in everyday life. This is the crisis management part of DBT. We'll talk about distress tolerance in Chapter 8.
- **Emotion Regulation**: Understanding and adjusting emotional responses in healthy ways. Whereas distress tolerance deals with distressing experiences, emotion regulation helps you keep your emotions on an even keel, reducing the need for distress tolerance skills. This is the everyday management of emotions part of DBT. We'll talk about emotion regulation in Chapter 8.
- **Interpersonal Effectiveness**: Skills that allow us to be effective in how we relate to others that we interact with. Interpersonal effectiveness allows us to communicate our needs, set boundaries, and respond to others

gracefully, with respect to others' needs and desires. We'll talk about interpersonal effectiveness in Chapter 9.

Running through all of DBT is the concept of **Wise Mind**: the integration of *Emotion Mind* (hot, reactive, feeling-driven) and *Reasonable Mind* (cool, logical, fact-driven).

We often find ourselves in *Reasonable Mind*, where we objectify everything in and around us and respond in what we perceive is the most logical way forward. This can be useful when there are problems to solve, but it can also discount how we might be feeling about the things that we face.

Alternatively, we might be in *Emotion Mind*, where we react to everything based on our feelings. This can be useful when we are interacting with other people, helping us to be empathetic to others, but it can result in illogical actions that cause more harm than good.

Wise Mind is a blend of *Reasonable* and *Emotion Mind*. We take into account both our thoughts and our feelings, finding the effective middle ground. Wise Mind isn't about finding a compromise between the two; it's about accessing a deeper knowing that includes both. Linehan described it as "that part of each person that can know and experience truth… grasping the whole picture when before only parts were understood." Importantly, Wise Mind has qualities that overlap with flow, including intuition, improvisation, present-moment responsiveness, and a sense of rightness about one's actions.

A clarification is helpful here: the *Observing Self* (from ACT) and *Wise Mind* (from DBT) are related but distinct constructs. The *Observing Self* is a perspective—the part of you that notices all your experiences without being any particular experience. It witnesses without evaluating. Wise Mind is an integration—bringing together *Emotion Mind* and *Reasonable Mind* to access a deeper knowing. Think of it this way: the Observing Self creates the space from which Wise Mind can emerge. When you step back and notice (Observing Self), you create room for that integrated wisdom (Wise Mind) to arise.

How does this help you cultivate Values-Flow? DBT skills help create the conditions for flow experiences to happen, which—when combined with values-based living—can lead to Values-Flow. For instance, Mindfulness helps you stay in the present moment, setting the conditions for flow to occur. Distress tolerance skills can keep you in the game even when frustration peaks, so you don't bail before flow has a chance to occur. Emotion regulation skills help you maintain balance, creating an openness for flow experiences. Interpersonal effectiveness skills help you navigate the social relationships and community that you are a part of. Wise Mind provides access to a state of integrated, intuitive responsiveness that both supports flow and shares its qualities. Dialectics are also central to Values-Flow, just as they are an integral part of DBT.

It is worth stating this overlap directly. When Linehan described Wise Mind functioning, she emphasised intuition, improvisation, present-moment responsiveness, and a felt sense of rightness about one's actions. These qualities are phenomenologically very close to what Csikszentmihalyi documented when he studied flow. Recall from Chapter 1 that Linehan spoke of "speed, movement, and flow" as central to how therapy and life itself should work. What she intuited experientially through decades of clinical practice, Csikszentmihalyi documented empirically through decades of research across cultures and activities. DBT's Wise Mind and Flow Theory's optimal experience may well be describing the same state from different vantage points, one from clinical wisdom and one from empirical observation. This convergence is not coincidental; it reflects something genuine about what integrated, fully engaged human functioning looks and feels like.

Flow Theory

From **Flow Theory**, we gain the structure of absorbed engagement and the understanding of the conditions that create optimal experiences. Csikszentmihalyi discovered that people across many areas of life (for instance, climbers, artists, and surgeons) described a "timeless, energising focus." He called it flow because they often said it felt like "being carried by a current."

Flow is often described using nine dimensions. Three are commonly treated as preconditions: challenge–skill balance, clear goals, and unambiguous or immediate feedback. These set the stage for the flow experience. The remaining six dimensions describe the felt experience of flow: action–awareness merging, total concentration, a sense of control (felt control over one's actions, not guaranteed outcomes), loss of self-consciousness, transformation of time, and autotelic enjoyment (where the activity feels rewarding in itself). More specifically:

- **Clear Goals**: Knowing exactly what you're working towards in the moment.
- **Immediate Feedback**: Real-time info about how you're doing (e.g., each brush stroke on a canvas).
- **Challenge–Skill Balance**: The sweet spot between "too easy," resulting in boredom, and "too hard," resulting in anxiety.
- **Merging of Action and Awareness**: You're so focused that self-conscious chatter quiets down. What you are doing and what you are aware of become one seamless activity. You are no longer a person thinking about painting; you are simply painting. This merging of doing and knowing is distinct from the other dimensions described here, although it often accompanies them.
- **Total Concentration**: Your attention is completely absorbed by the activity. Distractions fade into the background, and you are able to give your full focus to what you are doing. This deep concentration is both a condition for flow and one of its most recognisable features.
- **Sense of Control**: You experience a feeling of being in control of your actions and the situation. This is not a guarantee that everything will go perfectly, but rather a felt confidence that you can handle whatever the

activity demands. It is the sense that your skills are adequate for the challenges you face.
- **Loss of Self-Consciousness**: The inner critic goes quiet. You stop monitoring how you appear to others or evaluating your own performance. Your sense of self recedes from awareness, not because you have lost yourself, but because your attention is so fully invested in the activity that there is no room left for self-evaluation. Paradoxically, many people report feeling a stronger sense of self after a flow experience precisely because they were free of self-consciousness during it.
- **Transformation of Time**: Time feels different during flow. Hours can pass in what feels like minutes, or a single moment can seem to stretch and expand. This altered sense of time is one of the most commonly reported features of the flow experience, and it reflects the depth of absorption in the activity.
- **Autotelic Enjoyment**: The activity becomes intrinsically rewarding. You are doing it because the experience itself is worth having, not because of any external reward or outcome. This is what Csikszentmihalyi meant by the autotelic quality of flow. The activity is its own goal. We explore this dimension further in Chapter 6, where we discuss the autotelic personality and the concept of serious play.

These nine dimensions have been identified across dozens of countries and cultural contexts. Researchers have documented the same structure of experience in Italian farmers, Indian yoga practitioners, Korean teenagers, Japanese motorcycle enthusiasts, Navajo shepherds, and many other populations. While the structure of the flow experience is remarkably consistent across cultures, the activities that produce flow and the values that guide engagement towards it are culturally shaped. What produces flow for a rock climber in the Swiss Alps may differ from what produces flow for a calligrapher in Kyoto, but the quality of the experience – the absorption, the merging of action and awareness, the autotelic reward – is recognisably the same. This cross-cultural consistency suggests that flow reflects something fundamental about human psychological functioning rather than being an artefact of any particular cultural context.

Flow is different from distraction, where time is passing by in a meaningless way. Not sure if you're in flow or just zoning out? Ask: "Am I gaining something (insight, skill, meaning), or simply numbing myself?"

It is also important to note that flow is consistently associated with peak performance. Research across domains, from sport to surgery to creative work, shows that people perform at their best during flow states. This makes sense. You are giving an activity your full cognitive and emotional resources, with no energy diverted towards self-doubt, distraction, or resistance. This connection between flow and performance is relevant to the Values-Flow framework because it means that the skills described in this book are not only about feeling good; they are about functioning at your best in the activities that matter most to you.

People who experience flow indicate that it's a positive experience, even if they don't feel positive during the activity itself. Regular experiences of flow have several advantages, including:

- **Engagement over Avoidance**: If a person finds a truly absorbing activity, they're less likely to engage in unhealthy coping strategies.
- **Sustainable Motivation**: Flow experiences spark an "I want to do this again" drive.
- **Builds Resilience**: Regular flow experiences foster a mindset that says, "I can handle more than I thought."
- **Frees Up Energy**: As less mental energy is used to fight thoughts and emotions, there is more bandwidth for creativity, problem-solving, meaningful engagement, and good relationships with others.
- **Better Mental Health and Wellbeing**: Flow often feels good and contributes to positive states of mental health.

Flow isn't just about feeling good. It often involves real effort or challenge. Think of painting for hours or learning a complicated dance routine. Frustration might pop up, yet you keep going because you're so immersed in the activity. That sense of total engagement increases meaning and satisfaction.

Compare it with an hour of doomscrolling: you also lose track of time, but you often emerge drained or worried, and unfulfilled. Flow typically leaves you feeling more alive, not less.

Other misconceptions of flow include:

- "Flow is only for the artist or athlete."
  Absolutely not. Scientists, teachers, managers, parents—anyone can access flow if skill meets challenge and it's a personally meaningful activity.
- "It's euphoria."
  Flow can be pleasurable, but it's often more about serious play, focused effort that feels deeply rewarding.
- "Flow can solve all my problems."
  It's not a magic wand. Serious mental or physical health issues often need professional care. But flow is a powerful supplement to building a meaningful life.
- "Flow is a Western construct."
  While the term "flow" comes from Western psychological research, the experience itself has been documented across cultures worldwide and has parallels in concepts such as the Taoist wu wei (effortless action) and the Hindu concept of sahaja (spontaneous naturalness). As noted above, researchers have identified the same nine dimensions in populations across Asia, Europe, the Americas, and beyond. The cultural context shapes which activities produce flow, but the underlying experience appears to be a universal feature of human psychology.

Flow rarely just happens on its own. It needs the right conditions, both within and beyond the person. You can have the skills that enable flow experiences but be in a very distracting environment. You can have an environment that is well suited to flow experiences and not have the skills needed to experience flow.

ACT's concept of values as "freely chosen directions" maps onto the autotelic quality of flow. When you act from freely chosen values, the action itself becomes intrinsically meaningful. You are not doing it because someone told you to, or because you expect an external reward, but because the activity expresses something you genuinely care about. This is precisely the autotelic orientation that Csikszentmihalyi described as an activity that is its own reward. The convergence here is significant, because it suggests that values-aligned living, as ACT conceives it, naturally creates the motivational conditions that Flow theory identifies as essential for optimal experience.

Importantly, we suggest that practising ACT and DBT skills increases your chances of staying in that challenge–skill sweet spot, thus creating the conditions for flow experiences to occur.

How does this help you cultivate Values-Flow? Flow Theory provides a vivid illustration of what optimal engagement, meaningful existence, and the life well lived feel like. If you've never experienced the life well lived, then how would you know when you have achieved that?

Importantly, in Values-Flow, flow is not the goal. Flow is an experience that sometimes happens when conditions are right, when you're genuinely absorbed in a meaningful challenge that stretches your skills without overwhelming them. When flow arrives, it can be a wonderful experience. When it doesn't show up, you continue anyway, with willingness and persistence. That willingness to keep showing up, whether or not you feel "in the zone," is as important as any flow state. We don't pursue flow directly; we pursue meaningful challenges with openness and skill. Flow sometimes visits along the way.

Points of Convergence and Creative Tension

Before we bring these approaches together, we want to be explicit about where they agree and where they hold genuinely different positions. The dialectical tensions between these approaches are part of the richness of Values-Flow.

Where ACT and DBT Converge:

- Both emphasise acceptance as foundational, acknowledging reality as it is.
- Both value present-moment awareness (mindfulness).
- Both target behavioural change aligned with what matters to you.
- Both recognise that fighting internal experience often creates more suffering.
- Both use metaphor and experiential exercises rather than purely didactic teaching.

Where ACT and DBT Hold Creative Tension:

- Can emotions be directly changed?
  ACT emphasises changing your relationship to emotions, not the emotions themselves. DBT's *opposite action* explicitly aims to change emotions that don't fit the facts.
- Is targeting positive states legitimate?
  ACT is cautious about making any emotional state a goal. DBT explicitly includes "building positive experiences" as a therapeutic target.
- How structured should interventions be?
  ACT emphasises psychological processes that can be achieved in many ways. DBT provides concrete, teachable skills with acronyms and protocols.
- What is the self?
  ACT's Observing Self is a perspective of witnessing without evaluating. DBT's Wise Mind is an integration, bringing together emotion and reason to access knowing.

How Values-Flow Holds These Tensions

Rather than choosing sides, Values-Flow works with these tensions dialectically:

- Sometimes acceptance of emotion is what's needed. Sometimes changing the emotion through skilful action is what's needed. Wisdom lies in discerning what the most effective goal and action is, when, and under what conditions.
- Flow is not the goal, AND creating conditions for engaged living is legitimate and skilful.
- Psychological processes matter, AND concrete skills provide the means to enact those processes.
- The Observing Self creates the space from which Wise Mind can emerge.
  This is the dialectical heart of Values-Flow: holding creative tensions rather than resolving them prematurely.

Bringing Things Together: The Values-Flow Synthesis

ACT, DBT, and Flow Theory each provide important contributions to the life well lived. Think of each one as a toolkit with specific tools to address psychological distress, challenging circumstances, and the constant onslaught of stimuli that overwhelms our senses. But it's when we bring the three together that something valuable emerges. That's the heart of Values-Flow.

Here's how the synthesis works:

- **ACT Provides the Stance**: Psychological flexibility, willingness to have whatever internal experiences arise while moving towards what matters. ACT teaches you to unhook from mental clutter and reorient towards your values.

- **DBT Provides the Dialectical Frame**: Knowing when to accept and when to change. DBT provides concrete, teachable tools for when knowledge alone isn't enough, and when you need structured support to regulate intensity, tolerate distress, or navigate relationships.
- **Flow Theory**: Provides the experiential framework of what engaged living feels like and the conditions that make it possible. Flow gives us a shared language for the state we're cultivating.
- **Values-Flow**: Synthesises all three together, to help you live life well alongside the challenges that life brings. Sometimes you need the values clarification and acceptance of life's circumstances. Sometimes you need the skills and perspective of whether to accept or change things. And sometimes you need to know what optimal engagement feels like and how to create conditions that foster that engagement. This book is designed to help you know which to apply when.

Values-Flow Nudges (Actionable Tips)

Here are a few ways to start cultivating the conditions for Values-Flow to occur:

1. **Recall a Flow Moment**: Have you ever experienced flow? When did you last lose track of time doing something enjoyable or challenging? If so, what conditions made it possible to experience flow? What were you doing at the time? How did it feel? If you haven't experienced flow, then be on the lookout for flow experiences as you read through the pages ahead.
2. **Distraction Versus Immersion**: Next time you catch yourself numbing out or doomscrolling, ask: "Could I pick a more challenging activity that aligns with my interests?" Even working on a puzzle or reading a short article on a topic you care about might nudge you closer to flow than flicking through social media feeds.
3. **Sit Through Hard Moments**: Think about how you deal with challenges in your life. What makes it better or worse? Next time you face a challenge, consider how you can improve the moment and not make things worse.
4. **Identify What Thriving in Life Means to You**: Write down your definition of the life well lived. Return to the House of Functioning in Chapter 1. What floor are you at, and what would it look like to move to a different floor? Where is there room for improvement?
5. **Notice Which Approach Fits**: During one challenging moment this week, pause and ask: What do I need right now?
   - Am I fused or caught up with unhelpful thoughts? (Try ACT defusion)
   - Am I emotionally flooded or overwhelmed? (Try DBT distress tolerance)
   - Am I bored or underwhelmed? (Try increasing challenge)
   - Am I anxious about difficulty? (Try breaking down the task)

Notice that different moments call for different responses. That's the dialectical wisdom that Values-Flow cultivates.

Sound Bite Summary

1. **Acceptance, dialectics, and flow**: Three perspectives that converge in important ways and hold creative tensions in others. Bringing them together dialectically gives us **Values-Flow**.
2. **ACT** unhooks you from unhelpful mind chatter and grounds you in values. ACT provides the stance of psychological flexibility and the importance of values-aligned living.
3. **DBT** provides the dialectical stance of knowing when to accept and when to change. It provides concrete skills to regulate emotions, tolerate distress, navigate relationships, and connect with wisdom within yourself.
4. The **dialectical tensions** between ACT and DBT aren't problems to solve. They're resources for flexibility. Wisdom lies in discerning what's needed when.
5. **Flow** is a unique and personal experience that shows you what it feels like to live a life that's worth living.
6. **Values-Flow** holds these approaches in creative tension, recognising that sometimes you need acceptance, sometimes you need skills, and always you're oriented towards meaningful and absorbed engagement in life.

Final Word

No single approach has all the answers, but the dialectical integration of ACT, DBT, and Flow Theory packs a powerful punch. As you continue through this book, keep an open mind about which elements resonate most with you. Maybe defusion from ACT helps you handle self-critical thoughts, or DBT's emotion regulation keeps you steady in the heat of a challenging project.

The key is developing wisdom about what's needed when. Sometimes acceptance is what's needed. Sometimes change is the path forward. Sometimes the task needs to be harder. Sometimes it needs to be broken down. Values-Flow gives you the framework to discern, and the skills and perspectives to respond. Your daily routines can become opportunities for deeper engagement and greater satisfaction, not by forcing flow, but by creating conditions where engaged living becomes possible.

Above all, Values-Flow begins with the assumption that something remarkable is possible for you, regardless of where you currently stand in the House. You do not need to believe this. Belief comes and goes. But assumption is a choice. Even if you are reading this from the basement, even if the upper floors feel impossibly distant, we invite you to assume that more is possible than your mind tells you. That assumption will not guarantee anything, but it opens a door that resignation keeps firmly shut. In the chapters ahead, we will show you how to walk through it.

3 The Values-Flow Card

Chapter Overview

To help you engage with the Values-Flow framework, this chapter introduces the Values-Flow Card, which is designed to help you to track your functioning and skills practice across the week. The Card contains the *Values-Flow skills*, which we briefly overview here, with details provided over the next six chapters, along with a rating system. The chapter includes a detailed description of how to complete the Card.

Aligning with What Matters

Meet Poppy. She's 34, works in marketing, and feels…stuck. Not *depressed* exactly, but not thriving either. When her therapist asked what she truly values, Poppy drew a blank. "Um…success? Being a good person?" It's not that she doesn't care about anything—she cares about *everything*. But after years of just getting through each day—work deadlines, bills, social obligations—she'd lost touch with what *actually mattered* to her.

Sound familiar? Maybe you're crushing it at work but realise you haven't called your best friend in months. Or you value health but keep hitting snooze instead of going out for a morning walk. Or perhaps, like Poppy, you're not even sure *what* you value anymore. Life's been on autopilot for so long that your internal compass has gone fuzzy. You are living on the lower floor of the House of Functioning. Days are filled with a quiet desperation. You may feel invalidated by people or situations that have happened or are happening. Perhaps you're grieving or have intrusive memories from past experiences of trauma. Or perhaps you feel emotionally numb.

To support your quest for thriving in daily life—moving to the upper floors of the House—we'll rely on the **Values-Flow Card**, a portable helper that prompts you on the journey of practising acceptance, values, and skilful action. In the chapters ahead, we'll show you how you can use the Card to apply the concepts we cover to create meaningful change, helping you reach and stay on the upper floors of the House.

DOI: 10.4324/9781003771173-4

Think of the Values-Flow Card as your furniture-moving toolkit, the practical means by which you carry each piece of equipment up the stairs and arrange it on the upper floors of the House. The Card helps you track which floor you're on, what skills you're building, and whether you're moving towards or away from the life you want to live.

We'll describe this in more detail below, but take a moment to look at the Values-Flow Card (Figure 3.1). The front (Figure 3.1) contains the House of Functioning and asks you to consider where in the House you are today. The back (Figure 3.1) contains the Values-Flow skills (VIRTUE, INVOLVE, VITAL, ACCEPT, REGULATE, and RELATE), with the opportunity to rate how well you are using the skills, and reflect upon your values and goals. We also provide a summary rating scale (Figure 3.2).

We'll explain how to understand and cultivate each skill, as well as how to rate your use of each skill in the coming chapters. Here we provide a brief overview of the skills and rating system.

Values-Flow Practices

At the beginning of the week, reflect upon your goals for the week

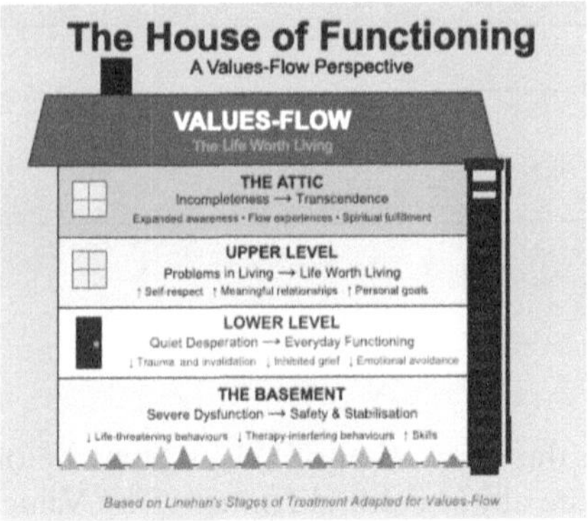

At the end of the week, reflect upon the following questions to honour the process:

- Did I show up for what mattered this week, regardless of the outcome?
- Was I willing to have whatever feelings arose?
- Did I act on my values even when it was uncomfortable?
- Did I continue even if flow didn't occur?

Daily Reflection: Where am I in the house today?

Monday
Tuesday
Wednesday
Thursday
Friday
Saturday
Sunday

Figure 3.1 The Values-Flow Card (Front, Left, Back, Right).

(Continued)

Values-Flow Skills

Each day, rate each Values-Flow Skill on the extent to which you practiced the skills, ranging from 0 (did not practice, was not on my radar) to 6 (reflected upon and used the skill, experiencing flow in the process). At the end of the week, rate the extent to which you practiced each Skill across the week (overall).

SKILLS	MON	TUE	WED	THU	FRI	SAT	SUN	OVERALL
VIRTUE SKILLS								
Core Values								
Strengths Use								
INVOLVE SKILLS								
Attending								
Reflecting								
Informing								
Acting								
VITALITY SKILLS								
Autotelic Engagement								
Serious Play								
ACCEPT SKILLS								
Willingness								
REGULATE SKILLS								
Emotion Regulation								
Distress Tolerance								
RELATE SKILLS								
Interpersonal Effectiveness								
Environmental Effectiveness								
Overall skills practice for the day								

Figure 3.1 (Continued).

The Values-Flow Skills

The Card contains the skills that form the foundation of Values-Flow. Before we describe the skills, an important note about cultural context. The Values-Flow framework draws on research conducted across dozens of countries. We believe the underlying processes are universal. However, how these skills are expressed, which values are prioritised, and what activities create meaningful engagement will look different depending on your cultural background, community, and life circumstances. In some cultures, values may be strongly oriented towards family obligation and collective harmony rather than individual growth. In others, spiritual practice may be central to regulation and acceptance in ways that differ from the Western therapeutic traditions we draw upon. We encourage you to interpret these skills through the lens of your own cultural context. Adapt them to honour the traditions and relationships that shape your life. There is no single version of the life well lived.

Values-Flow Skill Ratings

Skills	Meaning
Virtue	Live according to your core values and strengths
Involve	Align your actions to the ARIA (Attend, Reflect, Inform, Act) principles
Vitality	Activate the autotelic self and serious play
Accept	Willingness and acceptance
Regulate	Emotional regulation and distress tolerance
Relate	Relational objectives and skills, Environment demands

Daily Ratings (across the Values-Flow Skills)

Score	Meaning
0	Didn't reflect on or practice any of the skills. "The Values-Flow skills weren't on my radar at all today."
1	Reflected, but didn't attempt. "I thought about using one or more of the skills, but didn't take any action toward using them."
2	Reflected and attempted; felt confused or lacked significance. "I practiced one or more skill but wasn't sure why."
3	Reflected and attempted, but got bored or listless. "I practiced one or more skill but my goals felt too easy or not meaningful."
4	Reflected and attempted, but felt overwhelmed or anxious. "I tried to practice the skills, but it felt too big today."
5	Reflected and did the skills. It was enjoyable but I didn't experience flow. "The skills were interesting to do but I didn't lose myself in the experience."
6	Reflected and did the skills; experienced flow (enjoyable absorption). "The challenge was high yet meaningful—I lost myself in it in a good way."

End of Week Overall Rating (for each Values-Flow Skill)

Score	Meaning
0	Didn't reflect on or practice. "The skill wasn't on my radar at all today."
1	Reflected, but didn't attempt the skill. "I thought about it, but didn't take any action toward using the skill."
2	Reflected and attempted the skill; felt confused or lacked significance. "I practiced the skill but wasn't sure why."
3	Reflected and attempted the skill, but got bored or listless. "I practiced the skill but it felt too easy or not meaningful."
4	Reflected and attempted the skill, but felt overwhelmed or anxious. "I tried to practice the skill, but it felt too big today."
5	Reflected and did the skill. It was enjoyable but I didn't experience flow. "The skill was interesting to do but I didn't lose myself in the experience."
6	Reflected and did the skill; experienced flow (enjoyable absorption). "The challenge was high yet meaningful—I lost myself in it in a good way."

Track Without Attachment! The numbers aren't the whole story—and they're not a judgment of your worth or progress.

Figure 3.2 The Values-Flow Card Rating Scale.

VIRTUE: Live According to Your Core Values and Strengths

While there are different ways of defining Virtue, in the Values-Flow model, **VIRTUE** draws on Aristotle's concept of the Golden Mean while integrating the ACT understanding of values. In ACT, values are freely chosen directions. They're not about being a "good person" in some externally defined sense, but about identifying what genuinely matters to you. In Values-Flow, we use VIRTUE to honour both traditions: values are personal directions (as defined in ACT), which are expressed through strengths of character in ways that contribute to thriving (Aristotle).

The first part of VIRTUE is aligning your life with your core values. Values aren't goals you achieve and tick off; they're qualities of ongoing action. You can express kindness right now regardless of the outcome. You can be curious right now. You can show courage right now. When you live in accordance with your values, you are more likely to be engaged and interested in life, even when challenges arise. For instance, if you value health, you are more likely to experience a sense of thriving when you practise healthy habits such as getting regular exercise, sleeping well, eating healthy foods, and avoiding substances. Values-aligned living often contributes to those around you, but the primary measure is whether you're moving in directions that matter to you.

The second part of VIRTUE is strengths. These refer to capabilities for thinking and feeling that you are good at doing, which contribute to a life well lived. Putting your strengths into practice can help you feel good and can lead to virtuous behaviour, doing good for those around you. By bringing your best self to negotiate life's challenges, through both good and bad times, you can more effectively navigate the complex circumstances of everyday life.

INVOLVE: Align Your Actions to the ARIA Principles

The thriving life is action-oriented. It doesn't just happen, but rather requires that you **INVOLVE** yourself in everyday living. But the question becomes: what should you be involved in? Some activities promote the wellbeing of both you and those around you. Other activities are neutral. They pass the time but reflect existing rather than thriving in life. Then there are activities that detract from your own and/or others' sense of wellbeing. For instance, you might spend the afternoon playing games on your smartphone rather than achieving the goals that you have set for yourself for the day.

To help you engage in activities that are life-giving, we use the acronym ARIA, which stands for Attending, Reflecting, Informing, and Acting. This is a circular process that helps you experience Values-Flow (see Figure 3.3).

First, **Attending** refers to paying mindful attention to goals and challenges inside and outside of us. We spend much of our life on autopilot. Attending breaks us away from this and helps us to intentionally engage in each task that comes our way. As we will explore in Chapter 5, the key to effective attending is often to slow down. When we rush through our day, we miss the signals that could guide us towards more engaged living. Even a brief pause creates space for genuine awareness to emerge. It means that we first set goals for the day.

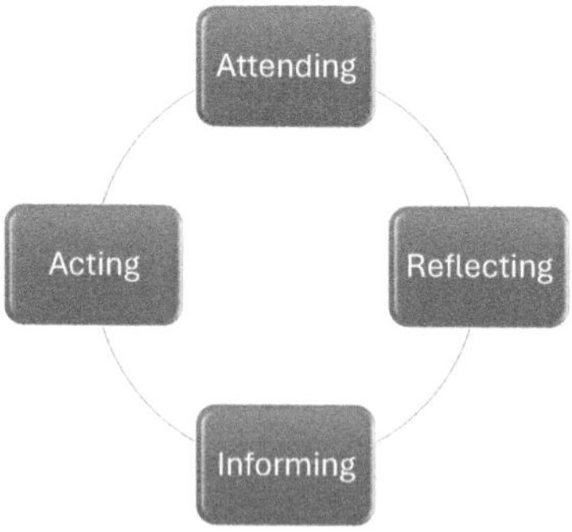

Figure 3.3 The ARIA Cycle of INVOLVE.

What are the small or big things that would feel good to cross off our to-do list today?

It also means that we are cognisant of possible challenges. *Inner challenges* are personal things that block us from achieving our goals, such as feeling anxiety about the activities that we plan to do, or having a busy, unfocused mind. *Outer challenges* are the many stressors that we face each day, such as people wanting us to do favours for them, traffic jams that make our commute longer than we anticipated, or trying to juggle the many activities that our children are engaged in. By mindfully acknowledging these challenges, we can identify ways to navigate those challenges so we can purposefully pursue the goals and intentions that we have set for the day.

Second, **Reflecting** refers to using both the Observing Self (from ACT) and Wise Mind (from DBT) to explore acceptance *and* change. Once we've identified our goals and challenges, we reflect upon the best way to address these, so that we can navigate the day effectively. By being in *Wise Mind*, we can learn to accept the things we cannot change, have courage to change the things we can, and have wisdom to know the difference, as described by the Serenity Prayer. So, **Reflecting** is all about pausing in the face of internal or external challenges and tapping into the *Observing Self* and *Wise Mind* to determine the next right action.

Third, **Informing** is about intentionally gathering feedback about our thoughts and feelings. This involves noticing signals from our body, the environment around us, and our own experiences in life, and then considering the extent to which these align with our values. This means that we are not acting on impulse, but rather being intentional about our actions, being mindful of but not overwhelmed by the perceived and real challenges of the day. We are looking to inform our next step based upon our values and strengths.

Finally, **Acting** refers to taking flexible, values-based steps to adapt, engage, or invent new solutions, while incorporating our strengths. After we have paused, reflected on the situation, and identified the next step that is most aligned with our values and strengths, Action brings values-based living to fruition. Because we are not acting on impulse but instead being mindful in our approach, it allows us to respond rather than react to situations that arise throughout our day.

When you cycle through Attending → Reflecting → Informing → Acting, you keep attention, insight, feedback, and behaviour in constant interaction. This helps you to live on the upper floors of the House. This cycle prevents two common traps: (1) *autopilot*, where you act without awareness and drift into boredom, and (2) *analysis-paralysis*, where you reflect endlessly but never translate insight into movement (also known as *procrastination*), both of which are common in the lower floors of the House. Using the full ARIA loop helps you calibrate challenge and skill in real time, making flow experiences and progress towards living according to your values far more likely.

For instance, start by setting a goal for the day that is time-limited (I can complete this today), specific (e.g., "I will run 1 km" rather than "I want to improve my fitness"), and stretches you just beyond your comfort zone (I can run ½ km now, but it'd be nice to run a full km). Reflect upon what you need to accept and what you can change (e.g., I accept that running 1 km is challenging and pushes my limits, but it may be possible if I give it a go). Go for a run and notice how well you achieve your goal (I made it 0.6 km before I had to stop and rest, but then walked the final 0.4 km). Identify what actions are needed to reach your goal (tomorrow I will try to run 0.8 km before I walk).

Or perhaps you need to address a dicey issue with a colleague at work. Attend to the goal of having a conversation with your colleague and finding a resolution that will work for both of you. Pause for a few minutes before the conversation, tapping into both your Reasonable Mind (there is a clear problem that needs a solution) and Emotion Mind (both I and my colleague feel passionate about our own solutions). Mindfully listen to your thoughts and emotions—what are they telling you and how might they get in the way of attaining a mutually supportive solution? Let this inform how you approach the situation. Then act intentionally, having the conversation with your colleague, owning your perspective and role, but also listening and being willing to compromise to reach a good solution.

VITAL: Cultivating the Autotelic Personality Through Serious Play

Csikszentmihalyi described the **autotelic personality** as a person who does things for their own sake, because the experience itself is the main goal. Think of a child completely absorbed in building a sandcastle. They are not building it because anyone told them to or for a grade, but because they enjoy doing it. The doing is its own reward.

That's the spirit of **VITAL**. It's what Kevin Rathunde called **serious play**—approaching challenges with the kind of absorbed, intrinsically motivated engagement that children bring to play, combined with the purposefulness that connects activities to deeper meaning. When you approach a difficult conversation with genuine curiosity about the other person's perspective, or treat your morning walk like a small expedition, that's the autotelic personality in action. VITAL is about cultivating this orientation, bringing a quality of playful seriousness to everyday life that transforms going through the motions into genuine engagement, and helping you reside on the upper floors of the House.

The autotelic orientation is closely connected to one of the key preconditions for flow that we identified in Chapter 2: the challenge–skill balance. The autotelic person naturally seeks to calibrate challenges to match their developing skills. They neither settle for tasks that are too easy nor become overwhelmed by tasks that are too difficult. This ongoing calibration, combined with the intrinsic motivation that serious play provides, creates the conditions where flow experiences are most likely to emerge.

ACCEPT: Having the Willingness to Accept Life on Life's Terms

As we travel along the journey in life, we often encounter situations or people that challenge us. These can be hard situations, which we might try to avoid because they cause us discomfort or other negative emotions. **ACCEPT** means that we are willing to accept the people and circumstances that come our way, despite the discomfort that they causes. This means that we don't fight against life, but we accept the things that happen that we cannot change.

For instance, when faced with a situation that you are not happy about, especially when facing strong emotions or interpersonal friction, notice what you are feeling without trying to push it away. You may still feel stressed, and that is acceptable. The goal is not to eliminate the stress but to change your relationship to it. Acknowledge that it is present. Allow it to be there. Then choose how to respond based on your values rather than on the urgency of the emotion.

This is different from simply deciding not to be stressed, which is a form of the control agenda that ACT identifies as part of the problem. This also does not mean that you become a doormat or that you approve of or like the circumstance. There are times that we need to stand up to other people or actively change the circumstances that we are facing. This is especially true when circumstances grate against our values. This is where making changes to either your mindset or the situation is important. Acceptance means that we take responsibility for the things that are within our control and let go of the things that are beyond our control.

Both ACT and DBT emphasise willingness—the readiness to have whatever internal experiences arise while moving towards what matters to you. This isn't resignation or passive acceptance; it's an active opening to experience. Further, willingness sometimes needs support from concrete skills. For example, when emotions are intense, distress tolerance techniques can help you stay willing.

At the heart of both Values-Flow and DBT is knowing when to accept and when to change. Drawing on both ACT and DBT, you might:

- Accept when the situation cannot be changed OR fighting reality is creating more suffering than the situation itself OR acceptance would free up energy for values-aligned action elsewhere.
- Change when the situation can be changed AND the emotion's intensity doesn't fit the facts AND change would move you towards values rather than away from discomfort.

This isn't always clear-cut. That's where Wise Mind comes in. Wise Mind, as we described in Chapter 2, is not simply a compromise between emotion and reason. It is a deeper form of knowing that integrates both. It taps into an intuitive sense of what the situation requires. When you are unsure whether to accept or change, pausing to access Wise Mind rather than reacting from pure emotion or pure logic often reveals the most effective path. ACT reminds us that the struggle to control internal experiences often backfires. DBT reminds us that emotions that don't fit the facts can be changed through skilful action. Both are true; wisdom lies in discerning which applies when.

REGULATE: Optimal Self-Regulation

An important part of daily life is understanding and managing the myriad array of emotions that we experience. Due to a combination of our biological nature, personal experiences in the past and present, the environment that we are in, and our current mental and physical state, at times we are able to handle a lot of stress and pressure, whereas at other times those become overwhelming. Rather than shutting down and ignoring our emotions, **REGULATE** provides skills primarily based on DBT that help you understand and regulate your emotions, both in everyday life and when life becomes overwhelming. For instance, *opposite action* is a strategy that helps you approach a challenging situation when you'd rather flee.

ACT adds strategies to accept the emotions that we feel when the emotions that we are experiencing fit the facts. For instance, if you are feeling anxious about giving a speech, you can pause, notice the anxiety, and allow it to be present, not judging yourself for feeling anxious.

A helpful way to think about regulation is through the concept of the *window of tolerance*, which we explore in Chapter 8. Each of us has a range of emotional arousal within which we can function effectively. When arousal exceeds this range, we enter what is called hyperarousal (the *panic zone*). We become overwhelmed and effective engagement becomes impossible. When arousal drops below this range, we enter hypoarousal (the *shutdown zone*). We become numb and disconnected. The REGULATE skills help us stay within our window, or return to it when life pushes us out. This window is also where flow experiences become possible. Flow requires enough activation to be fully engaged but not so much that you become overwhelmed.

It's important to gently acknowledge your thoughts and emotions, noticing them with curiosity rather than judgement. Avoiding or denying these parts of you can keep you stuck. Noticing them is the first step towards meaningful movement. This is a key message that comes from both ACT and DBT: only by acknowledging and accepting our inner experiences can we make room to respond differently.

The next step is where ACT and DBT offer different but complementary perspectives. ACT suggests that the goal isn't to change inner experiences but to change your relationship to them. When you notice the thought "I'm a failure," you don't need to argue with it or replace it. You can simply notice it as a thought, create some distance from it (defusion), and act on your values anyway. The thought can come along for the ride.

DBT adds that sometimes, particularly with intense emotions that don't fit the facts of the situation, direct change strategies are appropriate. If you're feeling crushing shame about a minor mistake, *checking the facts* and using *opposite action* can help the emotion shift. The key distinction is that we're not trying to never feel difficult things; we're developing flexibility in how we respond.

Both approaches share a commitment to not letting inner experiences run the show. Whether you change your relationship to the experience (ACT) or change the experience itself (DBT), the result is greater freedom to live according to your values.

RELATE: Optimal Interpersonal and Environmental Regulation

As human beings, we are relational creatures. We need other people in our lives and to feel like we are valued and cared about by others. However, relationships also bring a number of challenges, such as effectively expressing our needs, maintaining a positive relationship with others despite having differing viewpoints, and maintaining a sense of self-respect. The **RELATE** skills draw on the interpersonal effectiveness module of DBT to improve our relationships with others.

As we interact with the world around us, we can also come across barriers in our environment that make it a lot harder for us to focus on and achieve our goals and live according to our values. Time and resources are perhaps the biggest barriers that we face. We only have so much time in the day, and only the privileged few are blessed with endless resources. But other challenges include toxic environments, the endless noise of modern life, and political dynamics. External challenges are a lot harder to change because a lot of external factors are outside of our control. The key is to acknowledge and let go of the things that are beyond our control.

Values-Flow doesn't happen in a vacuum. It occurs within the constraints of real life, so acknowledging real-world demands helps us adapt or negotiate with our environment. As you prepare for your day, it's helpful to identify what external barriers you might face, such as time constraints, social obligations, and the demands and expectations of other people, which impact upon your day. By acknowledging them, it's easier to accept and work within the constraints that are there.

Sustaining Your Values-Flow Practice

The Values-Flow skills are most impactful if you regularly incorporate them into your everyday life. The exercises we describe in this book only take a few minutes to do, so they can easily be inserted into your day. Schedule a time each day to practise one or more Values-Flow skills. If you miss a day, notice what barriers got in the way of your practice. If you engage in the skills, notice what made it easier to do the practice.

Importantly, some of the exercises will be easy for you to do and others will be hard. Play with the exercises, see what works and what doesn't work for you. If you struggle doing one of the exercises, then accept that it might not be the best fit for you, but don't give up there. Try a different exercise or come up with your own ideas. There's no one right way to practise the skills, but to fully access Values-Flow, it's important that you regularly put the skills that work for you into practice. The more you practise the skills, the easier and more automatic they will become, making it more likely that you will experience flow.

That being said, the journey towards Values-Flow is bound to be met with the inevitable ups and downs of life. Every adventurer knows that learning to use a compass is one thing; navigating through storms, fog, and challenging terrain is quite another. The same holds true for your Values-Flow practice.

Using the Values-Flow Card

Now that you've learned about the different skills on the Values-Flow Card, how do you use the Card to help you practise the skills and make it possible to experience Values-Flow? The skills become reality when you put them into daily practice. You are more likely to practise skills when you track your use of those skills, as writing them down makes you more accountable. So the Card helps you to reflect on the skills that you used during the day and week.

First, at the beginning of the week, on the front of the Card, use the box at the top to describe your goals or target behaviours that you have for the week. This provides a sense of meaningful purpose for approaching the week.

Second, each day of the week, start by looking at the House. Rate where you are today (the basement, lower floor, upper floor, or the attic). Write this down on the Card.

Third, go through your day. Try to apply the skills that we've just described and will elaborate on in subsequent chapters. Then, at the end of the day, on the back of the Card, consider the Values-Flow skills. Go through each skill. Rate your skill practice, using the ratings provided in the chapters to come. You might have used only one or two skills or all of the skills.

Fourth, at the bottom of the Card, rate your overall skill practice for the day, using the 0–6 scale described in Table 3.1.

Table 3.1 Daily Rating Scale

Score	*Meaning*
0	Didn't reflect on or practise any of the skills. "The Values-Flow skills weren't on my radar at all today."
1	Reflected, but didn't attempt. "I thought about using one or more of the skills, but didn't take any action towards using them."
2	Reflected and attempted; felt confused or lacked significance. "I practised one or more skills but wasn't sure why."
3	Reflected and attempted, but got bored or listless. "I practised one or more skills, but my goals felt too easy or not meaningful."
4	Reflected and attempted, but felt overwhelmed or anxious. "I tried to practise the skills, but it felt too big today."
5	Reflected and did the skills. It was enjoyable, but I didn't experience flow. "The skills were interesting to do, but I didn't lose myself in the experience."
6	Reflected and did the skills; experienced flow (enjoyable absorption). "The challenge was high yet meaningful—I lost myself in it in a good way."

A note on recognising flow. When the scale refers to "experienced flow," it means more than simply feeling good or losing track of time. As we described in Chapter 2, flow involves a specific cluster of experiences. Your attention is fully absorbed. Your actions and awareness merge into a seamless activity. Self-consciousness recedes. You feel a sense of control over what you are doing. Time seems to pass differently. The activity feels intrinsically rewarding. You do not need all nine dimensions to be strongly present to rate a 6. But the experience should feel qualitatively different from ordinary enjoyment. It is the difference between liking an activity and being completely absorbed by it.

Fifth, **at the end of the week**, use the **0–6 rating scale** (Table 3.2) to rate how well you used each skill in working towards your goals.

Finally, at the end of the week, read through your Card. On the front of the Card, write down any thoughts or reflections you have about the skills. Reflect on how the skills might have helped you navigate situations and experiences to make Values-Flow possible. Reflect upon the following questions:

- What goals did I have this week? Which ones did I achieve or make progress towards?
- Which Values-Flow skills did I use?
- How often did I use the Values-Flow skills?
- Were there any differences between the days that I used the skills and the days that I didn't?
- Did I have any flow experiences through using the skills?
- Were there times I showed up with willingness and engagement but flow didn't arrive? How did I respond?
- What goals do I want to set for next week?

In the following chapters, we will keep returning to the Card to show you how you can practically use the Card in everyday life to make it more likely that

Table 3.2 Weekly Rating Scale

Score	*Meaning*
0	Didn't reflect on or practise. "The skill wasn't on my radar at all today."
1	Reflected, but didn't attempt the skill. "I thought about it, but didn't take any action towards using the skill."
2	Reflected and attempted the skill; felt confused or lacked significance. "I practised the skill but wasn't sure why."
3	Reflected and attempted the skill, but got bored or listless. "I practised the skill, but my goals felt too easy or not meaningful."
4	Reflected and attempted the skill, but felt overwhelmed or anxious. "I tried to practise the skill, but it felt too big today."
5	Reflected and did the skill. It was enjoyable, but I didn't experience flow. "The skill was interesting to do, but I didn't lose myself in the experience."
6	Reflected and did the skill; experienced flow (enjoyable absorption). "The challenge was high yet meaningful—I lost myself in it in a good way."

you'll experience flow. Make it a practice to take a few minutes at the end of each day to fill out the Values-Flow Card. That way you capture your thoughts and behaviours when they are fresh, rather than trying to remember what you did and how you felt.

Track Without Attachment! There is no right or wrong answer in completing the Card and reflecting upon these questions. These are just data, which help inform you in how often you are using the Values-Flow skills, setting and achieving goals, what challenges you are finding in the practice, and whether you are having any flow experiences as a result of working the skills. The numbers aren't the whole story. They are not a judgement of your worth or progress. Alongside your ratings, we encourage you to ask yourself some questions that honour the process, not just the product:

- Did I show up for what mattered today, regardless of the outcome?
- Was I willing to have whatever feelings arose?
- Did I act on my values even when it was uncomfortable?
- When flow didn't come, did I continue anyway?

A day of low scores isn't a failure; it's simply information. Take time to reflect upon the conditions that made engagement difficult. Consider what might help tomorrow. The Card is a mirror for reflection, not a scorecard for judgement. If you find yourself getting attached to the numbers, that's worth noticing too. Can you hold the tracking with lightness, using it as information rather than evaluation?

This orientation towards tracking connects to a fundamental insight from ACT. Values are about process, not outcome. The point of using the Card is not to achieve a particular score. It is to build a practice of noticing how you are engaging with what matters to you. The act of reflecting each evening is itself a values-aligned behaviour, regardless of what the reflection reveals. A week of low scores that prompts genuine curiosity and adjustment is more valuable than a week of high scores that goes unexamined.

The Rhythm of the Seasons

One of the problems that arises from many self-help books is that there's an underlying pressure to always be improving. This same problem can occur if you focus on continually improving your Values-Flow scores. There are two problems with this. First, on a 0–6 scale, there is only so much room for improvement. Second, the goal is not to constantly be performing at your peak level. It's about being present in the everyday. There is no right or wrong score; each day you are simply documenting how things went.

Remember from Chapter 2 our garden metaphor: just as different gardens thrive under different conditions and in different seasons, your Values-Flow practice will naturally cycle through different phases. Understanding and accepting these rhythms prevents the discouragement that comes from expecting perpetual peak performance.

Spring seasons in your practice feel like discovery. For instance, the ARIA cycle reveals new insights each time you engage with it. Attending shows you things you've never noticed. Reflecting opens unexpected insights about patterns you've carried for years. Informing connects dots between disparate experiences, revealing resources you didn't know you had. Acting feels fresh and experimental, each values-based step teaching you something new. During spring seasons, document everything. Write down what works, what surprises you, and what challenges you. These records become invaluable resources during leaner times.

Summer brings the full flowering of your practice. Your use of the Values-Flow skills hums along smoothly, almost effortlessly. For instance, you find yourself naturally attending throughout the day, reflection becomes automatic, you instinctively know what information you need, and your actions align with your values without conscious effort. The danger in summer is assuming this ease is permanent. Summer is the perfect time to deliberately challenge yourself. Focus on one of your lesser used skills. Try applying Values-Flow skills in new domains, teach someone else the practice, or consciously increase the difficulty of the challenges you engage in.

Autumn in your practice might appear as a gradual sense of staleness or boredom. The skills that felt so alive now seem mechanical. This isn't failure. Rather, it's a signal that you're ready for evolution. Perhaps your values have shifted, requiring new expressions. Maybe you've outgrown your current challenges. Autumn invites experimentation with new approaches to each Values-Flow skill.

Winter seasons can feel like the practice has died. You might abandon your Values-Flow skills for days or weeks, unable to muster the energy for conscious attending or structured reflection. Yet if you keep trying to use these skills, you are creating the conditions for future growth to occur. Even then, integration is happening below the threshold of consciousness. When spring returns, you'll find your practice has developed new depths you couldn't have achieved through constant summer conditions.

Values-Flow Nudges

Here are a few ways that you can start putting the Values-Flow Card into practice:

1 **Morning Card Check**: Right after breakfast, look at the House of Functioning and ask where you are today. Then, glance at the Skills on your Values-Flow Card. Which skill feels most relevant today given your position in the House?

2 **Evening Reflection**: At night, rate each skill that you used on the 0–6 scale. Don't judge your scores as good or bad. You are simply collecting information.
3 **Micro-Moment Awareness**: Next time you sense boredom (skill > challenge) or anxiety (challenge > skill), see if you can gently adjust the task or your approach. For instance, if it's too easy, add a fun twist. If it's too hard, break it down or ask for help.
4 **When Flow Doesn't Come**: Notice a time this week when you engaged fully but flow didn't arrive. Explore the day. Did the circumstances of the day provide an opportunity for flow? Did you show up? Did you act on your values? Were you willing? If you can say yes to these questions, that's success, regardless of whether or not you experienced flow.

Sound Bite Summary

Key points to remember from this chapter:

1 **Values-Flow** is about observing your challenges, reflecting wisely, and acting from a place of openness and creativity, guided by your values.
2 The **Values-Flow Card** is a practical, portable method to *notice*, *reflect on*, and *actively engage* with daily challenges in alignment with what matters to you.
3 **The Card includes Six Skill Domains**: VIRTUE, INVOLVE, VITAL, ACCEPT, REGULATE, and RELATE.
4 You can actively use the Card each day by rating yourself on a **0–6 scale**. This practice encourages daily mindfulness, fosters personal insights, and allows you to adjust challenges to help you move to the upper floors of the House.
5 **Track without attachment**: The numbers are information, not judgement. Reflections about your willingness, values alignment, and showing up matter as much as the numerical ratings.
6 **Your practice will move through seasons**, including spring discovery, summer ease, autumn staleness, and winter dormancy. Each season serves a purpose in your growth. Notice and lean into each season rather than resisting or fighting them.

Final Word

By integrating these **Values-Flow Skills** into your routine, including morning check-ins, evening reflections, and in-the-moment awareness, you're more likely to discover **meaningful engagement** in everyday life. Whether it's choosing a new challenge, handling obstacles with compassion, or leveraging your strengths in a creative way, these Cards and skills form a roadmap for thriving in life.

And remember: flow doesn't always arrive, even when you create the conditions for flow. That's not failure; that's the nature of optimal experience. What you can control is showing up, engaging with willingness, and acting on your values. Flow sometimes visits under those conditions. But the showing up is the success, whether or not flow comes. That willingness to keep showing up for what matters, with or without the reward of flow, is not a consolation prize. It is itself an expression of your deepest values. Values, as ACT reminds us, are about process rather than outcome. Every moment you engage with what matters, you are living according to your values.

In the next few chapters, we'll delve deeper into what each skill is and how to put them into practice as you navigate the ups and downs of life. Over time, through ongoing practice, you can be well on your way to the life well lived.

Part 2

Skills to Help You Thrive in Life

4 VIRTUE

The Core of Values-Flow

Chapter Overview

This chapter describes the first Values-Flow skill: VIRTUE, which occurs as you live in alignment with your core values and strengths. Values are the deep-seated principles that reflect what is important to you, guide your behaviour, and influence how you feel and function in life. Strengths are things that we are good at. Together, the VIRTUE skills keep you oriented towards what truly matters and leverage your natural abilities to help you live the life well lived.

What Do You Value?

Meet James. At age 42, he's finally made it. He's been promoted to senior manager, lost 20 pounds, bought a house with a nice yard, got married, and had a few kids. So why does Sunday evening feel so hollow? He's scrolling through his phone, another weekend gone, and can't remember the last time he felt genuinely *alive*—not just productive, but deeply engaged in something that mattered.

His therapist asked him a simple question: "What do you actually *value*?" James froze. "I value…success?" Even as he said it, he knew it sounded empty. He'd been chasing goals—the promotion, the weight loss, the perfect family, the house—but never stopped to ask why. What did he truly value? Achievement? Sure. But achievement towards what? Connection? Growth? Contribution? He honestly didn't know. James's rapid answer of "success" was not genuine contact with his values. It was a protective strategy, a well-worn narrative that kept him from having to sit with the vulnerability that he longed for. As we will explore in Chapter 5, this kind of protective response is common. Touching what you most yearn for carries enormous risk. It is often easier to stay on the surface with socially acceptable answers than to go deeper into what genuinely matters.

Sound familiar? You can crush every goal on your list and still feel like something's missing. That's because **goals are finish lines; values are directions**. This chapter is about **VIRTUE**: identifying what truly matters to you

DOI: 10.4324/9781003771173-6

(your values) and harnessing your natural strengths so that your daily actions feel purposeful, not just productive.

VIRTUE captures the *why* behind the things that we do. Values-Flow doesn't come from checking boxes. It comes from aligning what you do with who you want to be.

Growing a Meaningful Life

Remember our garden metaphor from Chapter 2? Just as gardens need the right seeds planted in spring to flourish in summer, VIRTUE is your planting stage. It is the act of choosing and cultivating your core values and strengths so that you can thrive, not merely survive. You're not just pulling weeds; you're actively choosing what to grow.

This is not to say that distress is unimportant. Distress is like weeds in the garden. We need to manage distress, just like we need to manage weeds if we want our garden to thrive. We'll talk more about managing distress in Chapter 8. But a weed-free garden is simply bare ground if we haven't planted and cultivated seeds. So, this chapter is all about planting seeds, setting the foundation for a thriving life, helping you move to the upper floors of the House.

What Is VIRTUE?

In Values-Flow, VIRTUE occurs as you live in alignment with your core values and strengths.

A clarification is necessary here. We use the term "VIRTUE" to honour the wisdom tradition stretching back to Aristotle, but we want to be clear about what we mean and what we don't mean.

In classical virtue ethics, virtues are character traits that make someone a "good person," such as courage, temperance, justice, and wisdom. These are often seen as objective goods that everyone should cultivate.

In ACT, values are something different: they're freely chosen directions that give your life meaning. They're not about being a "good person" in some externally defined sense. They're about identifying and living according to what genuinely matters to you. Your values aren't goals you achieve and tick off; they're qualities of ongoing action you can express in any moment.

Values-Flow holds both perspectives: values as personal directions (ACT) that can be expressed through character strengths (positive psychology) in ways that contribute to building a life worth living (Aristotle). But the foundation is ACT's insight that values are chosen, not imposed, and that you can live them now, not someday when conditions are right.

VIRTUE in Values-Flow has Two Elements:

1 **Core Values**: Values are like a compass pointing towards what truly matters to you. They are not a destination you arrive at, but what guides you in

which direction you travel. When you value connection, conversations become an opportunity to express that value. When you value growth, challenges become a chance to learn. Values aren't achieved; they're enacted, moment by moment.

2 **Strengths Use**: Character strengths are trait-like positive characteristics that contribute to the life well lived when put into action. They are the things that you are good at doing, such as being a kind person, leading others, or sticking with things even when it gets hard. All of us have strengths; the challenge is to identify and use your strengths in everyday life.

To thrive, VIRTUE says that it is necessary to know and live according to our values and our strengths. We need to know ourselves, not just what we do wrong or things that we don't like about ourselves, but also what we are good at, what we care about, and the person that we want to be.

Core Values

To live according to your values, the first step is to identify what you value in life. In Values-Flow, values are what you really care about at the core of your being. These are not just personal beliefs. Beliefs are influenced not only by your values but also by your experiences and circumstances. Values are the deep-seated principles that reflect what is important to you, guide your behaviour, and influence how you feel and function in life. They inform what you believe is right and wrong. They arise from a combination of the culture you live in, your experiences in life, and who you are as a person. They are inherently good in nature—contributing to the good of you, those around you, and society in general.

A note of honesty is needed here. The claim that values are inherently good reflects the Aristotelian tradition, where virtues are understood as objective goods. ACT takes a different position. In ACT, values are freely chosen directions. They are not evaluated as good or bad by an external standard. They are simply what matters to you. Values-Flow holds both perspectives in creative tension. We honour the Aristotelian insight that values-aligned living tends to contribute to the broader good. We also honour the ACT insight that the power of values comes from their being freely chosen, not externally imposed. In practice, most people find that their deepest values do contribute to the wellbeing of themselves and others, but that contribution emerges from authentic choice rather than from obligation.

Values are personal in nature, so different people have different values. Table 4.1 organises common values into six motivational families. The grouping draws on Shalom Schwartz's cross-cultural research on basic human values, and on the values tradition in ACT as articulated by Russ Harris. Values overlap, and any single value can sit in more than one family.

Table 4.1 Common Values

Family	*Motivational Core and Example Values*
Care and connection	*Caring for the wellbeing of those close to us, and extending that care outward into wider community.* Love, kindness, compassion, generosity, caring, friendliness, loyalty, forgiveness, intimacy, connection, cooperation, supportiveness, reciprocity, hospitality, filial piety, respect for elders, community harmony.
Justice and integrity	*Acting fairly and honestly, treating others as equals, and standing for what is right.* Honesty, fairness, justice, equality, trust, authenticity, responsibility, respect, open-mindedness, tolerance, accountability, dignity, courage, assertiveness.
Growth and mastery	*Developing knowledge, skill, and self-understanding through ongoing learning and effort.* Self-development, learning, curiosity, creativity, discipline, persistence, skilfulness, wisdom, self-awareness, reflection, industry, excellence, freedom of thought, independence.
Vitality and adventure	*Engaging life with energy, openness, and a willingness to seek out novelty and pleasure.* Adventure, excitement, playfulness, humour, fun, pleasure, sensuality, spontaneity, exploration, vitality, sexuality, romance.
Stability and wellbeing	*Looking after physical, emotional, and relational health, and maintaining the conditions for steady living.* Health, safety, self-care, order, reliability, resilience, patience, peace, contentment, balance, mindfulness, security, calm, organisation.
Tradition and spirituality	*Connecting to something larger than the self, whether through faith, heritage, gratitude, or service.* Spirituality, spiritual devotion, reverence, gratitude, humility, meaning, purpose, tradition, heritage, ancestral connection, service, faith, devotion, acceptance.

Read through the list and highlight the ones that resonate with you. You might find a lot of them resonate, or only a few. There is no right or wrong answer. If a value that is central to you is missing, add it in.

Your **core values** are the beliefs that are most critical to your identity and drive what you do and what you care about. Go back to the list above and circle the five values that are most important to you. These are your core values. Secondary values are things that you care about but are less central to your identity (the rest of the values that you highlighted). For Values-Flow, both primary and secondary values are important to identify.

From Goals to Values: A Key Distinction

Many people **aim for goals** (e.g., get a promotion, lose 10 pounds) without reflecting on the *values* underneath (e.g., personal growth, wellness, creativity, collaboration). Goals are tangible, tick-off-the-list achievements. Values are ongoing qualities of action:

- **Goal**: "I want to run a marathon."
- **Underlying Values**: "I value health and self-discipline."

Once that marathon is over, your training might stop. But the values "health and self-discipline" keep guiding your choices every single day. You might have personal (individual), social, and/or cultural goals. You might have work goals or family goals. They might be short term (I want to start running), medium term (I want to run a marathon), or long term (I want to become a regular runner). But they are things that you can make progress towards and achieve.

Values, in contrast, never expire. They are a core part of who you are as a person and are your deeply held beliefs. They are things that you care about simply because that is part of you as a person. They simply are...you.

Aligning Your Actions with Your Values

Once you've identified your core and secondary values, the challenge is to live your life in ways that align with your values. A lot of misery can arise from living in a way that is counter to what you value. For instance, if you really value your family, but you sacrifice all of your time that you could spend with them to work at your job, over time your quality of life might diminish. In contrast, if you prioritise spending time with your family and then adjust your work around your family time, you are more likely to experience a sense of thriving. Ask yourself, how can I align my everyday actions with my values?

Character Strengths

Character strengths are the things that we are good at. Research suggests that there are lots of benefits of identifying and using our strengths on a regular basis. You might think that it is best to focus on your weaknesses, but research suggests that there's a greater benefit of focusing on your strengths.

There are different strengths that have been identified in the literature. A very popular list of strengths was developed by the Values in Action (VIA) Institute on Character. VIA identified 24 different strengths that appear in people to varying degrees regardless of background, beliefs, or culture (see Table 4.2). Which ones do you identify with?

Table 4.2 Character Strengths Identified by the VIA Institute

Appreciation of Beauty	Bravery	Creativity	Curiosity
Fairness	Forgiveness	Honesty	Humility
Judgement	Kindness	Leadership	Love
Love of learning	Perspective	Perseverance	Prudence
Self-regulation	Social intelligence	Teamwork	Zest
Gratitude	Hope	Spirituality	Humour

As with the values list above, the VIA framework was developed primarily within Western psychological research. Some strengths that are highly valued in particular cultural traditions may not be well captured by these 24 strengths. If you come from a background where strengths like collective responsibility, spiritual discipline, or relational attunement are central to how you understand good character, you may want to supplement the VIA list with strengths that feel more culturally resonant. The goal is self-knowledge, not conformity to any particular framework.

You might notice that some of the core values and character strengths have the same names. Values are personal beliefs that drive you, whereas character strengths are traits that help you put your values into action. For instance, you might value kindness (reflecting the core belief that other people are worthy of care), so you draw on your strength of kindness (one of your character traits) to do kind acts for others.

The VIA Institute has developed a survey that you can take to identify your top character strengths and learn how to put these strengths into action. Go to www.viacharacter.org. A box will come up to get you started. Complete the survey, which takes 10–15 minutes to complete. At the end of the survey, you will get a report identifying your top strengths. Write these down in a prominent place, so that you'll remember them.

If the survey sounds too overwhelming, then simply review the list of 24 strengths above. Which ones resonate the most with you? These are likely your top strengths.

The next step is to learn more about your top strengths. On the VIA website, click on the top tab "Character Strengths." This will bring up a page with the 24 strengths. Click on the ones that you identified as your top strengths. This will give a lot more information about the strength—what it is, and how it can be manifested in everyday life.

While it's helpful to know what your strengths are, research shows that the real benefit arises from putting your strengths into action. So, a critical step is to *use* your strengths. The VIA website includes ideas on how to use your strengths. As we put our strengths into action, it helps us live in accordance with our core values, leading to a meaningful and engaged life. For instance, if one of your top strengths is gratitude, then you might start each day by writing a gratitude list. If one of your top strengths is teamwork, then you might ask your boss to work on group projects rather than solo projects.

Why Focus on VIRTUE?

When you combine values and strengths, you engage with life in ways that feel both purposeful and natural, helping you reside on the upper floor of the House. Think of VIRTUE as your **internal compass**. Even if storms hit (e.g., stress, anxiety, conflict), you can reorient to your "true north" and keep going by putting your strengths into practice and staying true to your core values.

One reason why VIRTUE is so important is that it helps us engage in things that we are internally motivated to do. We do things for different reasons. Some things we are not motivated at all to do. This is **amotivation**. For instance, you might have no motivation to exercise, and it's not important to you, so you don't exercise. Other things are motivated by our circumstances or the people around us. This is **external** or **extrinsic motivation**. For instance, your workplace might offer a monetary reward for regularly exercising, regardless of whether or not you want to exercise. So, you exercise to get the money. Then there are the things that you do because they are really important to you. This is **internal** or **intrinsic motivation**. For instance, you might view yourself as an athlete, and staying physically fit is an important part of your identity, so you regularly exercise just because you want to. When your actions align with your deeply held values, you're fuelled by intrinsic motivation. You become less reliant on external "have-tos" and more focused on your personal "want-tos."

A second reason that VIRTUE is important is that it gives us **clarity in tough times**. Distress, doubts, and obstacles can make it hard to function. We might shut down and not do anything, or we might avoid doing tasks that are unpleasant. It becomes easier to navigate hard times when you remember *why* you're doing what you do. That's core values at work. For instance, you might be having behavioural problems with one of your children. But you care deeply about your child, which connects with your value of love. So you discipline them in a loving manner, letting them know what is and is not acceptable to do, and showing that you are putting this boundary in place because you love them.

A third reason that VIRTUE is important is that it promotes **resilience** and **personal growth**. Remember that VIRTUE is your compass, pointing you where you should go regardless of what is happening in or around you. Drawing on personal strengths helps you handle curveballs more flexibly, fostering a sense of ongoing growth.

From a DBT perspective, knowing your values also supports the emergence of Wise Mind. When you are clear about what matters to you, Wise Mind has an anchor. In moments of confusion or emotional intensity, where Emotion Mind pulls you one way and Reasonable Mind pulls you another, your values provide the reference point from which Wise Mind can discern the most effective path forward. Values clarity does not remove the difficulty of navigating complex situations. But it gives Wise Mind something solid to work with. Without values clarity, Wise Mind is navigating without a compass.

Importantly, living by your values doesn't require feeling good first. This is a crucial ACT insight. You don't have to wait until anxiety passes, until you feel confident, or until conditions are perfect. You can act on your values right now, with whatever feelings are present. The feelings can come along for the ride. This is the opposite of the *control agenda*, the belief that you need to fix your internal state before you can live well. Values-based action says: move towards what matters and let your internal experiences be what they are.

Another important distinction from ACT is worth noting here. Values are not the same as rules. Rules prescribe specific behaviours rigidly. "I must exercise every day" is a rule. "I value health" is a value. The rule can be broken, producing guilt and self-criticism. The value cannot be broken, because it is a direction, not a standard. If you miss a day of exercise, you have not violated your value of health. You have simply had a day where you did not move in that direction. Tomorrow you can move in that direction again. This flexibility is what makes values so powerful compared to rules. Rules create rigidity. Values create direction with room for the inevitable variability of being human.

VIRTUE and Flow: A Natural Match

Recall how flow is more likely to occur when challenge meets skill. Aligning tasks with your values and using your strengths ensures you're motivated, engaged, and open to the natural feedback loops that spark flow. For example:

- If one of your top values is "wisdom," and you have the strength of "curiosity," you might immerse yourself in reading about new strategies that can be applied to your work. The challenge is high enough to keep you engaged, and drawing on your strength keeps you on task, creating the conditions that make flow more likely to occur.
- If one of your top values is "connection," and you have a strength of "kindness," you might volunteer at a community centre. You're challenged to find ways to connect with community members, and your kindness provides a pathway to foster connection, again creating conditions for flow to occur.

Notice how values contribute to several of the nine flow dimensions we described in Chapter 2. When an activity connects to something you genuinely care about, you are more likely to give it your total concentration. Self-consciousness recedes more easily because your attention is invested in the activity rather than in monitoring how you appear. The activity feels intrinsically rewarding (the autotelic dimension), precisely because it expresses a freely chosen value. And challenge–skill balance becomes easier to calibrate because intrinsic motivation keeps you willing to stretch rather than retreat. Values do not guarantee flow. But they create the fertile ground from which multiple flow dimensions can emerge.

Bringing VIRTUE into Practice

Bringing this all together, how can you put VIRTUE into practice? First, identify your core values (see Table 4.1). Jot these down and place them in a visible spot, so that you can reconnect with your core values on a daily basis. Also identify your secondary values, which offer additional directions to focus upon.

Do not rush this step. Values clarification is not something to be ticked off a to-do list. It requires genuine contact with what matters to you, and that contact often involves vulnerability. If you find yourself quickly selecting values that sound socially desirable, pause. Take a breath. Ask yourself whether these are truly your values or whether they are what you think you should value. As we described in the opening of this chapter, James's quick answer of "success" was a protective response, not genuine values contact. Give yourself permission to sit with uncertainty. The values that matter most are often the ones that take the longest to name.

Second, identify your top strengths (see Table 4.2). Take the VIA survey. Reflect upon your top strengths that are identified. Do they resonate with you? If so, how can you use these strengths in your everyday life? If they don't resonate with you, read through the other strengths on the VIA site and identify which ones do resonate. If you're unsure, check with a family member, friend, or colleague. What strengths do they see in you?

Third, put your values and strengths into practice. The VIA site gives some examples, but consider what this practically looks like for you, tying your values to your strengths. For instance, if you value "contribution," and your strength is "leadership," maybe you can host a neighbourhood clean-up. If you value "authenticity," and your strength is "humour," your next presentation can include a personal anecdote or light-hearted story.

Fourth, track your progress using the Values-Flow Card. Under "VIRTUE," rate the extent to which you put your values and strengths into action on a 0–6 scale (Table 4.3).

Finally, observe your thoughts and feelings associated with using your VIRTUE skill. Did you have glimpses of flow? Did the task challenge your skills or prompt you to learn something new? What worked and what didn't work? How can you live more aligned with your values and strengths tomorrow?

But also ask: Did I act on my values today, regardless of how it felt? Did I use my strengths in service of what matters? These questions honour the process, not just the experience.

Table 4.3 Rating Scale for Your VIRTUE Practice

Score	*Meaning*
0	Didn't reflect on my values and strengths or practise them.
1	Reflected on my values or strengths, but didn't attempt to put them into practice.
2	Attempted to put my values and strengths into practice, but it had no effect on how I felt, thought, or acted.
3	Attempted to put my values and strengths into practice, but got bored or listless.
4	Attempted to put my values and strengths into practice, but felt overwhelmed or anxious.
5	Put my values and/or strengths into practice. It was enjoyable, but I didn't experience flow.
6	Put my values and/or strengths into practice and experienced flow (enjoyable absorption).

Flow Nudges

Here are a few ways that you can put VIRTUE into practice:

1 **Mini-Values Check**: Before starting any meaningful activity, ask: *"Which value would I like to express here?"* or *"Which strength can help me show up fully?"* This quick mental note connects you to VIRTUE, helping you to reside on the upper floors of the House.
2 **Celebrate Small Wins**: At the end of a day, note a moment when you lived in line with your values. Maybe you listened patiently instead of rushing through a conversation, or used creativity to solve a problem. Acknowledge that you showed up for what mattered, not because it felt good, but because it was meaningful to you.
3 **Mini-Shift for Alignment**: If you realise a task feels dull or forced, see if you can tie it back to a core value or incorporate a personal strength. Turn "data entry" into "improving organisational efficiency for my team" (aligned with the core value of contribution) using your strength of "self-regulation."

Sound Bite Summary

Key points to remember from this chapter:

1 **VIRTUE** keeps you oriented towards what truly matters and leverages your natural abilities.
2 **Values** are freely chosen directions that give life meaning. They are not goals to achieve, but qualities of action to express.
3 **Strengths** are the personal capabilities that help you enact those values.
4 **Flow** is far more likely to occur when tasks align with your core values and personal strengths, and you successfully negotiate the challenges at hand. But remember that flow is not the goal, values-aligned engagement is. Flow is what sometimes happens along the way.
5 On the **Values-Flow Card**, use the VIRTUE section to note daily reflections and whether you showed up for what mattered, regardless of how it felt.
6 **Revisit** your core values and top strengths often, especially when tasks feel stale or meaningless.
7 **You can act on your values right now**, with whatever feelings are present.

Final Word

Living in alignment with your values and strengths transforms everyday routines from chores into opportunities. By weaving VIRTUE into your daily decisions, you create the conditions for Values-Flow to occur. You are consistently fuelling your sense of purpose and wellbeing, helping you reside on the upper floors of the House of Functioning.

And on the days when engagement feels flat, when you're going through the motions, when flow is nowhere to be found, remember that you can still express your values. That's the quiet victory: showing up for what matters, not because it feels good, but because it is good. That's VIRTUE in action.

Notably, you will never finish values work. Values are not a destination you arrive at and then move on from. They are a lifelong practice of returning, again and again, to what matters. Some weeks you will live in close alignment with your values. Other weeks you will drift. The drifting is not failure. It is simply what happens in a human life. The practice is in the noticing and the returning. Every time you notice that you have drifted and gently redirect yourself towards what matters, that noticing is itself a values-aligned act.

Next, we'll explore **INVOLVE**, focusing on how we *attend*, *reflect*, *inform*, and *act* when life's challenges appear, so that even the trickiest moments become stepping stones towards deeper engagement.

5 INVOLVE

The ARIA Skills

Chapter Overview

This chapter describes the second Values-Flow skill: INVOLVE, which transforms mere activity into meaningful engagement through the ARIA (Attending, Reflecting, Informing, and Acting) cycle. We describe the ARIA skills and give practical ways that you can practise these skills. Sustained practice of the ARIA skills gets you through challenging seasons and has positive ripple effects for the communities that you are a part of. The INVOLVE skills focus on *how* to put values into action.

The Vulnerability Beneath the Values

Meet Vecky. She's 38 years old, a project manager at a tech company, and she knows something is missing. It's not that she doesn't know what she values. When her coach asked what she truly valued, Vecky easily responded: "I value achievement, being a reliable worker, being fit and healthy, and spending time with my family." But then her coach asked her how she was living according to her values. She froze. "I don't know. I'm trying to be everything to everyone. But in the process, I'm not truly there for my family or as reliable a worker as I'd like to be."

Vecky isn't unusual. Most people spend little time thinking about what is most important to them on a deep, personal level. If they do consider their values, they hardly live according to them. They live according to what they perceive as others' expectations of them, rather than what truly matters to them. They spread themselves too thin, and then break down when it all becomes too much.

Why do we so easily sacrifice our own values to fit the desires of others? Beneath our values lies immense vulnerability. Touching what you most yearn for in life carries with it a huge amount of risk. In living according to your values, you must accept that others may not approve of your actions, you might not get the things you long for, or even lose what you value most, and that you might be better off where you are now. Known suffering is less risky than facing the unknown. There is something safe about keeping things the

DOI: 10.4324/9781003771173-7

way they are, to the point where change can feel unnecessary, dangerous, or even impossible.

People have a host of strategies for insulating themselves against this vulnerability. Some of these might seem familiar: resistance to exploring what matters to you, laser focus on surviving life, chronic "stuckness," endless "I don't know" responses, insistences that "nothing matters," or elaborate stories about why you can't reach for something more. On the surface, these behaviours look different. But functionally, they are the same. They are protection in the form of what ACT calls *fusion* and *avoidance*.

From an ACT perspective, these protective strategies serve the same function. They reduce contact with what matters to reduce the pain of potentially losing it. This is experiential avoidance in action. The ARIA cycle is designed to gently interrupt this pattern, not by attacking the avoidance directly (which often strengthens it) but by creating the conditions under which a different relationship to vulnerability becomes possible. Each ARIA step cultivates a different facet of *psychological flexibility*. Attending cultivates present-moment awareness. Reflecting cultivates defusion and self-as-context. Informing cultivates acceptance of what is present. Acting cultivates committed action in the direction of values. Together, they form a complete psychological flexibility practice.

Here's the surprising opportunity: there is a light in those dark moments when you feel most stuck. In that darkness, you can see a glimmer of something longed for, something that might even be more powerful because it's so tightly bound and protected. You can use your own protective strategy as an entry point to find your way to the heart of your deepest concerns and desires.

Recall from Chapter 4 that VIRTUE captures your *why*—the core values and character strengths that guide a life well lived. **INVOLVE** focuses on the *how*. It's the bridge between your deepest intentions and the tangible ways you show up in the world. Think of INVOLVE as the engine that transforms values from abstract ideals into lived experiences, creating the conditions where optimal experiences can naturally emerge.

The Power of Doing

This chapter is about INVOLVE, but not the kind of involvement that skims over vulnerability. INVOLVE is about showing up for what matters in a way that honours both the longing and the risk. It's about transforming mere activity into meaningful engagement through a cycle we call **ARIA**: **A**ttending, **R**eflecting, **I**nforming, and **A**cting.

But here's what we need to be clear about from the start. Insight is not the fuel of values work, but rather it's the exhaust. We're trying to facilitate a creative approach to life that's disruptive of the protective mindsets that keep us stuck on the lower floors of the House.

In developing the ARIA framework, we have drawn heavily on the work of Kelly G. Wilson, one of the original developers of ACT and a master clinician.

Wilson articulates five principles that guide transformative engagement with what matters most to a person. Each element of ARIA corresponds to one of Wilson's principles, helping us move *through* protective barriers rather than around them:

- **Attending** embodies Wilson's "Slow is Fast."
- **Reflecting** embodies Wilson's "Small Is Big."
- **Informing** embodies Wilson's "Meet Yourself in the Work."
- **Acting** embodies Wilson's paradox: sometimes, "Taking Action Off the Table" is what allows genuine movement to emerge.

Wilson's fifth principle—"Assume Magnificence is Possible"—runs through the entire ARIA cycle, reminding us to hold unrelenting curiosity for what remarkable changes might be possible, even when we feel the most stuck.

What Is INVOLVE?

In the Values-Flow framework, INVOLVE represents a dynamic cycle of engagement with life through four interconnected skills. These aren't just discrete actions to check off a list; they form a continuous loop of awareness and response that keeps you connected to both your inner experiences and the outer world. When these four elements work in harmony, they create a rhythm of engagement that makes flow experiences more probable.

Whether you're navigating a difficult conversation with your teenager, tackling a complex project at work, or simply trying to be more present during your morning routine, these four skills provide a framework for meaningful engagement in life. They transform potentially overwhelming situations into manageable sequences of attention, understanding, learning, and action.

Importantly, the ARIA cycle describes universal processes of human engagement, but how these processes are expressed will vary across cultures. In some traditions, attending may involve tuning into the group rather than to individual feelings. Reflecting may be done through storytelling, prayer, or consultation with elders rather than through private introspection. Informing may draw on collective wisdom and ancestral knowledge rather than on individual strengths alone. And acting may prioritise communal wellbeing over individual values expression. These cultural variations are not departures from the ARIA framework. They are expressions of it. The underlying cycle of awareness, understanding, learning, and action is universal. The forms it takes are diverse.

Attending: Slow Is Fast

Attending means paying mindful attention to what's happening right now, both inside you (your thoughts, emotions, behaviours, and sensations) and around you (your current context, other people, and the environment).

It's the foundational skill that prevents you from sleepwalking through life on autopilot, lost in worries or daydreams about the future or ruminations about the past.

Here's the crucial insight from Wilson's work: moving slowly is the fastest, and often the only, way to do this work.

When you ask yourself questions about what you long for in life, very often you'll launch into a well-worn narrative about who you are, how you've tried and failed before, and what you're allowed to have. This story is typically full of words like "always," "never," and "should."

We can do something very simple and gentle to disrupt that protective repertoire: slow down. Literally slow your internal pace to the point where you can hear the space between the words. Don't answer questions about what matters right away. Take a deep breath and sit with each question. Don't just visit the question, inhabit it.

Slowing down destabilises the protective armour you've put up around what you care about. Sometimes emotion surfaces simply from that change of pace. It allows other responses to emerge that might otherwise be denied breathing room. And it has a flavour of acceptance, because moving slowly requires sitting with experiences rather than skimming over them with the problem-solving mind.

Attending builds upon core concepts in both ACT and DBT. In ACT, mindfulness is emphasised in *Contact with the Present Moment*, the ongoing, non-judgemental contact with psychological and environmental events as they occur. In DBT, mindfulness is the foundation from which the other core modules (distress tolerance, emotion regulation, and interpersonal effectiveness) are built. Both therapies place mindfulness at the centre of being able to accept our current circumstances, our experiences, and ourselves.

For flow, attending creates one of the essential conditions: concentrated attention on the task at hand. Csikszentmihalyi found that flow requires what he called "total concentration." But here's the paradox: you can't *force* concentration. You create conditions for it by slowing down, removing distractions, and allowing attention to settle naturally onto what's before you. This is Wilson's "Slow is Fast" in action.

Why It Matters. Without awareness, we slip into autopilot, get lost in daydreams or worries, or find ourselves ruminating about the past. Without genuine attending, we miss crucial information that could guide our responses. We might fail to notice the subtle tension in a colleague's voice that signals misunderstanding, or the tightness in our own chest that warns of mounting stress. Attending allows us to show up in life, for ourselves and for those around us.

How to Practise. There are numerous brief mindfulness-based exercises that put Attending into practice. Some are informal, intentionally placing your attention on something within or around you. Others are formal meditations using techniques like paced breathing or imagery.

- **Micro Mindfulness Moments**: Pause for a breath and notice your posture, your next inhalation, and the feel of your feet on the floor. These moments of reconnection can happen while waiting for your coffee to brew or sitting at a red light.
- **Caring Attention**: Approach your observations with warmth. For instance, "I'm noticing tightness in my chest. Let me gently check in with that. What is it telling me?"
- **5-4-3-2-1 Grounding**: Identify 5 things you can see, 4 things you can hear, 3 things you can touch, 2 things you can smell, and 1 thing you can taste. This sensory grounding is particularly helpful when anxiety threatens to pull you out of the present moment.
- **Box Breathing**: Slowly breathe in to the count of 4, hold for 4, exhale for 4, hold for 4. As you do this, your nervous system settles and your attention naturally sharpens.
- **Mindful Hands**: Hold out a hand and carefully observe the colours, lines, and contours of each finger and palm. Stretch your hand wide and watch how the colours change.
- **The Slow Question**: Following Wilson's principle, when facing a values question, don't answer immediately. Take three deep breaths. Let the question settle. Notice what arises in the silence before the words come.

Reflecting: Small Is Big

Reflecting involves stepping back to think about what you're experiencing, rather than immediately reacting to the situation. Your thoughts might be spinning out of control, or you might be feeling a series of negative emotions. When this happens, we often react in automatic ways. A person criticises you and you snap back a harsh comment. Someone cuts you off in traffic and you scream at them with rage. Reflecting involves purposely pausing to transform raw sensory and emotional data into meaningful understanding.

The principle here, drawn from Wilson's work, is to *get granular*. Fusion and avoidance thrive in abstractions and generalisations, but values live in the details. This is what Wilson means by "Small Is Big."

If you find yourself persistently returning to a vague sense of dissatisfaction at work, in relationships, or with life itself, there's usually an unfulfilled value behind that. But rather than attacking that dissatisfaction directly, to get at it, you need to take a step back and observe the texture of that dissatisfaction. Don't stay at the level of "I feel unfulfilled." Go to a specific instance: "Last Tuesday, when my colleague dismissed my idea in the meeting, I felt my chest tighten and I thought 'What's the point?'" Then go slowly, examining the circumstance frame by frame. What thoughts, emotions, and sensations showed up? Rather than breezing over these, take the time to reflect upon them, and ask yourself what they might be telling you.

In those granular experiences, you'll find both loss and longing. The dismissal hurt because being heard matters to you. The "What's the point?"

thought was protecting you from the vulnerability of caring about contribution. Even seemingly superficial concerns can yield something meaningful if you go into the details.

Reflecting also arises from what ACT calls the *Observing Self*. As we described in Chapter 2, this is the part of you that can notice your thoughts, feelings, behaviours, and sensations without judgement, simply observing what is there. The Observing Self is the "you" that has been present throughout your life. When you tap into the Observing Self, you create space from which you can examine experience like a precious object, turning it over, noticing its details, rather than being consumed by it.

ACT introduces *defusion* techniques that can help you create space between your thoughts and emotions and how you respond to them. Instead of saying to yourself "I'm a failure," purposely shift the thought to "I'm having the thought that I'm a failure." This creates distance from the thought itself, allowing for clearer reflection on what's actually happening versus what your mind is constructing.

From a DBT perspective, Reflecting is where *Wise Mind* becomes most accessible. As we described in Chapter 2, Wise Mind is not a compromise between emotion and reason but a qualitatively different state that transcends both. When you slow down (Attending) and then step back to observe your experience without judgement (Reflecting), you are creating the conditions under which Wise Mind can emerge. The "Relax into Wise Mind" exercise listed below is one of the most direct pathways into this state. But the entire Reflecting step, when practised with the slow, granular attention that Wilson describes, is itself a form of Wise Mind practice. You are holding both what you think and what you feel, allowing a deeper knowing to surface.

How to Practise:

- **The Specific Instance**: Embodying Wilson's "Small Is Big," when something feels important or painful, ask: "Can I recall a specific moment when this was particularly true?" Then explore that moment in granular detail—what you saw, heard, felt in your body, and thought.
- **Curious Lens**: Pause and ask yourself where you are at in the current moment, with an attitude of curiosity. Ask open questions like, "What might this feeling be telling me?" or "What options do I actually have here?"
- **Find the Middle Ground**: Strive for a balanced perspective that honours both reason and emotion. Ask yourself, "What do I want?" "What do others want?" Identify where the two meet and proceed mindfully.
- **Relax into Wise Mind**: Sit in a comfortable position. Breathe in saying "wise" and breathe out saying "mind." This grounds you, pulling you out of overwhelming emotions or reminding your reasonable side to check in with your feelings.

- **Defuse from Your Thoughts**: Say to yourself "I'm having the thought that I am stressed," rather than ruminating that "I am stressed."
- **Appreciating the Value**: Once you glimpse a value beneath the details, don't rush past it. Spend time simply appreciating it, examining it like a precious object, and exploring its details.

Informing: Meet Yourself in the Work

Informing means actively gathering relevant information, both from your past experiences and your present environment, to shape your next step. Whereas Reflecting is about noticing your thoughts and feelings, Informing is about gathering evidence of your skills, internal and external strengths and resources, and a realistic picture of the situation you're in to determine what the most effective action might be.

The principle here, adapted from Wilson, is: "meet yourself in the work." Wilson originally framed this as "meet clients in the work" for therapists, but the principle can be equally applied to our own inner work.

This means putting yourself fully in the work as a participant observer. Not as a detached observer cataloguing data, but as someone willing to be affected by what you discover. Ask yourself searching questions about what your thoughts, emotions, sensations, or behaviours are telling you. For instance, if you notice resistance or stuckness, ask yourself what it might be telling you. Don't treat it as an obstacle to overcome. Don't make yourself go where you don't want to go. There are other ways in. Just notice the resistance, accept that it is there, and be curious.

Informing draws upon the *Acceptance* part of ACT and DBT. From ACT, it's important not only to acknowledge the current circumstance we are in and the challenges that situation might be causing, but also to allow those challenges to be present. We are not trying to change them. We are simply identifying and documenting in our mind what is present. DBT builds on this by suggesting that we cannot change until we have accepted our current circumstances; our thoughts, emotions, behaviours, and sensations; and what the most effective pathway moving forward might be.

This is where Flow Theory makes a distinctive contribution. Csikszentmihalyi identified immediate feedback as one of the essential conditions for flow. You need real-time information about how you're doing to stay engaged and adjust your approach accordingly. But in values work, feedback isn't just about task performance, it's about noticing what your reactions are telling you about what matters. The protective behaviours themselves are information. If you find yourself going blank when asked about what matters to you, that blankness is data, perhaps telling you that you are not clear on what your values are. If you notice yourself launching into a rapid-fire narrative about your values, that speed is data, perhaps telling you that you are afraid of being vulnerable enough to share your values. If you feel the urge to change the subject or dismiss something as unimportant, that urge is data. All of it points towards something worth protecting, which means something worth caring about.

How to Practise:

- **Strengths Check**: In Chapter 4, we explored character strengths. Return to these strengths now. Ask yourself, "What are my strengths?" and "What strengths could I draw on right now to effectively manage the situation?" Perhaps your creativity could help you reframe a problem, or your perseverance could carry you through a difficult patch.
- **Context Scan**: Do a quick scan of the current context: "Is this environment safe?" "Is there something in this context I'm missing?" "Is there someone who could offer a different perspective?"
- **Previous Wins**: Think back to times when you succeeded in the past: "When did I face a similar challenge? What helped me succeed or manage it last time? How could I apply that to the current situation?"
- **Real-Time Sensor Reading**: Pause mid-task to scan your body (posture, breathing, muscle tension) and the immediate environment. Treat the micro-cues that you observe as live data that can suggest an on-the-spot adjustment that can pull you closer to values-based behaviour.
- **Resistance as Information**: When you notice yourself shutting down, going blank, or wanting to move on quickly, pause. Ask: "What might I be protecting here? What's the longing beneath this defence?"
- **Check in on the HALTS**: Are you meeting your basic needs? Are you Hungry, Angry, Lonely, Tired, or Sad/Stressed? Addressing the HALTS can play a key role in helping us function effectively.

Acting: Take Action Off the Table

Acting means taking a step, whether small or significant, that is aligned with your values and guided by the insights from Attending, Reflecting, and Informing. This is where the rubber hits the road, where intentions transform into reality. Without Action, the previous three steps remain an interesting internal exercise. With Action, they become a pathway to growth and meaningful engagement.

Here's the paradox at the heart of ARIA's Acting component, drawn directly from Wilson's clinical wisdom: *sometimes the most powerful thing you can do is take action off the table.*

Values are about process rather than outcome. But when a value starts to become clear, there's a strong pull to jump straight into committed action. When we do this too quickly, we place values in the future as a goal to achieve, instead of grounding them in the present as a process to experience. And the future can be a scary place! If you have a thick layer of protective avoidance, just thinking about action will trigger your defences. The inevitability of needed action often prevents you from even opening the door to the possibility of change. Fear leads to procrastination, preventing you from moving towards values-based living.

In many cases, taking action off the table entirely and explicitly can be an important first step in being present with what matters. Instead of "What should I do about this?", spend time simply appreciating a value, examining it, exploring its details, as described in the previous ARIA skills. Rest in the present moment, moving slowly, getting granular. From that space of appreciation, the next thing to do often reveals itself naturally. Committed action becomes a choice, not a "have to" or "should."

This is the heart of ACT's *committed action*, which involves taking *effective* steps guided by your values, even when difficult thoughts and feelings show up along the way. The word "committed" implies choice, not obligation. DBT's emphasis on effective behaviour means doing what works to build a life worth living, residing within the upper floors of the House of Functioning, not doing what you "should" do just because someone said so or you feel like you have to do it.

A key dialectic emerges here that sits at the centre of both ACT and DBT. Sometimes the right action is *acceptance*: acknowledging reality as it is, making room for difficult experiences, and letting go of the struggle to control what can't be controlled. Other times, the right action is *change*: taking steps to modify your situation, your behaviour, or even your emotional state when it doesn't fit the facts. Wisdom lies in knowing which approach fits which moment. This is the accept-and-change dialectic that runs through both DBT and Values-Flow.

Furthermore, DBT's distress tolerance skills are relevant here. There are moments in the ARIA cycle when the most effective action is simply to tolerate the discomfort of not yet knowing what to do. Wilson's "Take Action Off the Table" is, in many ways, a form of *radical acceptance* applied to the uncertainty of values work. You do not yet know what action to take. You can sit with that not-knowing. You can tolerate the distress of caring about something without immediately needing to fix, change, or achieve anything. This tolerance is not passivity. It is an active, skilful choice to remain present with vulnerability rather than fleeing into premature action. The REGULATE skills that we explore in Chapter 8 provide tools for managing the emotional intensity that this kind of deep values work can produce.

Thriving and optimal performance don't happen when you stay in your head. They arise when you take action: experiment, create, play, help, move, speak. When we engage with the world and test our skills against real challenges, flow becomes possible. Acting doesn't mean rushing forward blindly. It means moving with intention, guided by awareness and understanding, even when the outcome remains uncertain. Every action becomes an experiment that generates new data for the next cycle of Attending, Reflecting, and Informing.

How to Practise:

- **Permission to Not Act**: Embodying Wilson's "Take Action Off the Table," when a value becomes clear, explicitly give yourself permission to not do anything about it yet. Say to yourself, "I don't have to act on this today.

I can just sit with it and appreciate that it matters, taking action towards it when I am ready."

- **Small Steps When Ready**: When action does feel right, break it into manageable pieces. Instead of "write the report," try "open the document and write one sentence." These small steps build momentum and often lead into greater engagement.
- **Anchor to a Value Prompt**: Before acting, name out loud the value it serves (e.g., "Connection" or "Growth"). Remember from Chapter 4 that values are directions, not destinations. Saying "I'm doing this for connection" reinforces motivation and keeps the action value-aligned.
- **Time-Box the First Move**: If you're ready but hesitant to take action, set a short timer (e.g., 5 minutes) and start. It doesn't matter what you do. Perhaps you only write one sentence on the page. But you've begun. A tight window lowers resistance, builds momentum, and often ushers you into deeper engagement even after the timer ends.
- **Be Open to Feedback**: Pay attention to how your action lands. Did it bring you closer to your value or prompt new insights for adjustment? Staying open to feedback means treating each action as data rather than as a final verdict on your capabilities.
- **Assume Magnificence is Possible**: This is Wilson's fifth principle, which runs across the entire ARIA cycle. Sometimes you might try to convince yourself that you're just stuck, that nothing could change. But belief comes and goes. Assumption, however, is a choice. Choose to assume that more is possible, even when you feel completely defeated.

The ARIA Cycle in Motion

When INVOLVE operates at its best, the four ARIA steps flow seamlessly into one another, creating a continuous cycle of meaningful engagement with life. You attend to a sensation of restlessness during a meeting. Reflecting, you realise you have something important to contribute but fear looking foolish. Informing yourself, you remember previous times when speaking up led to valuable discussions, and you notice others seem to be waiting for input. Acting, you offer your perspective with conscious vulnerability. This action immediately generates new data to attend to. How did others respond? How do you feel now? And then the cycle continues.

When Vecky first encountered the ARIA cycle, she tried to use it the way she approached everything else: quickly, efficiently, looking for the right answer. It didn't work. The "I don't know" kept coming back.

Her coach asked her to slow down (Attending—Wilson's "Slow is Fast"). Not to answer the question about what mattered, but just to notice what happened in her body when the question was asked. Vecky felt her shoulders tense. Her breath got shallow. She noticed an urge to launch into a story about success at work and providing for her family.

Then something shifted. She was invited to reflect on a specific instance (Reflecting—Wilson's "Small Is Big"). "Can you think of a moment in the last month when you felt something like longing, even briefly?" Vecky remembered standing in her backyard the previous weekend, watching her daughter chase the cats. For just a moment, she'd felt something open in her chest. Then she'd remembered the emails waiting, and the feeling closed back down.

Going frame by frame through that moment, Vecky found something: a longing for presence, for being fully in her life rather than always racing ahead to the next thing. The "I don't know" wasn't emptiness, it was protection around something tender.

As she sat with this recognition (Informing, meeting herself in the work), Vecky noticed tears forming. She felt the vulnerability of caring about presence when her whole life was structured around productivity. She noticed the part of her that wanted to dismiss this as impractical, to move on to something more "actionable." She held that resistance with curiosity rather than with judgement.

And then, crucially, action was taken off the table (Acting, Wilson's paradox). She wasn't asked to change anything, to make a plan, or to commit to being more present. She was just invited to appreciate what she'd discovered, to sit with it, to let it be enough for now. From that space of non-demand, something surprising happened: Vecky found herself naturally wanting to put her phone away during dinner that night. Not because she "should," but because presence had become real to her.

INVOLVE and Flow

Flow experiences often feel effortless, but they usually rest on a foundation of attention, reflection, real-time feedback, challenge–skill balance, and bold action. By repeatedly cycling through the ARIA steps, you create the conditions where flow experiences become more likely because:

- You're present (Attending)
- You pause to process (Reflecting)
- You stay informed by immediate feedback (Informing)
- You act in line with your values (Acting)

Repeatedly cycling through these four steps fosters a rhythmic dance that matches increasing challenges with the development of adequate skills in a values-based direction. That's the pathway towards experiencing Values-Flow.

Consider how the ARIA cycle maps onto the nine flow dimensions we described in Chapter 2. Attending cultivates total concentration. Reflecting supports the emergence of action-awareness merging, because when you have genuinely paused to understand your experience, your subsequent engagement becomes more seamless. Informing provides real-time feedback about how you are doing and helps you calibrate the challenge–skill balance by assessing your resources against the demands of the situation. Acting, when guided by values, creates the conditions for autotelic enjoyment, because you are doing what matters for its own sake. And the entire ARIA cycle, practised with Wilson's slow, granular attention, naturally produces loss of self-consciousness and transformation of time. These are not add-on benefits. They are the natural consequences of full engagement through the ARIA process.

Navigating Life's Upheavals

There will be days, perhaps weeks, when your carefully cultivated INVOLVE practice seems to evaporate—the ARIA winter. Life has a way of throwing unexpected storms our way, such as a health crisis that rocks your family, work demands that explode beyond manageable limits, or a relationship that anchored your world suddenly dissolving. During these times, you might find yourself unable to attend to anything beyond the immediate crisis, too overwhelmed to reflect, too exhausted to seek information, and reduced to being reactive rather than taking intentional action. In terms of the House of Functioning, you might find yourself back in the basement when you thought you'd made it to the upper floors. Practising the REGULATE skills (see Chapter 8) can be helpful when you are struggling to get you back into a state of mind where you can engage with the INVOLVE skills.

Times of struggle are precisely when the deeper wisdom of Values-Flow reveals itself. The INVOLVE cycle doesn't require perfection. Rather, it requires presence. When life becomes overwhelming, you might only manage one conscious breath of attending in an entire day. That single breath matters. You might only reflect for 30 seconds before bed, realising "Today was about survival, and I survived." That recognition matters. Your informing might be as simple as remembering "I've been through hard things before," and your acting might be just getting up to face another day. During crisis, these micro-applications of INVOLVE can be more powerful than elaborate practices during summer periods.

The ARIA skills can be as involved or simple as needed. The key thing is that you give them a go. Try them out when things are going okay, and then they become core to survival when life goes awry. This is Wilson's "Assume Magnificence Is Possible" in action. Even in the darkest moments, there is value in holding space for the possibility of meaningful engagement to occur.

Building Your Practice Community

The INVOLVE cycle is an internal practice, small actions that you incorporate into your everyday life. However, sustaining its long-term benefits often requires external support. This doesn't mean everyone needs to understand Values-Flow terminology or practise the ARIA skills explicitly. But it means surrounding yourself with people who support your growth, challenge your perspective, and model their own forms of engaged living.

Practice partners can offer invaluable support for sustaining INVOLVE. Meeting regularly with someone else who's exploring these skills creates accountability and shared learning. You might practise attending together, sitting in silence for five minutes, then sharing what you noticed. You can reflect on each other's experiences, offering perspectives that would be impossible to achieve alone. Informing becomes richer when you can tap into another person's knowledge base. And acting with a witness adds both courage and feedback to your values-based steps.

Sarah and Jennifer, two nurses at the same hospital, discovered this mutually beneficial power. They started meeting for coffee before their shifts, initially just to vent about workplace stress. But when Sarah introduced Jennifer to the INVOLVE concept, their meetings transformed. They began with three minutes of silent attending, noticing their internal states before the chaos of their shifts. They'd reflect together on the previous day's challenges, helping each other see patterns and possibilities. They'd share information. Sarah might describe a communication technique she'd learned, while Jennifer offered insights from a conflict resolution podcast. Then they'd each commit to one values-based action for their shift. This simple routine transformed their individual practices, helping them each to meaningfully engage in the workplace.

The Ripple Effect of Sustained Practice

As you consistently practise INVOLVE over time, it can begin to influence the people around you. When you consistently cycle through ARIA, you create what researchers call "positive contagion." Others unconsciously begin to mirror these capabilities.

In families, parents practising INVOLVE often notice their children developing greater emotional awareness and thoughtful response patterns. Children see their parents pause to attend before responding to frustration. They witness reflection happening out loud: "I'm noticing I'm getting overwhelmed. Let me think about what would help." They observe information gathering: "Remember when we handled something like this before?" And they experience values-based action: "Even though this is hard, we're going to respond with kindness."

Workplaces can shift when team members bring INVOLVE energy to their interactions. Meetings become more productive when even one person models genuine attending—putting away devices, making eye contact, and listening fully. Reflection spreads when someone says, "Let's pause and think about what we're really trying to achieve here." Informing becomes collaborative when people share relevant experiences and resources rather than hoarding knowledge. And acting with clear values creates a culture of intentional rather than reactive decision-making.

Using INVOLVE with Your Values-Flow Card

Here's how to use the INVOLVE section with your Values-Flow Card. On the Practice side of your Card, under "INVOLVE," note moments where you applied these four steps, even partially, rating with 0–6 (Table 5.1).

At the end of the week, reflect upon how well you used each ARIA skill, and rate your practice in the Overall column. Reflect upon your successes and challenges with using the skill and allow that data to inform your ARIA cycle the following week.

Values-Flow Nudges: INVOLVE in Action

1 **The Slow Question Practice**: Embodying Wilson's "Slow is Fast," once this week, ask yourself a values-based question, such as "What really matters to me?". Don't answer for a full minute. Notice what happens in the silence. Notice the urge to fill it with familiar words. Stay with the not-knowing.
2 **The Specific Instance Exploration**: Following Wilson's "Small Is Big," when you notice a dissatisfaction or longing, take it to a specific moment. Go frame by frame through that moment. Find both the loss and the longing in the details.
3 **Micro-Pause Before Taking Any Key Action**: Take three deep breaths (Attending). Ask, "What am I feeling? What's my immediate feedback?" (Reflecting). Decide which skill or knowledge is relevant (Informing). Then either pause or step forward, depending on what the most effective action is (Acting).
4 **Resistance as a Doorway**: When you notice yourself shutting down, going blank, or wanting to move on quickly, pause with curiosity. Ask: "What might I be protecting here?" The resistance is information about what matters to you.

Table 5.1 Rating Scale for Your INVOLVE Practice

Score	*Meaning*
0	Didn't think about the ARIA skills.
1	Considered the ARIA skills but did not try them out.
2	Gave one or more of the ARIA skills a go but it had no effect on how I felt, thought, or acted.
3	I used one or more of the ARIA skills but got bored or half-checked out.
4	I used one or more of the ARIA skills but felt overwhelmed or anxious.
5	I practised all of the ARIA skills and felt some benefit. It was enjoyable, but I didn't experience flow.
6	I used the ARIA skills to the fullest. I experienced a sense of flow or deep involvement.

5 **Action-Free Appreciation**: Following Wilson's "Take Action Off the Table," when a value becomes clear, spend at least one full day simply appreciating it without any pressure to act. Notice how this changes your relationship to it.
6 **Involve Others**: Share your INVOLVE practice with friends or colleagues. Shared reflection can spark fresh ideas, fuelling more effective action.

Sound Bite Summary

Key points to remember from this chapter:

1 Beneath our values lies **vulnerability**. Our protective behaviours, such as saying "I don't know," the feeling of stuckness, or rapid-fire narratives, are types of fusion and avoidance. But there is light in those moments of stuckness, which can be found by going through the ARIA cycle.
2 **Drawing on Kelly Wilson's transformative principles**, ARIA embodies: Attending (Slow Is Fast), Reflecting (Small Is Big), Informing (Meet Yourself in the Work), and Acting (Take Action Off the Table). Wilson's "Assume Magnificence Is Possible" infuses the entire cycle.
3 **Slowing down** destabilises protective armour. **Getting granular** reveals both loss and longing in the details. **Meeting yourself in the work** with kindness allows vulnerability to be touched. **Taking action off the** table allows committed action to become a choice rather than a "have to" or "should."
4 By **repeatedly cycling through the ARIA steps**, you deepen engagement, refine your approach, and create a rich environment for Values-Flow to emerge.

Final Word

When you bring the ARIA principles into your daily practice, you can enter completely different conversations with yourself than you would otherwise have. You can unravel fusion, break through avoidance and procrastination, and see options beyond running from the things you care most about.

By being willing to go where it's dark and sit with yourself in that territory, you're more likely to do the kind of inner work that makes movement possible. This is how you climb from the ground floor towards the attic: not by forcing your way up, but by making genuine contact with what matters, one slow, granular, kindly-met moment at a time.

And remember Wilson's fifth principle running through it all. Assume magnificence is possible. Not as a belief you must hold, but as a choice you make. Even when the basement feels permanent, even when stuckness feels like identity rather than strategy, choose to assume that something remarkable might be available to you. That assumption does not guarantee anything. But it opens a door that cynicism keeps shut. The ARIA cycle gives you the skills to walk through that door.

When you combine INVOLVE with VIRTUE (Chapter 4), you start to live your best intentions through consistent, skilful effort. Attending to your life's moments, Reflecting on what they mean, Informing yourself with feedback, and Acting in harmony with your values is how you turn daily tasks into opportunities for flow experiences, optimal performance, and thriving in life.

In the next chapter, we'll explore VITAL—the autotelic personality and serious play that helps you say "yes" to life's mysteries and challenges, fuelling sustained engagement even when the path is uncertain. If INVOLVE is about how you show up for what matters, VITAL is about the spirit with which you show up. Together, they create something powerful: the capability to engage fully with life as it is, not as you wish it would be.

6 VITAL

Cultivating the Autotelic Personality Through Serious Play

Chapter Overview

This chapter describes the third Values-Flow skill: VITAL, which provides the creative energy and orientation that transforms going-through-the-motions into genuine engagement. VITAL represents the spirit with which you engage in life, the autotelic orientation that finds intrinsic reward in activities themselves, and integrates playfulness with purposefulness. We describe how to deal with flatness and resistance, and how you can create autotelic contexts through the 5Cs. VITAL helps create conditions for flow by removing resistance (through intrinsic interest), maintaining motivation (through serious playfulness), and enabling the challenge–skill balance where absorption becomes possible.

The Spirit of Engagement

Meet Boris. He's a 45-year-old accountant who came to therapy after what he called "hitting the wall." For 20 years, he had done everything right—built a successful practice, provided for his family, and earned the respect of colleagues. Yet somewhere along the way, the fire had gone out. "I know what I should be doing," he told his therapist. "I even know *why* it matters. But I can't seem to make myself care anymore. Everything feels like I'm just going through the motions, unmotivated to do anything."

Boris knew his core values and character strengths from the VIRTUE work in Chapter 4. He understood the INVOLVE cycle from Chapter 5. He had been practising his ARIA skills diligently. Yet something essential was missing. Not the *why* of VIRTUE or the *how* of INVOLVE, but the *spirit* with which he engaged.

This is the challenge that **VITAL** addresses. You can have perfect technique and still feel dead inside. You can know your values and still experience life as drudgery or boredom. You can cycle through all the right skills and still find yourself stuck on the lower floors of the House. You might feel like you're experiencing a midlife crisis and slip into a deep depression. Or perhaps you are not in the burning basement of crisis, but are trapped in the grey lower floor of quiet desperation, where everything works but nothing really matters.

DOI: 10.4324/9781003771173-8

VITAL is what moves you into the upper floors, towards the space of transcendence and optimal experiences.

Steven C. Hayes, one of the founders of ACT, observed that therapists and coaches have become quite good at helping people identify what matters and even at teaching the skills of committed action, but there's a "content vacuum" when it comes to sustaining meaningful change over time. How people engage with daily challenges in creative and adaptive ways has been left to "the creativity of the therapist and the spontaneous comments of the client." In other words, we've been teaching people *what to do* without adequately addressing *how to bring that doing into everyday life*.

VITAL fills that vacuum. VITAL represents the creative energy and orientation that transforms going-through-the-motions into genuine engagement. It's what Hayes was pointing towards: the creative, adaptive capability that allows values work to become sustainable meaningful engagement rather than another set of obligations to fulfil.

From an ACT perspective, the autotelic orientation can be understood as a particular expression of *psychological flexibility*. The psychologically flexible person can hold multiple perspectives, shift fluidly between acceptance and change, and engage with difficult experiences without being dominated by them. The autotelic person does something very similar, but in the domain of engagement rather than distress. They hold playfulness and seriousness simultaneously. They shift between challenge-seeking and skill-building as the situation requires. They engage with difficulty as interesting information rather than as a threat. This is not a separate capacity from psychological flexibility. It is psychological flexibility applied to the task of living fully.

What Is VITAL?

In the Values-Flow framework, VITAL captures the quality of engagement that makes flow experiences possible. It represents what Csikszentmihalyi called the **autotelic personality**, which involves having the capacity to find reward in the activities themselves rather than only in their external consequences or benefits. The word *autotelic* comes from the Greek *auto* (self) and *telos* (goal): an autotelic person does things for their own sake, because experiencing the activity itself is the main goal.

Think about the difference between two musicians approaching their daily practice. The first sits at the piano because they know they should. Their teacher expects progress by next week, and falling behind would be embarrassing. They work through scales mechanically, watching the clock, counting down until the obligation is fulfilled. The practice session yields improvement, but something essential is missing. The second musician sits at the piano because they cannot wait to discover what will emerge. They are curious about how a particular phrase might sound with different dynamics, excited to explore the edge of their current ability. Time dissolves as they become absorbed in the interplay between challenge and skill. Both musicians are practising. Both are improving. But only the latter is cultivating the autotelic personality.

Kevin Rathunde, a scientist who collaborated extensively with Csikszentmihalyi, captured this quality through the concept of **serious play**. The most engaged learners, the most creative achievers, the most fulfilled individuals share something in common: they experience their activities as simultaneously challenging and enjoyable, meaningful and pleasurable, serious and playful. This integration—being playful and serious at the same time—represents not merely optimal learning but optimal living.

VITAL is about cultivating this autotelic orientation through serious play. It involves approaching life with dual qualities that make sustained engagement possible: the playful curiosity that finds interest and enjoyment in the moment, and the serious purposefulness that connects activities to deeper meaning and skill development. When these qualities combine, something powerful emerges: what Rathunde called *undivided interest*, the state where spontaneous enjoyment and goal-directed engagement become one. The term VITAL also nods to what Jeanne Nakamura and Csikszentmihalyi called vital engagement, a relationship to the world where flow and meaning meet.

The Autotelic Personality

What distinguishes people who regularly experience flow from those who struggle to find engagement? The answer isn't talent or circumstance. It's a particular orientation towards experience that can be deliberately cultivated.

Autotelic individuals demonstrate genuine curiosity and interest in life. They approach situations with questions rather than assumptions, finding fascination in areas that others dismiss as boring or routine. While Boris saw his accounting work as an obligation, an autotelic person sees the same work as a journey of discovery. They might wonder: What patterns am I noticing in this data? How might I solve this problem more elegantly? What would happen if I approached this client conversation differently? This curiosity isn't passive wondering but active engagement. It is a drive to understand, to explore, to discover what lies beneath the surface of ordinary experiences.

Autotelic individuals also show remarkable persistence when pursuing challenges that interest them. This persistence differs from grim determination or white-knuckled endurance. It flows naturally from the intrinsic reward of engagement itself. When you find an activity genuinely interesting, continuing isn't effortful, it's what you *want* to do. The autotelic person persists not because they should but because the experience itself is rewarding. Behaviours are intrinsically motivating. You want to do it because it matters to you, not because someone else wants you to do it.

Importantly, autotelic individuals display low self-centredness during activities. This doesn't mean they lack self-awareness but rather that their attention flows outward to the task rather than inward to self-evaluation. They aren't constantly monitoring how they appear to others or comparing their performance to some standard of adequacy. This reduced self-consciousness is both a prerequisite for and a consequence of flow states. You cannot be fully absorbed in an activity while simultaneously standing outside yourself in judgement.

Notably, autotelic individuals hold seemingly opposing qualities in tandem, returning to the power of *dialectics*. They possess both curiosity and a need to achieve, both enjoyment of the process and persistence towards outcomes, both openness to novelty and the capacity for narrow concentration, both independence and cooperation. Rather than resolving these tensions in favour of one pole or the other, they contain multitudes, being able to shift fluidly between complementary modes as the situation requires. This is what Csikszentmihalyi called the "dynamic, dialectical tension" conducive to optimal development. It's also what Hayes was pointing towards when he emphasised creativity as essential for sustainable values work: the capacity to hold and integrate apparent opposites rather than being trapped by either extreme.

From a DBT perspective, this capacity to hold opposites is the essence of dialectical thinking as we introduced in Chapter 2. Linehan's entire therapeutic framework rests on the ability to hold acceptance and change simultaneously, to validate the reality of suffering while also working to build a life worth living. The autotelic person does something similar in the domain of daily engagement. They hold play and purpose, ease and effort, enjoyment and discipline in a fluid integration that neither collapses into one pole nor splits into alternation.

This is also *Wise Mind* applied to living. When you are in *Wise Mind*, you are not choosing between emotion and reason. You transcend both. Similarly, when you are in autotelic engagement, you are not choosing between play and seriousness. You are accessing a state that transcends both. The parallels are not coincidental. They reflect the same underlying human capacity for integration.

The Serious Play Integration

The philosopher John Dewey observed that the dichotomy between playful enjoyment and serious effort represents a false choice. Understanding this integration, and what happens when it breaks down, illuminates why Boris felt so stuck despite doing everything "right."

Consider what happens when we separate playfulness and seriousness. Pure play without the anchor of purpose becomes what Dewey called *fooling*—jumping haphazardly from interest to interest without accumulating skill or knowledge. The person caught in fooling enjoys the moment but never develops mastery. They start many projects but finish few. They have bursts of enthusiasm that fade quickly when the initial novelty wears off. Without the seriousness that connects activity to meaning and growth, play degenerates into distraction. In terms of the House, fooling keeps you wandering the lower floors, never finding the stairs to the attic.

Conversely, pure seriousness becomes *drudgery*—going through the motions on tasks recognised as important but experienced as joyless obligation. This was Boris' predicament. He knew his work mattered. He understood its value to his clients and family. But the *knowing* had become disconnected from the *feeling*. Achievement brought relief rather than satisfaction. Each completed task simply revealed the next obligation. Without the playfulness that makes activities intrinsically rewarding, seriousness degenerates into grinding duty. In the House, drudgery traps you on a treadmill of the lower floor of quiet desperation, expending enormous energy without ever climbing higher.

Rathunde's longitudinal work with talented teenagers revealed something striking: those who approached their talent areas with undivided interest—simultaneously experiencing high intrinsic enjoyment and high goal-directed engagement—demonstrated significantly greater mastery than their peers, regardless of initial ability levels. The highly engaged students reported undivided interest more than twice as often as those who disengaged from their talents.

For Values-Flow, this suggests that the *quality* of engagement matters more than the *quantity* of effort. Working hard at something you find meaningless often produces worse results than working hard at something that captivates you. And enjoying something without connecting it to purpose often produces worse results than enjoying something that stretches your capabilities towards valued ends.

The serious play integration involves holding both spontaneous interest (the playful qualities of excitement, openness, and intrinsic enjoyment) and goal-directed interest (the serious qualities of perceiving the activity as important, challenging, and relevant to your future) together. When both are simultaneously present, attention becomes both involuntary (spontaneously drawn to the engaging qualities of the activity) and voluntary (purposefully directed towards skill development and meaningful goals). This creates the efficient use of cognitive resources and generates the momentum that is more likely to trigger flow experiences. It's also part of the creative response functions that Hayes identified as missing from most approaches to values work, the living energy that makes commitment sustainable.

Cultivating Autotelic Engagement

Here's the good news: the autotelic personality isn't a fixed trait that you either do or do not have. It can be cultivated deliberately through practices that strengthen your capacity to find intrinsic reward in activities and to integrate playfulness with purposefulness. The mark of the autotelic personality, Csikszentmihalyi suggested, is the ability to manage a rewarding balance between the play of challenge-finding and the work of skill-building. This balance is learnable.

The cultivation begins with how you frame activities. Consider the difference between approaching your morning routine as a set of obligations to complete versus as opportunities for small experiments with presence and efficiency. The orientation transforms the experience. In the former, you mindlessly or even begrudgingly go through your routine. In the latter, every part of your routine is an opportunity for engagement, playfulness, and growth. The person who wonders *How might I bring more awareness to making breakfast?* or *What would happen if I tried this routine in a different order?* is cultivating autotelic engagement. They are finding challenge where none was externally imposed and creating the conditions for intrinsic reward to appear.

Several practices support this cultivation. First, set clear goals and review them each morning, not as a burden of expectation but as an invitation to engage. When you know what you're trying to accomplish, your attention has somewhere to go. The goal provides structure within which play can occur. This connects directly to the ARIA cycle from Chapter 5: goals inform your Attending and Reflecting, giving shape to what might otherwise be formless experience.

Second, allow yourself to become genuinely immersed in activities rather than holding yourself at a distance. You are mindfully engaged in the present moment, not ruminating on the past, judging yourself in the present, or worrying about the future. Immersion requires surrender, a letting go of the part of you that evaluates and judges yourself and allowing yourself to enter fully into what you're doing.

Third, learn to control your attention, not through forcing concentration through willpower alone but by training the capability to purposefully direct awareness. Every time you notice your attention has wandered, gently guide it back to your chosen focus, mindfully returning to the present moment. Each time you do this, you strengthen the attentional muscles that make sustained engagement possible. Over time, this training allows you to become absorbed more readily and maintain absorption for longer periods.

Fourth, learn to enjoy your immediate experience. This sounds simple but often requires deliberate development. Many of us have learned to either defer enjoyment in anticipation of some future reward, or to deny ourselves enjoyment as we don't feel worthy of it. The autotelic orientation reverses this pattern, finding reward in present activities rather than postponing or denying satisfaction. This doesn't mean abandoning future goals, but rather discovering that the journey can be as rewarding as the destination. Remember Wilson's principle from Chapter 5: sometimes taking action off the table is what allows genuine engagement to emerge. The same applies here. Sometimes releasing the grip on future outcomes is what allows present enjoyment to arise.

Ultimately, the goal is to make most of the day consist of tasks you look forward to. This might sound impossible given the realities of work obligations and daily responsibilities. But the autotelic approach transforms how we relate to those obligations. It's about changing our orientation towards our everyday behaviours. It's not about escaping to preferred activities but about bringing the qualities of curiosity, challenge-seeking, and intrinsic reward to whatever activities life presents. This is the creativity that Hayes identified as essential. Not creativity in the artistic sense, but the creative capacity to transform how we engage with what's in front of us.

The Challenge-Skill Dance

Central to both Flow theory and serious play is the dynamic relationship between challenge and skill. Flow emerges in a particular zone where challenges are high enough to require full attention (the stretch zone), but not so high as to overwhelm our current abilities (the panic zone). When challenges are too low relative to your skills, we enter the boredom zone. There's nothing to engage attention. The sweet spot occurs when challenge and skill are both elevated and roughly balanced.

What makes this insight particularly important for VITAL practice is recognising that finding this sweet spot is an ongoing dance, rather than being a one-time achievement. As your skills develop, challenges that once stretched you become routine. Yesterday's growth zone becomes today's comfort zone. Maintaining engagement requires continuously recalibrating, seeking new challenges as old ones are mastered, adjusting the difficulty of tasks to match your evolving capabilities. In terms of the House, this calibration is how you keep climbing the stairs rather than camping on one floor.

The autotelic person excels at this calibration. When they notice boredom creeping in, they intuitively seek ways to increase challenge: adding constraints, setting more ambitious goals, attempting more difficult variations. When they notice anxiety rising, they find ways to build supporting skills or break complex challenges into manageable components. This ongoing adjustment keeps them operating in the stretch zone where flow becomes possible.

This is also where serious play becomes practically relevant. The *playful* aspect involves approaching challenge-seeking as exploration and experiment rather than as grim duty. The *serious* aspect involves connecting these experiments to genuine skill development and meaningful outcomes. The combination produces engagement that is both enjoyable in the moment and productive over time.

VITAL in Daily Life

Let's return to Boris. His breakthrough came not from learning new techniques but from shifting his orientation towards the techniques he already knew. His therapist invited him to approach one routine task—reviewing monthly financial statements—with genuine curiosity rather than obligation. "Pretend you're a detective," she suggested. "What story are these numbers telling? What patterns might you notice if you were seeing them for the first time?"

At first, Boris found this ridiculous. He'd been reviewing financial statements for two decades. What could possibly be new? But he chose to challenge his assumptions and to try a different orientation to the same tasks. Something shifted when he stopped trying to get through the task and started trying to get *into* it. He noticed anomalies he'd been glossing over. He found himself curious about a client's spending patterns. He began asking questions he hadn't thought to ask in years. The statements hadn't changed, but his engagement with them did.

"It's like I remembered why I got into this work in the first place," Boris said in a later session. "Back then, I loved being a kind of financial detective—figuring out what the numbers revealed about how people and businesses actually worked. Somewhere along the way, I forgot to be curious. I was so focused on getting things done efficiently that I squeezed all the interest out of doing them."

This is autotelic engagement in action. Boris didn't change his job or reduce his responsibilities. He changed the spirit with which he met them. And that shift from drudgery to serious play began moving him up through the House, from the grey lower floor towards something more like the attic he'd experienced in his early career.

The workplace offers countless opportunities for autotelic engagement and serious play. That meeting you've attended dozens of times might become a laboratory for observing communication patterns or practising skills of attention. The routine report might become an experiment in efficiency or clarity. The colleague who usually annoys you might become a curiosity. What's really driving their behaviour? What might you learn from trying to understand their perspective?

Relationships particularly benefit from serious playfulness. Long-term relationships can fall into predictable patterns where genuine curiosity fades. We assume we know what our partners will say, how our children will react, or what our friends need. VITAL practice involves approaching familiar people with fresh interest. What if you were meeting your partner for the first time today? What would you notice? What questions would you ask? What assumptions would you not yet have formed? This curious, open stance revitalises connections that have grown stale through familiarity.

Even difficult situations can be engaged with the autotelic spirit. A health challenge might become an opportunity to learn about your body and develop new coping skills. A financial setback might become an experiment in resourcefulness and creativity. A professional disappointment might become a chance to discover what you truly value in your work. This isn't about denying difficulty or pretending everything is wonderful. It's about recognising that even in hardship, there are opportunities for growth and engagement that suffering alone would miss.

Creating Autotelic Contexts

While the autotelic orientation is something you cultivate within yourself, it doesn't develop in isolation. Certain environments systematically support or undermine the development of the autotelic personality and a serious playfulness mindset. Understanding these conditions allows you to shape your environments and to recognise when your environment is working against your VITAL practice.

Rathunde's comparison of different educational environments provides striking evidence for environmental effects. Students in Montessori settings experienced undivided interest during 40% of academic time compared to only 25% for students in traditional settings. The traditional students showed a characteristic pattern of high salience (recognising the importance of schoolwork) combined with low intrinsic motivation (not enjoying it). This is the drudgery quadrant. The difference wasn't in the students but in how the environments were structured.

Rathunde suggests that five characteristics (**the 5Cs**) distinguish contexts that support autotelic development:

1. **Clarity**: People know what's expected of them, what the goals are, and how their efforts connect to larger purposes. This clarity provides the structure within which play can occur. Without it, anxiety and confusion crowd out engagement.
2. **Centring**: Attention focuses on present concrete experiences. This doesn't mean ignoring the past or future but rather grounding engagement in the here and now. This is the essence of mindfulness, as emphasised by both ACT and DBT.
3. **Choice**: People feel they have possibilities to choose from, that their actions are self-determined rather than imposed. Autonomy is essential for intrinsic motivation. When choice is removed, engagement becomes compliance. When choice is present, even challenging activities can be experienced as self-chosen adventures.
4. **Commitment**: Others in the environment provide genuine attention and engagement to what people say or do. This attention signals that the person's engagement matters, reinforcing the value of investment.
5. **Challenge**: The environment provides increasingly complex opportunities for growth. Autotelic contexts don't make things easy. They provide appropriate difficulty that stretches capabilities without overwhelming them. This progressive challenge keeps engagement alive as skills develop, preventing the stagnation that occurs when environments remain the same.

You can use these five characteristics to assess and improve your own environments in areas where you have some degree of control. Does your workplace provide clarity about goals and expectations? Does it centre attention on present engagement or only on future results? Do you have genuine choice in how you approach your work? Do others offer committed attention to your efforts? Are challenges appropriately calibrated to your developing skills? Where these elements are missing, you might work to strengthen them, advocate for creating them, or recognise that the environment itself is working against your capacity for autotelic engagement.

Importantly, the 5Cs were identified primarily in Western educational and workplace settings. Cross-cultural research on flow suggests that autotelic contexts take different forms across cultures but still occur. In collectivist societies, commitment may look more like group solidarity than individual attention. Choice may operate within tighter social expectations but still be experienced as meaningful self-determination within those expectations. Challenge may be framed as contribution to family or community rather than personal achievement. The autotelic experience itself, as research across dozens of countries has shown, is consistent across cultures, but the contexts that produce it are shaped by cultural values and social structures. If the five characteristics listed above do not fully capture the conditions that support your own engaged living, consider what additional characteristics matter in your cultural context. What does an autotelic environment look like for you?

VITAL and Flow

Flow states don't arrive on demand. They can emerge when conditions are right. VITAL creates many of those conditions. The autotelic orientation removes the resistance that blocks flow by transforming activities from external demands into intrinsic interests. Serious playfulness provides the intrinsic motivation that sustains interest through challenge. The ongoing calibration of challenge and skill maintains the balance where flow is possible.

Consider what happens when you approach an activity with genuine VITAL energy. Your autotelic orientation means you're not holding back or protecting yourself from full engagement, as you've found something genuinely interesting in the activity. Your serious playfulness means you're intrinsically motivated while also connecting the activity to skill development and meaningful outcomes. Your challenge-skill calibration means you're operating at the edge of your ability, where full attention is required. These conditions create fertile ground for flow to naturally emerge. Remember: flow does not automatically arise when the conditions are right, but without the right conditions, opportunities for flow disintegrate.

The relationship between VITAL and flow is bidirectional. Not only does VITAL cultivation increase the likelihood of flow states, but flow experiences themselves strengthen the autotelic orientation. Each flow experience teaches you that engagement is rewarding, that curiosity leads to discovery, that challenges met with the right spirit become growth opportunities rather than threats. These positive experiences create upward spirals: VITAL cultivates the conditions for flow experiences, and flow reinforces the autotelic quality and serious play central to VITAL. Each flow experience is a step in the staircase leading upward in the House.

Professional athletes often describe this relationship intuitively. They talk about "staying loose," "enjoying the game," "seeing what happens." These aren't merely mental tricks but recognition that peak performance emerges from a particular psychological stance rather than from grinding effort or rigid control. The basketball player who's curious about what defensive formation the opponents will try next responds more creatively than one anxiously trying to remember set plays. The rock climber who engages fear as interesting information rather than being dominated by it maintains the fluid movement that challenging routes require. In both cases, the autotelic orientation creates the conditions for excellence.

Working with Flatness and Resistance

Despite understanding the value of autotelic engagement, there will be seasons when playfulness evaporates, curiosity dies, and life feels flat. These experiences aren't character flaws or failures. They're natural responses to depletion, overwhelm, or genuine misalignment that deserve understanding rather than judgement. Working with these flat states, rather than fighting them or surrendering to them, is part of VITAL practice.

It is worth recognising that flatness can also be a protective strategy. As we explored in Chapter 5, people develop a host of strategies for insulating themselves against the vulnerability beneath their values. Boris's "I can't make myself care anymore" may look different from Vecky's "I don't know" in Chapter 5, but functionally they serve the same purpose. Both protect against the pain of caring about something that feels unreachable. If you recognise this pattern in yourself, the ARIA skills from Chapter 5, particularly slowing down and getting granular, may help you discover what the flatness is guarding.

Flatness often signals that something important needs attention. Before trying to force autotelic engagement, it's worth investigating what the flatness might be communicating. Remember from Chapter 5: there is gold in stuckness. The flatness itself contains information.

At times, the engagement that once came naturally has faded because the *why* has disappeared. In these cases, VITAL practice means returning to VIRTUE (Chapter 4), reconnecting with your values and reconsidering whether your current activities serve them. No amount of playfulness will create genuine engagement with activities that conflict with your deepest purposes. In the House metaphor, this is like realising you've been climbing towards an attic you don't actually want to reach.

At other times, flatness comes from a sense of overwhelm. Here, a gentler approach is needed. Rather than demanding full autotelic engagement, you might look for tiny sparks of curiosity. Is there anything about this situation, however small, that interests you? Even minimal interest provides a foothold from which larger engagement might grow.

At still other times, flatness comes from depletion, stress, or exhaustion. Here, you might lower your challenge level for a period of time, giving yourself easier wins that rebuild confidence, energy, and motivation. Sometimes the best course of action is to rest (remember Wilson's "taking action off the table" principle in Chapter 5).

While flatness feels empty, resistance feels active, a pushing back against engagement. You might notice yourself avoiding activities you know would be valuable, procrastinating on important projects, or feeling inexplicably irritated by invitations to engage. Resistance often protects something vulnerable, as we explored in Chapter 5.

The autotelic orientation can help with resistance precisely because it doesn't demand any particular outcome. When you approach resistance with curiosity, you may ask questions such as: *What is this resistance about? What might it be protecting?* This allows you to transform the resistance itself into an object of playful investigation. This paradoxically often dissolves the resistance, because the fight against engagement was itself creating the problem. When you stop demanding that you overcome resistance and instead become curious about it, the conditions shift.

Using the Values-Flow Card to Enhance VITAL

Here's how to use the VITAL section with your Values-Flow Card. On the Practice side of your Card, under "VITAL," rate the quality of your engagement on a 0–6 scale (Table 6.1).

The VITAL row on the Values-Flow Card invites daily reflection on the quality of your engagement, not just whether you completed activities but how you showed up for them.

When rating your VITAL practice with the 0–6 scale, consider several questions. Did you approach activities with genuine curiosity, finding something interesting even in routine tasks? Did you experience moments of undivided interest where enjoyment and purpose combined? Did you calibrate challenges appropriately, neither avoiding difficulty nor overwhelming yourself? Did you find intrinsic reward in activities themselves rather than only in their outcomes?

Remember that scores are information, not judgement. A week of low VITAL scores might indicate genuine depletion requiring recovery, a mismatch between activities and values requiring reconsideration, or simply a difficult season that will pass. Patterns matter more than individual days. If you notice VITAL is consistently low despite adequate rest and meaningful activities, that pattern invites investigation. What is blocking autotelic engagement? What might need to change?

Table 6.1 Rating Scale for Your VITAL Practice

Score	*Meaning*
0	Felt completely flat or resistant and disengaged from the day.
1	Went through the motions of my day without engagement.
2	Tried to genuinely engage in activities but all felt effortful.
3	Tried to genuinely engage in activities but got bored or half-checked out.
4	Tried to genuinely engage in activities but felt overwhelmed or anxious.
5	Genuinely engaged in activities and felt some benefit. It was enjoyable, but I didn't experience flow.
6	I fully engaged in activities. I experienced a sense of flow or deep involvement.

Some practitioners find it helpful to note the balance of fooling, drudgery, and undivided interest in their daily reflections. Looking back over the day, were your actions purposeful? Did you experience a sense of enjoyment? What conditions supported the integration between seriousness and playfulness? These notes build understanding of your personal patterns and the contexts that support or undermine your VITAL engagement.

Flow Nudges: VITAL in Action

1 **The Curiosity Spark**: When facing a task that feels like drudgery, pause and ask: *What is one genuinely interesting question about this situation?* Finding even a small spark of curiosity can shift the entire quality of engagement.
2 **Challenge Calibration Check**: Notice when you feel bored or anxious. Boredom signals challenges that are too low. Ask: *How might I make this more interesting or difficult?* Anxiety signals challenges that are too high. Ask: *How might I break this down or build supporting skills?*
3 **The Integration Question**: Before beginning significant activities, ask yourself: *Am I approaching this with both playfulness and purpose?* If only one quality is present, consider what might activate the other.
4 **The Autotelic Reframe**: For an activity you typically experience as an obligation, spend two minutes finding its intrinsic interest. What value does it connect with? What skill does it develop? What might you notice if you paid closer attention? What experiment might make it more engaging?
5 **Fresh Eyes Practice**: Approach one familiar person, place, or activity as if encountering it for the first time. What would you notice if you had no assumptions? What questions would arise?
6 **Celebrate the Process**: At least once today, pause *during* an activity (not after completing it) to notice what is rewarding about the activity itself. This builds the autotelic capacity to find reward in the process rather than only in the outcomes.

Sound Bite Summary

Key points to remember from this chapter:

1 **VITAL** represents the spirit with which you engage life, the autotelic orientation that finds intrinsic reward in activities themselves and integrates playfulness with purposefulness.
2 The **autotelic personality** is characterised by curiosity, persistence, low self-centredness, high concentration capacity, and a positive orientation towards challenges. Autotelic individuals hold complementary traits in dynamic tension, the creativity dialectics that make adaptive engagement possible.
3 **Serious playfulness** integrates spontaneous interest (excitement, enjoyment, intrinsic engagement) with goal-directed interest (perceiving

activities as important, challenging, and meaningful). Neither fooling (pure play without purpose) nor drudgery (pure seriousness without enjoyment) leads to sustainable engagement or movement up through the House.

4 **Undivided interest** is the state where both playfulness and seriousness are simultaneously present, which can lead to skill development, creative achievement, and sustained engagement far better than effort alone.
5 The **autotelic orientation can be cultivated deliberately** through practices of goal setting, immersion, attention training, and learning to enjoy immediate experiences.
6 The **challenge-skill dance** requires ongoing calibration as skills develop. Autotelic individuals naturally seek to increase challenge when bored and build skills when anxious, maintaining the stretch zone where flow is possible.
7 **Autotelic contexts** are characterised by the **5Cs**: clarity, centring, choice, commitment, and challenge. These environmental conditions support the development of serious playfulness.
8 VITAL helps create **conditions for flow** by removing resistance (through intrinsic interest), maintaining motivation (through serious playfulness), and enabling the challenge–skill balance where absorption becomes possible.

Final Word

Boris' transformation didn't come from learning new skills or changing his circumstances. It came from recovering something he'd lost: the capacity to find genuine interest in what was right in front of him. The autotelic orientation he cultivated didn't make his work easier, but it made his work more alive. The same challenges that felt like obligations became sources of curiosity and engagement. He began climbing the stairs of the House again, not through dramatic life changes but through a shift in how he met each day.

This is the promise of VITAL: not that life will become effortless but that it will become more vivid. The autotelic person doesn't need circumstances to be perfect before engagement becomes possible. They bring the conditions for engagement with them, transforming whatever they encounter into an opportunity for growth and discovery.

When you combine VITAL with VIRTUE and INVOLVE, something powerful emerges. You know what matters most to you (VIRTUE). You have practical skills for showing up moment by moment (INVOLVE). And you bring the spirit of serious playfulness that transforms engagement from duty into adventure (VITAL). Together, these capacities create a life marked by meaningful and fully engaged experience as a cultivated way of being.

Today, when you look at the VITAL row on your Values-Flow Card, remember that you're not just scoring the day's engagement. You're reconnecting with your capacity to find intrinsic reward in life itself. You're recommitting to approaching challenges with curiosity rather than dread.

You're choosing to integrate playfulness with purpose, and transforming ordinary activities into opportunities for flow.

And if you find yourself reading this and thinking that autotelic engagement sounds wonderful for other people but impossible for you, remember Wilson's principle from Chapter 5. Assume magnificence is possible. Boris assumed it was impossible to care about his work again. He was wrong. Vecky assumed she would never know what she truly wanted. She was wrong. The autotelic orientation is not reserved for naturally enthusiastic people. It is available to anyone willing to slow down, get curious, and discover what happens when they approach the next moment with fresh eyes. You do not need to believe this is possible. You simply need to choose to assume it. That assumption is enough to make a beginning.

In the next chapter, we'll explore ACCEPT—the willingness that fosters resilience when facing difficulty. Where VITAL provides the spirit of engaged challenge-seeking, ACCEPT provides the foundation of willingness and acceptance that allows you to remain present even when life becomes painful. If VITAL is what helps you climb the House, ACCEPT is what keeps you from falling when the stairs get steep.

7 ACCEPT

Cultivating Willingness as the Gateway to Engagement

Chapter Overview

This chapter describes the fourth Values-Flow skill: ACCEPT, which is the skill that allows you to remain present and engaged even when life becomes difficult, to transform suffering into manageable pain, and to find your way through the lower floors of the House without becoming trapped there. Acceptance involves *willingness*, where you accept what *is*, together with responding to that reality in an effective or appropriate way. Acceptance has the capacity to transform tragedy and trauma into meaningful experiences. Acceptance does not mean approving of what happens in life, but instead is a willing stance to accept and face what life throws at you. We describe strategies to practise ACCEPT, including turning the mind and embodied practices. ACCEPT gives you the capacity to remain present and engaged even when difficulty arrives, to work with what is rather than being defeated by what isn't.

Finding Genuine Acceptance

Meet Tatiana. She's 38, a high school teacher who came to therapy after what she described as "hitting a wall I didn't even know was there." For months, she'd been waking at 3 a.m. with her mind racing through everything she couldn't control, such as budget cuts threatening her department, her mother's declining health, and a relationship that felt increasingly distant. When her therapist asked her about her anxiety, Tatiana replied, "I keep trying to accept my circumstances, but I'm not very good at it. I tell myself I should accept the things that I'm facing that I can't change, but the anxiety rages on. And then I feel guilty for still being anxious."

What Tatiana had stumbled upon was a crucial distinction. She understood acceptance as a concept. She voluntarily acknowledged and consented to her present-day reality. However, she lacked something that is fundamental to true acceptance: the quality of willingness that makes acceptance possible. She was trying to force herself to accept her circumstances, which is like trying to force yourself to sleep. The very effort works against the goal. Tatiana needed to

DOI: 10.4324/9781003771173-9

discover not just what acceptance is, but the spirit with which genuine acceptance unfolds.

Tatiana's experience illustrates something central to ACT. Her attempts to "try to accept" were a form of the *control agenda* we introduced in Chapter 2. She was using acceptance as another strategy to make the anxiety go away. But acceptance used as a control strategy is not acceptance at all. It is another form of avoidance. Genuine acceptance, as ACT describes it, is not a technique for feeling better. It is a willingness to have whatever you are having, without needing it to change. This is a subtle but important distinction.

This is where **ACCEPT** enters the Values-Flow framework. Whereas VIRTUE provides your why and INVOLVE offers your how and VITAL supplies the spirit of engagement with challenges you choose, ACCEPT addresses how you work with the challenges that arise, the difficulties that occur, and the pain that comes simply from being alive and caring about people, circumstances, and things. ACCEPT is what allows you to remain present and engaged even when life becomes difficult, to transform suffering into manageable pain, and to find your way through the lower floors of the House without becoming trapped there.

The Autotelic Personality and Acceptance: A Vital Connection

In Chapter 6, we explored the *autotelic personality*. Csikszentmihalyi described this as a capability that "easily translates potential threats into enjoyable challenges, and therefore maintains its inner harmony." This capacity doesn't mean that autotelic individuals never face challenges or that they're somehow immune to pain. Rather, it means they've developed a relationship with challenges that is grounded in acceptance rather than resistance.

A person with a well-developed autotelic orientation who encounters a major setback doesn't waste energy fighting with the fact that the setback occurred. They acknowledge the reality, feel whatever pain comes with it, and then engage with the situation as it is, rather than with how they wish it was. The autotelic quality that allows them to find intrinsic interest in chosen challenges also supports their capacity to accept unchosen difficulties. Both capacities spring from a willingness to engage with reality as it presents itself rather than demanding that reality conform to their own preferences.

This is where VITAL and ACCEPT intersect. The autotelic person brings playful curiosity to challenges they seek (VITAL) and willing acceptance to challenges that they encounter (ACCEPT). Neither capacity functions well without the other. If you can engage with challenges with enthusiasm but fall apart when difficulty arrives, you'll spend enormous amounts of energy trying to control what cannot be controlled. If you can accept difficulty but lack the autotelic spirit of engagement, you might endure life without thriving, remaining stuck on the lower floor of the House. Together, VITAL and ACCEPT create resilience, the flexibility to bend without breaking and to meet both chosen and unchosen challenges without being defeated by either.

Tatiana's situation illustrates this integration. She had some capacity for engagement when things went according to plan (VITAL), but she lacked the accepting orientation (ACCEPT) that would allow her to maintain that engagement as life fell apart. Her work was meaningful when her job was secure, but threats to that security sent her into resistance and suffering. What she needed was to develop the accepting stance that would stabilise her engagement across the varying circumstances that life inevitably brought her way.

Tragedies Transformed: When Acceptance Matters Most

Csikszentmihalyi was careful to acknowledge that: "It would be naively idealistic to claim that no matter what happens to him, a person in control of consciousness will be happy. There are tragic events—the death of a child, the torture of a beloved person, terminal illness, the loss of one's life work in middle age—that no one can welcome as challenges." Acceptance isn't about pretending that terrible things are wonderful or that genuine tragedy should be met with a smile. Some events are devastating, and any approach that fails to acknowledge this fact is disconnected from the realities of life.

Yet Csikszentmihalyi and other researchers have also documented something remarkable for those who experience various traumas and tragedies: acceptance creates possibilities that resistance forecloses. One study compared people who had been paralysed in accidents with people who had won major lotteries. Surprisingly, after some time passed, the paralysed individuals reported happiness levels that were similar to the lottery winners.

Similarly, Antonella Delle Fave and her colleagues studied people who maintained wellbeing after acquiring motor disability. They found that people didn't approve of their condition or cease efforts to maximise recovery. They accepted that the disability had occurred. From that acceptance, they could channel energy towards rehabilitation, adaptation, and building meaningful lives rather than exhausting themselves in futile resistance to what had happened. For instance, one person discovered they could advocate for accessibility rights, finding purpose in helping others avoid the obstacles they had encountered. Another developed a deep meditation practice, discovering mental stillness that they might never have explored otherwise. A third built relationships that became profoundly meaningful, realising that their previous busy life had left little space for true connection. In each case, acceptance created the foundation from which transformation became possible.

Other studies by Richard Tedeschi and Lawrence Calhoun describe *post-traumatic growth*, in which individuals experience greater appreciation for life, improved relationships, a sense of self-worth, personal strengths, new possibilities, and existential growth following traumatic events. How is this possible?

For the lottery winners, winning the lottery brought an initial emotional high. But while lotto winners believed that having excessive amounts of money would solve their problems and create everlasting joy, the money brought new problems. This included fair-weather friends who were only there when they could financially benefit from the relationship, quickly burning through the money and then being back where they started, or getting used to a new lifestyle that over time lost its initial appeal. Researchers call this the ***hedonic treadmill***. We have a set level of happiness, and though our happiness levels vary up and down, they remain fairly stable over time and circumstances.

What about the paralysed individuals? They didn't deny their reality or view their disability as desirable. Instead, they accepted their reality completely and then explored what remained possible within that reality. They controlled what was within their control and let go of what was beyond their control. They found meaning in their accident, developed new skills, created new supportive relationships, and pursued valued activities, all within the constraints of their changed circumstances.

Likewise, individuals who experience post-traumatic growth reframe the situation that they experienced, connect with others for social support, and actively make sense of the trauma. They accept that the traumatic experience occurred. It is something they can't change, but they can weave the experience into a meaningful story. For instance, the father of a child that was run over by a drunk driver might become an advocate for road safety, leading to other lives being saved and providing a sense of meaning to the bereaved father.

This connects directly to the distinction between pain and suffering that we'll explore in this chapter. Pain is the result of a broken world. Disability and trauma bring real physical and psychological pain, loss of physical or psychological capacities, and grief for the life that had been. That pain is unavoidable. But suffering is something more. It is an anguish that comes from refusing to accept what is. Pain is inevitable, but suffering is optional. When someone stops fighting reality and accepts it completely, energy that is locked in resistance becomes available for engagement. This is what allowed some people facing disability or trauma to report genuine contentment despite devastating circumstances.

Csikszentmihalyi wrote that "the integrity of the self depends on the ability to take neutral or destructive events and turn them into positive ones." This isn't about positive thinking or pretending that bad things are good. When you stop fighting with what has occurred and accept it completely, you create space to ask: "Given that this is the reality, what can I build from here? What opportunities exist within these constraints? How might I grow through this challenge?"

The importance of acceptance applies at every scale. For Tatiana, her mother's declining health was genuinely painful. Fighting with the fact that decline was happening added suffering to that pain without changing the underlying reality. When Tatiana learned to completely accept that her mother was declining, the pain remained; she still felt sad, worried, and grieved the losses occurring. But the hellish quality of her 3 a.m. anxiety spirals diminished. She could be present with her mother rather than being consumed by resistance. She could make practical plans rather than being paralysed by the narrative that "this shouldn't be happening."

Willingness and Wilfulness: Two Ways of Meeting Life

According to DBT, **willingness** is accepting what *is*, together with responding to that reality in an effective way. It's doing just what is needed in the current situation or moment. Notice that willingness includes both acceptance and a response. It's not passive resignation or giving up. It's active engagement with reality as it is, rather than with reality as you wish it were.

Wilfulness is the opposite. You impose your will on reality, trying to fix everything, or refusing to do what is needed to accept the circumstance. As the psychiatrist Gerald May simply wrote, willingness is saying yes to the mystery of being alive in each moment, whereas wilfulness is saying no—or perhaps more commonly, "yes, but..."

This distinction between willingness and wilfulness illuminates what Csikszentmihalyi observed in people who transformed tragedy. Those who maintained wellbeing weren't imposing demands on reality, insisting things be different than they were, or fighting with what had occurred. Instead, they acknowledged reality completely and then chose how to engage with that reality effectively. The autotelic capacity to find intrinsic reward in activities supports this willing stance. When you can find interest and meaning in what's present rather than only in idealised preferences, acceptance becomes possible.

Think about how this might play out in daily life. You wake to rain on a day you'd planned an outdoor event. The wilful response is immediately strategic, such as mentally arguing with the weather, running through alternative plans, and feeling irritated that reality isn't cooperating with your preferences. The willing response acknowledges that it's raining and that your preference was for sun. From that acknowledgement, an effective response becomes possible. You might still change plans, but you do so from acceptance of reality rather than from resistance to it.

Or consider the example of someone being fired from their job. The wilful response involves being consumed by "this shouldn't have happened," replaying events looking for who was at fault, and imagining how things could have been different. This response keeps you stuck in the past, fighting with what already occurred. The willing response acknowledges "I was fired, this is what happened" and then asks "What does this make possible that wasn't possible before? Might this push me towards work I find more meaningful? What can I learn from this experience?" Notice that the willing response doesn't approve of being fired or pretend it's a positive experience. It accepts that it happened and explores what can be built from that foundation.

This connects back to the ***autotelic orientation*** from Chapter 6. Remember that autotelic individuals demonstrate genuine curiosity about life, approaching situations with questions rather than assumptions. They find fascination in domains that others dismiss as boring or routine. This curious stance supports acceptance because it creates interest in what's present rather than attachment to what is preferred. When Tatiana's department faced budget cuts, her wilful response was to be consumed by how unfair this was, how her work was undervalued, and how things should be different. Her willing response began when she became curious, asking: "Given these constraints, what creative solutions might exist? What does this challenge reveal about what I most value in my work? How might I advocate effectively rather than just complaining?"

Importantly, if you witness injustice, willingness doesn't mean accepting that injustice and allowing it to continue. If you face a health crisis, willingness doesn't mean passively accepting decline without seeking treatment. The difference is in the spirit of your opposition. Wilful opposition comes from refusing to accept that the situation is happening, being locked in a "this shouldn't be" mentality. Willing opposition comes from accepting that the situation is happening and choosing how to respond effectively. One wastes energy fighting reality, keeping you stuck in misery. The other channels energy towards effective change.

This is crucial for understanding what we mean by ACCEPT in the Values-Flow framework. **Acceptance is not approval**. You can fully accept that something is happening while simultaneously working to change it, opposing it, or protecting yourself from it.

The Baseball Game You Can't Control

ACT offers a vivid illustration for understanding willingness and wilful resistance. Imagine that life is like hitting baseballs from a pitching machine. Your job is simply to do your best to hit each ball as it comes. The machine keeps pitching. Sometimes fastballs, sometimes curveballs, sometimes pitches right in your sweet spot and sometimes way outside the strike zone.

Now imagine your wilful response. You refuse to accept that a difficult pitch is coming. You stand at the plate mentally arguing: "This isn't fair, the machine shouldn't throw curveballs, I didn't sign up for this level of difficulty, someone should fix this machine." Does your protest stop the balls from coming? Does your willpower, defiance, crying, or complaining make the machine adjust its settings to your preferences? Not remotely. The balls keep coming, whether you like it or not.

You have three options with each pitch. You can stand in the way of the ball and get hit—this is refusing to engage while being impacted anyway. You can stand there doing nothing and let the ball go by as a strike—this is passive resignation that also doesn't serve you. Or you can swing at the ball—this is willing engagement with what's coming towards you. Notice that swinging doesn't guarantee a hit. Sometimes you'll miss, sometimes you'll make contact but send the ball foul, and sometimes you'll hit a home run. But only by swinging—by willingly responding to the actual pitch rather than the pitch you wished you'd receive—do meaningful responses become possible.

Tatiana's 3 a.m. worry sessions were the equivalent of standing at the plate arguing with the pitching machine while the balls kept flying past her. Her mother's health was declining—that was the pitch being thrown. Tatiana could accept that reality and consider her options, such as talking with her mother about care preferences, researching resources, and adjusting her own schedule to provide support (the equivalent to swinging at the pitch) or she could lie awake mentally insisting this shouldn't be happening (the equivalent to letting the ball go by as a strike). The second option doesn't change her mother's health. It just adds suffering to an already painful situation.

Pain Versus Suffering: A Crucial Distinction

DBT makes a crucial distinction between pain and suffering. This distinction is older than DBT, coming from the Buddha, who taught it in what is known as the Sallatha Sutta, the discourse of the arrow. The image is simple. When pain arrives, the unwise person fires a second arrow into themselves. The first arrow is the pain itself. The second is what the mind does with that pain, the resistance, the arguing with what has already happened. Two arrows when there only needed to be one. The wise person feels only the first.

Linehan trained for years in Zen Buddhism, and she carried this distinction directly into DBT, where it became one of the foundations of distress tolerance. According to DBT, **pain** is part of living. It can be emotional or physical. Pain is nature's way of signalling that something is wrong or that something needs to be done. The pain of a hand on a hot stove causes you to move your hand away from the hot surface. People without the sensation of pain are at risk of experiencing physical injury without realising it. The pain of grief causes you to reach out for others who are lost, and without it there would probably be no societies or cultures. No one would look after those who are sick, would search for loved ones who are lost, or would stay with people who are difficult at times. The pain of fear makes you avoid what is dangerous. The pain of anger helps you overcome obstacles.

In this sense, pain serves important functions. It provides information, motivates protective action, and connects us to what we care about. Tatiana's anxiety about her mother contained the pain of loving someone whose mortality was becoming undeniable, the pain of facing her own limitations in controlling outcomes, the pain of anticipatory grief. That pain was honest and functional. It reflected her deep care for her mother.

Suffering is pain plus nonacceptance of the pain. Suffering comes when we are unable or refuse to accept pain. Suffering comes when we cling to getting what we want while refusing to accept what we have. Suffering comes when we resist reality as it is now. Pain can be difficult to bear, but suffering is even worse. The refusal to accept reality and the suffering that goes along with it makes pain worse.

Think about Tatiana's experience through this lens. She felt pain about her mother's declining health. That pain was unavoidable and reflected the depth of their bond. But she also felt suffering, arising from the mental anguish that came from refusing to accept that decline was happening, from comparing the mother who was to the mother who had been, and from projecting into imagined futures where the decline continued. The suffering didn't reduce her pain or help her mother. It just made the entire experience more difficult to bear while clouding her ability to respond effectively to what was happening.

This is where **radical acceptance** enters the picture. Radical acceptance means letting go of fighting reality. The term "radical" implies that the acceptance has to come from deep within and has to be complete. It is not partial acceptance or conditional acceptance or accepting-while-mentally-arguing. DBT suggests that radical acceptance is the only way out of hell and the lower floor of the House, the way to turn suffering that cannot be tolerated into pain that can be tolerated.

Radical acceptance transformed Tatiana's experience not by changing her circumstances but by removing the cloud of suffering that surrounded her pain. When she stopped fighting the fact that her mother was declining and accepted it completely, she could be present with her mother rather than being consumed by resistance. She could make practical plans rather than being paralysed by "this shouldn't be happening." She could feel her grief directly rather than being lost in suffering about the grief.

In the House metaphor, radical acceptance is what allows you to stop being trapped on a lower floor. The difficulty itself, the actual challenges you're facing, might keep you from immediately reaching the attic. But nonacceptance keeps you stuck, unable to move in any direction because all your energy goes into fighting where you are. Acceptance doesn't magically transport you to a higher floor, but it frees you to begin climbing the stairs again.

Willingness ≠ Approval: A Critical Distinction

Many people resist acceptance because they confuse it with condoning, approving, or surrendering to harmful situations. The confusion is understandable. In casual speech, we often use the word "accept" to mean "be okay with" or "agree with." But in the context of ACCEPT in Values-Flow, acceptance means something quite different.

Willingness actually demands opposition to destructive forces. You can willingly accept that injustice exists while opposing that injustice with every fibre of your being. You can accept that you're in pain while simultaneously seeking treatment and relief. You can accept that someone treated you badly while setting firm boundaries to prevent future mistreatment. The acceptance is of what has happened or is happening. The response to that reality remains entirely within your choice.

Think about this in terms of wilfulness and willingness. If Tatiana's workplace was genuinely toxic, her wilful resistance might look like mentally complaining about how awful it was while continuing to show up and tolerate mistreatment. She wouldn't be accepting the situation. She'd be fighting it mentally and at the same time not taking effective action to change it. Alternatively, Tatiana's willing acceptance would involve acknowledging that her environment was toxic, feeling whatever pain comes with that recognition, and then responding effectively. This might mean setting boundaries, seeking a transfer, looking for different employment, or organising with others for systemic change.

This distinction matters for situations involving actual harm or injustice. Acceptance doesn't mean becoming a doormat or tolerating the intolerable. It means seeing clearly what is happening, acknowledging the pain of it, and responding from that clear-eyed acknowledgement rather than from the cloud of suffering that comes from "this shouldn't be happening." Ironically, willing acceptance often produces more powerful opposition to harmful situations than wilful resistance does. When you stop wasting energy fighting with the fact that something is happening and redirect that energy towards an effective response, your opposition becomes more strategic and sustained.

Csikszentmihalyi's work supports this distinction. The people who transformed tragedy weren't passive in the face of difficulty. They were actively engaged in maximising recovery, building meaningful lives, and often advocating for others facing similar challenges. Their acceptance didn't mean approval of what had happened or resignation to remaining stuck. It meant acknowledging reality completely so that all their energy could go towards effective responses rather than towards futile fighting with what had already occurred.

The concept of acceptance has deep roots across many cultural and spiritual traditions, not only in Western psychology. Buddhist traditions have long emphasised equanimity and non-attachment as pathways to wellbeing. The Taoist concept of wu wei, or effortless action, involves accepting and working with the natural flow of events rather than forcing outcomes. Indigenous Australian concepts of "Dadirri" describe a deep, contemplative listening and acceptance of what is. Hindu philosophy speaks of "santosha" or contentment with what the present moment offers. The Stoic tradition in Western philosophy also emphasised acceptance of what cannot be controlled.

When we speak of ACCEPT in the Values-Flow framework, we are drawing on a universal human capacity that different cultures have understood and cultivated through different practices and languages. If your own cultural or spiritual tradition offers practices of acceptance, those practices may be powerful complements to the skills described here.

Making Order Out of Chaos

Csikszentmihalyi observed that "the ability to make order out of chaos is not the privilege of the educated or of the wealthy." This capacity appears across all circumstances and backgrounds. What distinguishes people who thrive despite adversity isn't their resources or advantages but their relationship with challenges. Those who transform challenges share a common orientation. They accept what has occurred completely and then ask what order can be created from that chaos.

This connects to a fundamental principle of life itself. Csikszentmihalyi commented that complex organisms exist by extracting energy from entropy (a disordered existence), by recycling waste into structured order. In a sense, acceptance is the psychological equivalent of this biological process. When you accept difficulty completely rather than fighting it, you become able to extract meaning, growth, and even beauty from experiences that initially appear only to be destructive. You transform chaos into order not by denying the chaos but by acknowledging it fully and then discovering what patterns can emerge.

The people with motor disabilities acquired through accident or disease who maintained wellbeing weren't denying the chaos that injury created in their lives. They acknowledged the profound disruption, everything from daily routines to life plans required reconfiguration. But they didn't stay stuck fighting with that chaos. They accepted it and then began creating a new order. They developed new routines that worked within their constraints. They discovered capabilities they hadn't known they possessed. They found meaning in dimensions of life they might previously have overlooked. The chaos was real, but order could be made from it through acceptance and creative engagement.

Likewise, those who experience post-traumatic growth don't deny the injustice of their trauma. They acknowledge that it played a transformational role in their life and forever changed their perspective on life, shattering core beliefs. But then they look for meaning and possibilities arising out of the trauma. This includes shifting their mindset to one that is different and more fulfilling than their pre-trauma levels, to one of adaptation, awareness, and sense of purpose in life.

The Acceptance Challenge

Acceptance is important, as it reduces the suffering that we experience due to our own resistance. However, it's also not easy to practise. There are several reasons why acceptance can feel difficult. At times we fear that accepting something means it will never change. If I accept my mother's declining health, does that mean I'm giving up on her getting better? This confuses acceptance with approval or with ceasing efforts to help. You can accept that decline is happening right now while still engaging in actions that improve and support her care. The acceptance is *of what is*, not *of what must be*.

At other times we've learned to not accept things as they truly are. Perhaps tantrums got us what we wanted as children. Perhaps refusing to accept limitations led to breakthroughs that wouldn't have occurred with passive acceptance. These experiences teach us that resistance sometimes works, making willing acceptance feel like giving in or giving up. Understanding these patterns helps explain why our mind keeps pulling us back towards resistance even when we know intellectually that acceptance would help.

At other times we fear that acceptance means being a passive observer. If I accept that my workplace is dysfunctional, will I just tolerate mistreatment and never advocate for change? DBT offers a helpful metaphor here. Imagine you hate the colour purple, and then imagine your room is painted purple. If you refuse to accept that the room is purple, you will never paint it the colour that you want. You'll be stuck in stubborn insistence that the room shouldn't be purple while living in a purple room. Only by accepting that it is currently purple can you take effective action to change it.

This metaphor captures something essential about the relationship between acceptance and change. *Acceptance is the foundation that makes effective change possible.*

Turning the Mind

Understanding that acceptance transforms suffering into bearable pain is valuable, but understanding doesn't automatically produce acceptance. This is what Tatiana discovered. She could intellectually grasp that acceptance would help, but finding herself at 3 a.m. with racing thoughts, intellectual understanding wasn't enough. She needed something more practical.

This is where the DBT skill of **turning the mind** is helpful. Turning the mind is where you consciously make a mental shift to accept a reality rather than resist it. It involves identifying when you are rejecting a situation, and then repeatedly and purposefully choosing to turn your focus to accept the present moment. It's a deliberate action, not an emotional state, and is action-oriented in nature. It requires repetition, as acceptance sometimes only lasts a moment or two. As you notice your mind moving back to rejection, you gently guide it back to acceptance again and again. The choice has to be made every day, sometimes many times a day, or even every hour or every minute.

Tatiana would wake at 3 a.m. with her mind racing about her mother's health. At that moment, she had a choice. She could follow her thoughts into future catastrophising and past regrets, or she could turn her mind towards acceptance. Turning the mind meant noticing she was suffering, recognising that suffering came from fighting reality, and choosing again to accept what was true in that moment. The choice didn't solve the problem immediately or permanently. A few minutes later, her mind would return to negative thoughts. So Tatiana had to turn her mind again, and again, and again. Not because she was doing it wrong or because acceptance wasn't working, but because this is simply how turning the mind functions. It's an ongoing practice, not a one-time achievement.

This connects back to the autotelic personality from Chapter 6. Remember that autotelic individuals demonstrate remarkable persistence when pursuing challenges that interest them. But this persistence flows naturally from intrinsic reward rather than from grim determination. The same principle applies to turning the mind. Each turning isn't forced endurance but rather a gentle redirection motivated by your values.

Turning the mind is also a pathway into *Wise Mind*. Recall from Chapter 2 that Wise Mind is not a compromise between *Emotion Mind* and *Reasonable Mind* but a qualitatively different state that transcends both. When Tatiana was caught in her 3 a.m. racing thoughts, she was operating from Emotion Mind (overwhelmed by anxiety) or Reasonable Mind (trying to problem-solve her way out of pain). Neither was effective. Turning the mind towards acceptance created a moment of stillness from which Wise Mind could emerge. In that stillness, Tatiana could access a deeper knowing that held both the reality of her pain and the wisdom of how to respond. Each time she turned her mind, she was not just choosing acceptance. She was choosing to access the integrated awareness that Linehan described as the foundation of effective living.

Embodied Practices

DBT also offers several embodied techniques that support the development of willingness, using the body to influence the mind and emotions. Studies in neuroscience demonstrate that your facial expressions, posture, and breathing patterns influence your emotional states, not just reflect them. The key insight is that acceptance isn't primarily intellectual. You don't think your way into acceptance; you embody your way there. The practices work with your neurobiology, not just your understanding. Your nervous system learns through repeated experience that you can be present with discomfort, that resistance isn't required, and that acceptance is possible. This learning gradually changes your default responses.

Half-Smiling

A first embodied practice that encourages acceptance is **half-smiling**. To practise it, relax your face, neck, and shoulder muscles, then half-smile with your lips while adopting a serene facial expression. Aim for a Mona Lisa–type expression. The key is remembering to relax the facial muscles. It's not forcing a grin but allowing just a slight upturn of the lips and a softening around the eyes and forehead.

Why does this work? Emotions are partially controlled by facial expressions. When you adopt a half-smile and a serene, accepting expression, you influence your emotional state towards acceptance and calm. You create a feedback loop. The facial expression signals to your nervous system that things are okay enough to soften, which helps things become more okay by reducing the stress response. This isn't about pretending everything is fine when it isn't. It's about using your body to support your capacity to sit with challenge without adding layers of tension and resistance.

You can practise half-smiling in various contexts. Try it when you first wake in the morning, setting an intention for willing acceptance before the day's challenges arrive. Try it during free moments, such as waiting in line or sitting at a traffic light, using these tiny gaps as opportunities to practise the accepting facial expression. Try it while listening to music, coupling the practice with something that you already find to be pleasant. If you want to challenge yourself, try it when you're irritated, using the physical practice to interrupt the tendency towards tension and resistance.

Tatiana found half-smiling particularly helpful during difficult conversations with her mother. When her mother talked about fears related to declining health, Tatiana's natural facial response was tension, with a worried frown, furrowed brow, and tight jaw. She noticed this expression amplified her anxiety and made it harder to stay present with her mother. By consciously adopting a half-smile, relaxing her face while maintaining engaged attention, Tatiana found she could be with her mother's fears without being overwhelmed by them. The practice didn't eliminate the pain of the conversation. It just removed some of the suffering that came from resisting the pain.

Willing Hands

A second embodied practice that helps foster acceptance is **willing hands**. To practise it, intentionally relax your body. Unclench your hands, turn your palms upwards, and let go of tension. This technique tells the brain that you are calm, reducing the suffering that you are experiencing through resistance. You can practise it when you are seated, standing, or lying down. If you are seated, rest your hands on your lap with your palms facing upwards, relaxing your fingers. If you are standing, keep your arms by your side, open up your hands, and have your palms face forward. If you are lying down, place your arms at your sides, unclench your hands, and face your palms up.

When Tatiana couldn't sleep at 3 a.m., she started to adjust her body posture. She noticed the anxious thoughts, let her arms fall by her side, lifted up her palms, and focused on relaxing her body. The physical position relaxed her body, helping her to drift off to sleep.

Breathing Practices

A third embodied practice focuses on the **breath**. Most major religions and spiritual disciplines include focused breathing as part of their contemplative practices. This is intended to help individuals accept and tolerate themselves, the world, and reality as it is. Focus on breathing is also central to relaxation training and treatment of panic attacks, since anxiety often involves fighting with your own physiological responses rather than accepting them.

There are many breathing practices, but the simplest is to just follow your breath. Pay attention to the natural rhythm of inhaling and exhaling without trying to change it. Notice the sensation of air entering your nostrils, filling your lungs, and leaving your body. When your mind wanders (and it will), gently bring your attention back to the breath.

This practice trains several capabilities simultaneously. You're practising directing attention and noticing when attention wanders. You are gently redirecting without self-criticism and being with your immediate experience rather than fighting it or getting lost in thoughts about it.

Tatiana discovered that just two minutes of breath focus when she woke at 3 a.m. helped shift her intense anxiety. Rather than immediately following her racing thoughts, she would notice her breath for a few cycles. This created a small gap between waking with anxiety and catastrophising. In that gap, she could turn her mind towards acceptance rather than being swept immediately into suffering.

Awareness Practices

Awareness exercises train acceptance through direct experience, by paying close attention to how your body is positioned in space. Are you sitting or standing? What are your hands doing? How is your weight distributed? Where do you notice tension or ease? This practise grounds you in physical reality, which is always only in the present moment. Your mind might be time-travelling to past regrets or future worries, but your body is only here and now. By bringing attention fully to bodily sensations, you anchor yourself in the present moment.

Simple daily activities become opportunities for awareness practice. For instance, as you make tea or coffee slowly and mindfully, you can pay attention to each step, observing as you fill the kettle, listen to the water boil, watch steam rise from your mug, and feel warmth through the mug. You might wash dishes with full attention to the sensation of warm water, the texture of each dish, and the movement of your hands. Taking a bath in slow motion involves noticing every sensation.

Tatiana found this practice helpful during her commute. Rather than using drive time to rehearse anxious thoughts, she would periodically bring full awareness to her body. She would notice how her hands gripped the steering wheel, how her body made contact with the seat, and how her foot felt on the accelerator. These small moments of embodied awareness interrupted the anxiety loops and gave her mind brief rests from suffering.

The practices work not by making challenges disappear but by training your nervous system to relate to those challenges in a different way. When Tatiana felt overwhelmed by her mother's decline, she couldn't immediately leap to complete acceptance. But she could wash dishes mindfully for three minutes. She could notice the positions of her body. She could take three conscious breaths. Over time, small practices created moments where she could be in a more accepting mindset.

ACCEPT and the House of Functioning

Returning to the House of Functioning, the ACCEPT practice is particularly relevant for two aspects of movement through the House. First, it's what prevents you from falling into the basement when difficulty arrives. When life throws you a curveball, including illness, loss, disappointment, and conflict, nonacceptance adds suffering to pain and can quickly overwhelm your capacity to cope. That overwhelm is what sends you to the lower floor or even the basement. Acceptance transforms the same difficult event into pain that, while still hard, remains within your capacity to bear. You might not immediately climb to the attic, but you don't crash to the basement either.

For instance, many people who experience post-traumatic growth have a period where they fall into the basement, as they experience *post-traumatic stress disorder* (PTSD). However, through radical acceptance, they come to accept the trauma that occurred, find meaning, and grow. This carries them to the upper floors, such that they come out the other side of trauma not as the same person they were before the trauma occurred, but as a more mature version of themselves, which is full of purpose and meaningful engagement in life.

Second, ACCEPT practice is what allows movement when you're stuck on the lower floor. Tatiana spent months trapped on the lower floor, functioning enough to get to work and fulfil her responsibilities, but not really engaged with life, just going through the motions. What kept her trapped wasn't the difficulty of her circumstances but her resistance to them. The wilful fighting with reality consumed energy that might otherwise have been available for engagement and growth.

When Tatiana began practising acceptance, something shifted. She didn't immediately leap to the attic. Her mother was still declining, and work was still stressful. But Tatiana found she had energy available that had been locked in suffering. She could be more present with her mother and more creative in responding to work challenges. The pain remained, but it no longer trapped her.

This is how ACCEPT interacts with the other elements of Values-Flow. VIRTUE gives you direction. INVOLVE gives you the moment-to-moment skills of attention and action. VITAL gives you the autotelic spirit of curious, engaged challenge-seeking. ACCEPT gives you the capacity to remain present and engaged even when difficulty arrives, to work with what is rather than being defeated by what isn't. Together, these create the conditions for thriving—not despite life's challenges, but through them.

It is worth being specific about the connection between ACCEPT and the flow dimensions we described in Chapter 2. Nonacceptance is one of the most powerful blockers of flow. When you are mentally fighting reality, your attention is divided between the task at hand and the internal argument about how things should be different. This divided attention prevents total concentration, one of the core experiential dimensions of flow. Nonacceptance also heightens self-consciousness, because the internal fight draws attention inward to evaluation and comparison rather than outward to the activity itself. And nonacceptance disrupts the sense of control that flow requires, because you are trying to control things that cannot be controlled rather than directing your energy towards things that can.

Acceptance clears these obstacles. When you stop fighting what is, your attention becomes available for full engagement. Self-consciousness recedes because you are no longer evaluating reality against an impossible standard. And your sense of control increases because your energy is directed towards what is within your influence. Acceptance does not produce flow directly.

But it removes several of the most common barriers that prevent flow from emerging.

Using the Values-Flow Card for ACCEPT

Here's how to use the ACCEPT section with your Values-Flow Card. On the Practice side of your Card, under "ACCEPT," rate the quality of your engagement, not just whether you completed activities, but also how you showed up for them, on a 0–6 scale (Table 7.1).

On the Values-Flow Card, the ACCEPT row invites daily reflection on your relationship with acceptance. Not just whether you practised specific techniques, but the quality of willingness you brought to the day's challenges.

When rating your ACCEPT practice with the 0–6 scale, consider several questions. Did you notice when you responded with wilfulness versus willingness today? When you caught yourself fighting reality, how quickly did you turn your mind towards acceptance? Did you practise embodied practices through half-smiling, willing hands, breathing, or awareness exercises? Most importantly, did you find moments where you transformed suffering into pain by letting go of resistance?

Remember that scores are information, not judgement. A week of low ACCEPT scores might indicate several things. Perhaps you're facing genuinely overwhelming challenges that make acceptance very difficult. An appropriate response might be to increase support rather than to criticise yourself for struggling with acceptance, using the skills that we describe in Chapters 8 and 9. Perhaps you're in a winter season of practice where acceptance feels far away. Trust that integration is happening even when you can't see it. Perhaps you've uncovered deeper layers of resistance that are ready to be worked with. Consider whether professional support might help.

Some practitioners find it helpful to note specifically what they practised accepting each day. "Accepted that my chronic pain was elevated today." "Accepted that the meeting went poorly without catastrophising about my job security." "Accepted feeling lonely without demanding my partner

Table 7.1 Rating Scale for Your ACCEPT Practice

Score	*Meaning*
0	Was completely dominated by wilfulness and did not try any ACCEPT skills.
1	Was dominated by wilfulness, but I did consider the ACCEPT skills.
2	Tried to practise willingness, but all felt effortful.
3	Tried to practise willingness, but got bored or half-checked out.
4	Tried to practise willingness, but felt overwhelmed or anxious.
5	Practised willingness and felt some benefit. It was enjoyable, but I didn't experience flow.
6	Completely led by willingness. I experienced a sense of flow or deep involvement.

immediately fix it." These notes create a record of your practice and remind you during difficult seasons that you do know how to accept, even when it feels like you've forgotten.

You might also track the relationship between acceptance and suffering. On days with higher ACCEPT scores, did you experience less suffering even when pain was high? This can reveal the truth that suffering comes from nonacceptance more than from pain itself.

Flow Nudges: ACCEPT in Action

Here are practical nudges to support your ACCEPT practice:

1. **The Willingness Check**: When you notice distress, pause and ask: Am I being wilful or willing right now? Am I fighting or accepting what is? This simple question can interrupt automatic resistance and create space for turning the mind.
2. **The Baseball Reminder**: When challenges arrive, remind yourself that life keeps pitching balls whether you like them or not. Your only real choice is whether to swing at what's coming or stand there arguing with the machine. This metaphor can cut through complex situations and clarify your options.
3. **The Pain-Suffering Equation**: When experiencing difficulty, get curious about the ratio. How much of what I'm experiencing is pain (the difficulty itself) versus suffering (my resistance to the difficulty)? This isn't to minimise pain, but to recognise where your resistance might be amplifying distress. Even small reductions in suffering can make pain more bearable.
4. **Morning Turning**: Before facing the day, spend two minutes consciously turning your mind towards willingness. Acknowledge what's challenging in your life right now. Practise accepting those challenges. Set an intention to catch yourself in wilfulness and gently redirect towards willingness.
5. **The Half-Smile Anchor**: Choose one recurring activity today, such as making coffee, starting your computer, or sitting down for a meal, and use it as a cue to practise half-smiling. Relax your face, soften into a slight smile, adopt a serene expression. Let your body teach your mind about acceptance.
6. **Willing Hands**: Sit for a few quiet minutes. Open your palms upwards. Take several deep breaths and relax your body. This kicks off the parasympathetic system in your body, settling the angst that you feel and allowing you to turn towards acceptance.
7. **Breathing Space**: Create three two-minute breathing spaces during your day. Set gentle alarms if helpful. During these brief pauses, just follow your breath. When thoughts arrive (and they will), gently return attention to breathing. You're training the muscle of acceptance, being with what is rather than fighting it.

8 **Awareness Anchor**: Choose one routine activity to perform with complete awareness today, such as washing dishes, taking a shower, or walking to your car. Bring full attention to sensations, movements, and sounds. When your mind wanders to worries or plans, gently guide your attention back to your immediate experience. This trains presence with what is.
9 **The Approval Clarification**: When resistance arises, remind yourself: Acceptance doesn't mean approval. I can accept that this is happening while still opposing it, working to change it, or protecting myself from it. This prevents the common confusion that stops people from practicing acceptance.
10 **Catching Wilfulness**: Notice your "shouldn't" thoughts today. Each "this shouldn't be happening" is a small act of wilfulness. You don't need to change the thought, just notice it. Awareness itself creates space for willingness to emerge.

Sound Bite Summary

Here are the key insights from this chapter:

1 The autotelic personality from Chapter 6 connects directly to ACCEPT through a **shared capacity**, translating potential threats into workable challenges while maintaining inner harmony. The autotelic person brings playful curiosity to chosen challenges (VITAL) and willing acceptance to unchosen difficulties (ACCEPT). Neither capacity functions well without the other, and together they create the roots of resilience.
2 Csikszentmihalyi's writing on the transformation of misfortune, Delle Fave and colleagues' research on flow and wellbeing in people with motor disabilities, and Tedeschi and Calhoun's work on post-traumatic growth revealed that even people facing extreme hardship such as acquired motor disability or trauma could maintain wellbeing through radical acceptance. The key wasn't denying difficulty or pretending catastrophe was wonderful, but accepting reality completely and discovering what remained possible within that reality. Those who regained a sense of wellbeing stopped fighting with what had occurred and channelled their energy towards building meaningful lives from their new foundation.
3 ACCEPT cultivates **willingness**—the orientation of saying yes to the mystery of being alive in each moment. Willingness involves accepting what is together with responding effectively to what is. **Wilfulness** is the opposite—imposing your will on reality, trying to fix everything, or refusing to do what is needed. The distinction shows up in quality of engagement more than in specific actions.
4 **Life is like a pitching machine** that keeps throwing balls whether you like them or not. Arguing with the machine, refusing to accept that difficult pitches are coming, or standing frozen while balls fly past do not stop the balls from coming. Only willing engagement with what's coming creates

possibility for a meaningful response. This is the wisdom of acceptance in action.

5 **Suffering equals pain plus nonacceptance**. Pain is inevitable and often functional. It reflects care, provides information, and motivates protective action. Suffering comes from fighting pain, from refusing to accept what is, and from resistance to reality.
6 **Turning the mind** is the practice of choosing acceptance, again and again. Acceptance often lasts only moments before the mind returns to resistance, so you often must keep turning the mind over and over. Every day, sometimes many times per day. Each turning strengthens the capacity for acceptance itself.
7 **Embodied practices** like *half-smiling*, *willing hands*, *conscious breathing*, and *awareness exercises* work with your neurobiology to support acceptance. Your facial expression influences your emotional state, not just reflects it. Your relaxed body opens you up to new possibilities. Your breath can anchor you in present reality rather than in the suffering your mind creates about reality. Awareness of immediate physical sensations grounds you in the here and now where acceptance is possible.
8 ACCEPT prevents you from falling into the burning basement when difficulty arrives and allows movement when you're stuck on the lower floors. It doesn't eliminate pain or make challenges disappear, but it transforms your relationship with difficulty so that challenges don't overwhelm your capacity to cope or consume the energy needed for engagement and growth.

Final Word

Tatiana's transformation didn't happen overnight. But gradually, she began catching herself in wilfulness sooner. She learned to recognise the quality of resistance and to turn her mind towards acceptance. She practised half-smiling during difficult conversations with her mother, practised willing hands to relax her posture, used breathing to anchor herself when overwhelmed, and brought awareness to small moments when her mind wanted to race towards catastrophe.

The pain didn't disappear. Her mother's health continued declining. Work remained stressful. But the suffering began to lift. Tatiana discovered she could be present with her mother's remaining good days because she wasn't consumed by resistance to the declining ones. She found creative energy for responding to work challenges because she wasn't exhausted from mentally arguing with budget realities.

This is the promise of ACCEPT. Not that life will become easy or pain-free, but that you will develop the capacity to be with challenges without adding layers of suffering that make everything worse. You'll learn to recognise the difference between pain and suffering, between willingness and wilfulness, between acceptance and approval.

Here is something that Wilson's work helps us see more clearly. Acceptance itself requires vulnerability. To accept that your mother is declining means to fully feel the pain of that decline without the protective buffer of denial or mental argument. To accept that your workplace is changing means to feel the uncertainty of that change without the false reassurance of "this shouldn't be happening."

Today, when you look at the ACCEPT row on your Values-Flow Card, remember that you're not just scoring the day's practice. You're reconnecting with your capacity for willingness, for being with what is rather than being consumed by what isn't. You're recommitting to transforming suffering into pain, to turning your mind towards acceptance again and again, to saying yes to the mystery of being alive even when that mystery includes challenges. You're choosing the perspective that acceptance isn't a passive resignation but an active engagement with reality as it actually presents itself.

When you combine ACCEPT with VIRTUE, INVOLVE, and VITAL, you have a system for thriving. You know what matters most to you (VIRTUE). You have practical skills for showing up moment by moment (INVOLVE). You bring the spirit of curious, engaged challenge-seeking to what you choose (VITAL). And you maintain the capacity to remain present and engaged even when difficulty arrives uninvited (ACCEPT). Together, these create resilience. Not the brittle kind that never bends, but the flexible kind that bends without breaking, that meets challenge without being defeated by it.

In the next chapter, we'll explore REGULATE, which is the dimension of emotion regulation and distress tolerance that creates the stable foundation flow requires. Where ACCEPT provides willingness to be with difficulty, REGULATE provides skills for managing the intensity of emotions when they threaten to overwhelm. If ACCEPT is what keeps you from falling into the basement, REGULATE is what helps you climb back up when you fall. Together, they create the emotional stability that makes sustained engagement with meaningful challenges possible.

8 REGULATE

Optimal Internal Regulation

Chapter Overview

This chapter describes the fifth Values-Flow skill: REGULATE, which provides the emotional regulation necessary for the deeper work of values-aligned engagement to become sustainable. Emotion regulation is the infrastructure that makes flow possible; you can't engage meaningfully when emotional intensity destabilises you. We describe emotion regulation and distress tolerance skills from DBT, as well as the ACT perspective that turns away from struggle and towards values-aligned living. We need to feel enough emotion to be engaged while staying regulated enough to function, which the REGULATE skills enable.

The Thermostat and the Weather

Meet Marcus, a talented software developer who loved the deep absorption of coding. When things went well, he could lose himself for hours in elegant problem-solving, emerging tired but satisfied. But Marcus had a problem: his emotions were unpredictable visitors who didn't knock before entering. A critical comment from a colleague could send him spiralling into self-doubt for days. A project setback might trigger frustration so intense he'd abandon work mid-task. Even good news such as a promotion or positive feedback could spike his energy so high that he'd take on too much, crash, and spend the next week struggling to get out of bed each day.

Marcus wasn't lacking in values or willingness. He desperately wanted to engage with meaningful work. He understood the importance of acceptance. But something kept knocking him out of the game. His emotional system seemed to have a mind of its own, hijacking his attention and derailing his best intentions.

His therapist offered a helpful metaphor. "Think of your emotional system like a thermostat," she said. "Right now, yours swings wildly between too hot and too cold. When it's too hot and your emotions run high, you're in the panic zone, and no meaningful engagement is possible. When it's too cold and you're emotionally shut down, you're stuck in apathy, disconnected from what

DOI: 10.4324/9781003771173-10

matters. Flow happens in the comfortable middle range, but you can't stay in that zone if your thermostat keeps malfunctioning."

This chapter is about calibrating your emotional thermostat, offering skills to help you create the stable foundation that Values-Flow requires. Just as a house needs a functioning climate control system before you can comfortably work inside it, your internal system needs adequate regulation before the deeper work of values-aligned engagement becomes sustainable.

The Window of Tolerance: Your Personal Flow Zone

The **window of tolerance** was developed by Dan Siegel and is an integral concept within DBT (see Figure 8.1). The idea is that we each have a window of tolerance—a degree of arousal within which a person functions effectively. You experience and process emotions without becoming overwhelmed or shutting down. You feel like you can handle what's happening in your life. There might be stress or pressure, but it doesn't bother you too much. Notably, flow is most likely to occur when you are within your window. Arousal is high enough to be engaging but not so high as to be overwhelming.

Above the window of tolerance lies **hyperarousal**. This is the panic zone, where emotions are too intense, you feel overwhelmed, your nervous system goes into overdrive, and effective functioning breaks down. Symptoms include anxiety, panic, rage, racing thoughts, and high agitation.

Below the window lies **hypoarousal**. This is the shutdown zone, where your system has collapsed into numbing, dissociation, or emotional flatness. Symptoms include depression, feeling as if thoughts are occurring in slow motion, and having no energy to do anything.

As we go through our day, our level of arousal moves up and down. If we are well-regulated, then this variation remains within our window. However, if we experience too much stress or anxiety, we become dysregulated, and either panic (hyperarousal) or shut down (hypoarousal).

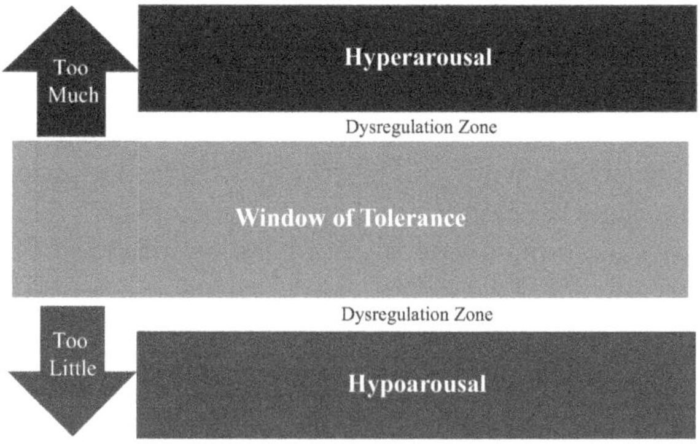

Figure 8.1 The Window of Tolerance.

In between the window of tolerance and the hyperarousal and hypoarousal zones is the **dysregulation zone**. This is where you are heading towards overwhelm or shutdown. If you recognise that you are becoming dysregulated, then you can take action to bring yourself back into your window before reaching complete panic or shutdown.

Importantly, different people have different sized windows. Some people have very wide windows. They can handle a lot of chaos, disorder, and stress without going into hyper or hypoarousal. They have high levels of *psychological flexibility*. Other people have very small windows. It doesn't take much to experience overwhelm. They have low levels of psychological flexibility. The size of the window varies based on your personality, the context, your personal history, everyday experiences, and the skills that you do or do not have.

Further, the size of your window of tolerance isn't fixed. Sleep deprivation, illness, and stress temporarily narrow the window; rest, nourishment, and safety expand it. Trauma typically narrows the window over a more prolonged period and to a greater degree, leaving less room for emotional variation before dysregulation occurs. Effective therapy, including DBT and ACT, gradually widens the window by building regulation skills and helping you to process traumatic experiences.

From a Values-Flow perspective, the window of tolerance is where you are most likely to experience flow. When you are within your window of tolerance, several flow preconditions become available simultaneously. Your attention can focus fully on the task (total concentration) rather than being hijacked by emotional overwhelm or numbed by shutdown. You can perceive and respond to feedback about how things are going (immediate feedback) because your cognitive processing is online. You can calibrate the challenge of what you are doing against your current skill level (challenge–skill balance) because you have the clarity to make that assessment. Action and awareness can merge because your awareness is not consumed by emotional firefighting. Self-consciousness recedes because you are not in the self-monitoring state that dysregulation produces. When you are outside your window, these dimensions are inaccessible. Regulation is the ground from which flow can emerge.

DBT offers two sets of skills to work with your window of tolerance. **Emotion regulation skills** keep you in the window of tolerance long enough for flow and meaningful engagement to emerge. **Distress tolerance skills** help you return to that zone when life's inevitable disruptions push you into dysregulation, hyperarousal, or hypoarousal.

The Dialectical Dance: Emotions and Flow

As we described in Chapter 2, at the heart of both DBT and Flow Theory lie fundamental *dialectics*. In DBT, the core dialectic is acceptance and change. We must fully accept ourselves and our circumstances while simultaneously working to change what can be changed. In Flow Theory, the core dialectic is challenge and skill. Optimal experiences occur when demands are high enough to require our full attention yet not so high that they overwhelm our capacity.

When we bring these two dialectics together, something powerful emerges. Emotion regulation becomes the art of maintaining a challenge–skill balance within our internal experience. Just as flow requires calibrating external challenges to match our abilities, emotional wellbeing requires calibrating our internal experiences to match our capacity to handle them. When emotional intensity exceeds our regulation skills, we tip into hyperarousal. When we over-regulate and suppress all emotional experience, we slide into hypoarousal.

Consider how this might play out in practice. Sanja is preparing for an important presentation. Some degree of anxiety is helpful. It sharpens her focus, motivates thorough preparation, and signals that the presentation matters to her. But if anxiety escalates beyond her capacity to manage it, then she will tip into hyperarousal, feeling a sense of panic and not being able to think clearly. Conversely, if she suppresses all anxiety and approaches the presentation with emotional flatness, she lacks the energetic engagement that makes for compelling communication. The goal isn't zero anxiety. It's having the right amount of anxiety to stay within one's window of tolerance. Challenging enough to be activating, regulated enough to be workable.

This is the dialectical dance of emotions and flow: we need to feel enough to be engaged while staying regulated enough to function. Too much emotional intensity overwhelms the cognitive resources needed for skilful action. Too little emotional activation leaves us disconnected and unmotivated. Optimal emotion regulation isn't about achieving a permanently calm state. It's about maintaining the emotional flexibility that allows us to meet life's varying demands.

Wise Mind plays a central role in navigating this dialectical dance. In the context of REGULATE, Wise Mind serves as the internal compass that tells you which regulatory strategy to deploy in a given moment. When your emotional intensity is so high that thinking has gone offline, Wise Mind might guide you towards the body-based *TIPP* and *STOP* skills to bring your arousal back within the window. When your emotions fit the facts of the situation, Wise Mind might guide you towards acceptance and making room for what's happening rather than trying to change how you feel. When your emotions do not fit the facts, Wise Mind might guide you towards *opposite action* or *problem-solving*.

The skills themselves are tools. Wise Mind is the wisdom that selects the right tool for the right moment. This is why mindfulness practice, which helps cultivate Wise Mind, sits at the foundation of DBT. Without Wise Mind, you have a toolbox full of skills and no way of knowing which one to reach for.

Notably, the right emotion regulation or distress tolerance skills to use varies across cultures and individual circumstances. In some cultures, communal meals with extended family serve both nutritional and social regulation functions. In others, spiritual practices such as fasting, meditation, or prayer serve regulatory purposes. Traditional practices such as yoga, tai chi, qigong, and various forms of breathwork have been cultivating emotional regulation for centuries, often integrating body, mind, and spirit in ways that Western psychological frameworks are only beginning to appreciate. If your own cultural or spiritual tradition includes practices that help you maintain emotional balance and stay within your window of tolerance, those practices are entirely compatible with the REGULATE framework. They may in fact be more powerful for you than the techniques described here, because they are embedded in a meaning system that resonates with your values and identity.

Understanding Emotions

Before we can regulate emotions effectively, we need to understand what emotions are and how they function. DBT offers a comprehensive model that treats emotions as valuable sources of information and energy.

Emotions arise from an intricate dance between what happens in our environment, how we interpret those events, and how our bodies and minds respond. A prompting event such as a sharp word from a friend, an unexpected bill, or a moment of recognition at work triggers the process. Our interpretation of that event, shaped by our history, beliefs, and current state, determines which emotion occurs and how intensely. The emotion then manifests in our bodies as sensations, in our minds as thoughts and urges, and in our behaviour as action tendencies.

DBT distinguishes between primary and secondary emotions. **Primary emotions** are our initial, often adaptive reactions to situations. For instance, you might feel a flash of fear when you sense danger, the warmth of love when you connect with someone you care about, or anger when your boundaries are violated. These primary emotions serve important functions. They communicate information, motivate action, and connect us with others.

Secondary emotions are our response to our primary emotions. According to DBT, this is where suffering originates. We feel anxious, a natural reaction to an uncertain situation, but then we feel ashamed of our anxiety, the secondary emotion that makes us feel bad about ourselves. We feel sad because we lose someone that we care about (a primary emotion), and then we feel angry at ourselves (a secondary emotion) for being sad. We feel angry because someone wronged us (a primary emotion), and then we feel guilty about our anger (a secondary emotion). These secondary emotions create emotional cascades that amplify distress far beyond what the original situation warranted, turning pain into suffering, as we described in Chapter 7.

Importantly, our emotional reaction to a situation or stressor (the primary emotion) is not good or bad. It's our emotional response to the primary emotion (the secondary emotion) which often causes us to suffer. Learning to recognise when we're in a secondary emotional spiral is a crucial regulation skill.

To effectively regulate our emotions, we first need to identify what emotion we are feeling, and determine whether it's a primary or secondary emotion. Table 8.1 lists some common emotions and the function they serve.

Table 8.1 Common Emotions and the Function They Serve

Emotion	*Function of the Emotion*	*Other Ways the Emotion Appears*
Joy	Tells us that things are going right in our world.	Happy, contented, excited, interested, pleased, peaceful, optimistic, trusting
Sadness	Tells us the brain needs to process loss or grief. There's something important to us that we've lost. It also helps us relate to others who are sad.	Depressed, bored, lonely, inadequate, miserable, vulnerable, hurt, disappointed, empty, isolated, abandoned
Fear	Helps us notice danger and protects us from harm.	Anxious, terrified, overwhelmed, worried, panicky
Anger	Tells us there is something wrong—an injustice or unfairness has occurred. Something might be blocking our way to getting what we want or need. It also tells us when something goes against our values.	Frustrated, hateful, rageful, annoyed, infuriated, mad, disrespected
Disgust	Protects us from physical, emotional, and social contamination. Helps us to withdraw from things that will pollute us.	Repelled, awful, disappointed, disapproving, horrified
Shame	Tells us when we've gone against the values of the society or community that we are a part of.	Rejected, embarrassed, anguished, humiliated, disgraced
Guilt	Tells us that we've gone against our own values, and that we have done something wrong.	Ashamed, remorseful, regretful, culpable
Envy	When we want something that someone else has. It can motivate us to work towards things that others have that we want.	Resentful, spiteful, ill-willed, greedy, malicious, distrustful, covetous
Jealousy	When we want to protect something that we fear we will lose. It tells us what is important to us.	Possessive, protective, domineering, suspicious, demanding
Love	Helps us to connect with others, tells us what or who is important to us, and allows us to put our needs below others whom we care about when they need it.	Liked, affectionate, passionate, devoted, respected
Surprise	Alerts us to unexpected change.	Startled, shocked, amazed

Think about times that you have experienced these different emotions. What caused the emotion? Was it a primary emotion (your natural reaction to a situation) or a secondary emotion (your response to the initial emotion)?

From a flow perspective, emotions serve as real-time feedback about our challenge–skill balance. Anxiety often signals that perceived challenge exceeds perceived skill, and that we're tipping towards the panic zone. Boredom signals that the challenge is too low for our skill level, and we're sliding towards disengagement. Frustration might indicate we're in the productive stretch zone but need to adjust our approach. Joy and absorption suggest we've found the sweet spot. When we learn to read our emotional signals this way, they become valuable navigational data rather than disruptive noise.

Regulating Emotions

Once you identify what emotion you are feeling and the reason why you are feeling the emotion, then you can regulate that emotion. If it is a primary emotion, what is it telling you? For instance, if you are angry, what boundary has been violated? If you are sad, what have you lost? If it is a secondary emotion, is the response serving you well? Or would a different response be more effective? At times, the most effective response is to accept the emotion that you feel. It might also help to be self-compassionate (treating yourself with kindness), especially if it's a negative emotion. At other times, the most effective response is to change the emotion, which is possible using one of the skills that we describe in this chapter.

The emotion regulation and distress tolerance skills that we discuss in this chapter are practical strategies for staying within or moving back into your window of tolerance. *Radical acceptance* keeps you from fighting battles that narrow your window. The *PLEASE* skills reduce vulnerabilities to help you stay within your window. *Building positive experiences* expands the window over time. *Opposite action* and *checking the facts* prevent unnecessary trips into the hyper or hypoarousal zones. The *TIPP* and *STOP* skills help you return to the window when you've moved into hyper or hypoarousal. The *ACCEPTS* and *IMPROVE the moment* skills help you strategically distract your attention or make some changes to weather the storms of life.

Radical Acceptance Revisited: The Foundation of Regulation

Chapter 7 introduced **radical acceptance**—choosing to accept an emotion or situation rather than fight it, which is different from approving of it or wanting it to continue. In the context of emotion regulation, radical acceptance takes on particular importance. We must radically accept our emotions themselves, not just our circumstances.

Many of us carry beliefs that certain emotions are wrong, shameful, or unacceptable. We believe we shouldn't feel angry, sad, or anxious. These beliefs create secondary suffering: we feel bad about feeling bad, anxious about feeling anxious, ashamed of feeling anything at all. Radical acceptance of emotions means acknowledging that feelings are neither good nor bad. We can feel angry without that making us a bad person. We can feel anxious without that making us weak. We can feel sad without that meaning something is wrong with us.

From a flow perspective, radical acceptance of emotions in response to a challenging task creates the psychological space where regulation and skilful negotiation of that challenge becomes possible. As long as we're fighting our feelings and trying to not feel what we feel, a portion of our resources is consumed by that internal battle, blocking conditions for flow to occur. When we accept that the emotion is present, we free those resources for more productive use, such as appropriately balancing the challenges of the situation with our available skills.

This connects to the core dialectic we discussed earlier: acceptance and change are partners. We accept that this emotion is here, right now, in this moment. And we also work to change our response to it, to regulate its intensity, or to prevent it from driving ineffective action. Both acceptance and change are true; both are necessary.

The Vulnerability Equation: The PLEASE Skills

Our capacity for emotion regulation isn't constant. It fluctuates based on what DBT calls **vulnerability factors**. When we're well-rested, nourished, and physically balanced, we have a wider window of tolerance and what ACT calls a greater capacity for *psychological flexibility*. When we're depleted, hungry, or physically stressed, even minor triggers can send us into emotional extremes. This is the vulnerability equation: the same external event plus different internal states equal vastly different emotional responses.

DBT's **PLEASE skills** address these vulnerability factors, helping us to stay within our window of tolerance. This creates what we might call "flow readiness"—a baseline state from which optimal experience becomes possible. No amount of sophisticated psychological techniques can compensate for severe sleep deprivation or chronic physical neglect.

Think of the PLEASE skills as maintaining your vessel. A ship with a solid hull, adequate provisions, and a rested crew can navigate choppy waters that would topple a poorly maintained vessel. Similarly, a body that's adequately rested, nourished, and cared for can handle emotional challenges that overwhelm a depleted system.

The **PL** is for **physical illness** or injury, which has a significant impact on our wellbeing. Studies have shown that our physical and mental health are closely linked. When we're fighting infection, managing chronic pain, or dealing with untreated medical conditions, we're drawing from a depleted well of resources. Before trying psychological intervention, it's helpful to work with your doctor to address or manage physical concerns.

The **E** is for **Eating**. Healthy eating maintains the blood sugar stability that supports emotional equilibrium. The research on the gut-brain connection continues to reveal how much our digestive system influences our mood and cognitive function. Skipping meals, relying on sugar and caffeine to survive the day, or eating in dysregulated patterns creates biological conditions that make emotional regulation harder. There are all sorts of dietary plans that you could follow, but in general, eating a well-rounded diet in moderation provides the best support for mental health.

The **A** is for Mood-**Altering** substances, including alcohol, recreational drugs, and even excessive caffeine. These can seem like helpful regulation tools in the moment but create greater amounts of dysregulation over time. The temporary relief of a drink to calm anxiety borrows from tomorrow's regulatory capacity while building tolerance that requires more and more of the substance to achieve the same effect. Rather than keeping us within our window of tolerance, mood-altering substances propel us into hyper or hypoarousal as we move from high-highs to low-lows.

The **S** is for **Sleep**, which is perhaps the most underrated emotion regulation tool we have. During sleep, our brains process emotional experiences, consolidate memories, and restore the neurochemical balance needed for next-day regulation. Sleep deprivation directly impairs the prefrontal cortex, which is the brain region responsible for emotional regulation. Furthermore, it leaves the amygdala, which is our emotional alarm system, hyperactive and overly sensitive.

Finally the **E** is for **Exercise**, which functions as both preventive maintenance and acute intervention for emotional regulation. Regular physical activity builds long-term resilience and regulatory capacity. Short bursts of movement can shift emotional states in the moment (as you'll see in the TIPP skill, described below).

When working with the Values-Flow framework, consider the PLEASE skills as your foundation maintenance. Before asking yourself why you can't seem to find flow or why emotions keep derailing your engagement, check your basics. Are you sleeping enough? Eating regularly? Moving your body? Managing physical health issues? Sometimes the most sophisticated-seeming psychological problems have surprisingly simple biological contributors.

Accumulate Positive Emotions: The Upward Spiral

Emotion regulation isn't just about managing negative emotions. It's equally about building positive ones. DBT emphasises the importance of **accumulating positive emotions**, both in the short term and the long term, as a proactive regulation strategy. This aligns beautifully with the Values-Flow framework's emphasis on engagement with meaningful activity.

Short-term pleasurable activities serve as emotional deposits into our wellbeing account, which helps us stay within our window of tolerance when negative experiences occur. *Jolts of joy*—simple actions that bring a sense of heartfelt positive emotion, such as a good cup of coffee, a walk in nature, a conversation with a friend, or a few minutes with a beloved hobby—aren't luxuries to be deferred until all problems are solved. They're regulation tools that build the positive emotional baseline from which we can better handle challenges. When we're running an emotional deficit, minor stressors become catastrophic. When we're emotionally resourced, we can absorb challenges without losing our footing. Simple positive activities inserted into the flow of life can also help us recover faster from negative interactions or experiences, helping us to stay within our window of tolerance.

Long-term positive experiences increase the size of our windows of tolerance, and arise from living a life aligned with our values. This is exactly what the VIRTUE component of Values-Flow addresses. When we act in ways that honour what matters most to us, we experience a sense of meaning and satisfaction. When we experience these positive emotions, we are more likely to keep engaging in those positive actions, creating a positive upward spiral.

From a flow perspective, each time we engage in an activity that's appropriately challenging and personally meaningful, we're not only enjoying the moment but also building the skill and confidence that makes future flow experiences more likely. The person who regularly experiences small moments of absorbed engagement develops a capacity for such experiences that compounds over time.

A common barrier to building positive experiences is the feeling that we don't deserve enjoyment until we've solved all our problems or accomplished all our obligations. This is a trap. Waiting until everything is perfect to experience positive emotions is like waiting until you're no longer hungry to eat. Positive experiences are nutrition for our emotional system, not rewards to be earned. Scheduling pleasant activities—even when (or especially when) things feel hard—is a strategic regulation move, not self-indulgence.

Cope Ahead: Preparing for Adversity

At times, stressful events, feelings, and experiences catch us off guard, pitching us into dysregulation. That's where distress tolerance skills are useful, as described below. But part of keeping ourselves on an even keel involves recognising activities and events that we expect to be stressful and engaging in the DBT skill of **cope ahead**. This involves acknowledging the discomfort that an event or situation will bring, and making a plan on ways that we can care for ourselves before, during, and after the stressful event.

For instance, if you struggle with social anxiety and are scheduled to go to a social event, you might spend time before the event resting and engaging in self-care (remember the PLEASE skills!). Make a plan for the event, including when you will arrive, how you will interact with other people, what will make the social event more manageable (e.g., perhaps you have a friend you can go with who you can talk to, instead of interacting with a lot of strangers), how long you will stay, and how you can graciously excuse yourself after an appropriate length of time. Then, after you get home, engage in a nice activity that you find soothing in nature (again, remember the PLEASE skills!).

By coping ahead, stressful events become not only manageable but can even be fun. You do positive things before the event, feel more in control of the situation, are more relaxed during the event, and have something positive to look forward to after the experience ends. By coping ahead, you are more likely to stay in your window of tolerance, and it's even possible to experience flow as you skilfully manage the stressful experience.

Check the Facts: Reality Testing for Emotional Balance

To begin regulating our emotions, DBT recommends that we **check the facts**. This is a systematic process of examining whether an emotional response fits the actual situation. This isn't about invalidating emotions or arguing ourselves out of feelings, but about ensuring we're responding to reality rather than to our interpretation of reality.

Check the facts involves asking several key questions: What is the prompting event—what actually happened? What are my interpretations and assumptions about this event? Are there other possible interpretations? What is the threat or outcome I'm imagining? How likely is that outcome? If the worst did happen, could I cope? Would a reasonable person have the same emotional response at this intensity?

This process directly supports the challenge-skill calibration essential for flow. When we check the facts, we're often discovering that we've overestimated the challenge ("This is impossible!") or underestimated our skills ("I can't handle this!"). By bringing our perceptions into closer alignment with reality, we create more accurate assessments of where we stand relative to the challenge, which allows more skilful action.

Consider Marcus from our opening story. When he received critical feedback on his code, his emotional system screamed "Catastrophe! You're incompetent! You're going to be fired!" If he'd checked the facts, he might have noticed that the feedback was about one function in one file, not his entire body of work. His manager had also praised several aspects of the project. No one had mentioned job security, and previous critical feedback had led to improvements, not termination. The emotional intensity didn't fit the facts of the situation.

Check the facts isn't the same as minimising or dismissing genuine concerns. Sometimes when we check the facts, we discover that the situation really is as serious as our emotions suggest, in which case our task is to respond effectively to a real challenge, not to regulate away a justified response. The point is accurate perception, not forced positivity.

Opposite Action: The Dialectical Intervention

One of DBT's most powerful emotion regulation techniques is **opposite action**—deliberately acting contrary to an emotion's action urge when that emotion doesn't fit the facts or when acting on it would be unskilful. This technique embodies the dialectical synthesis of acceptance and change: *we accept that the emotion is present while choosing to change our behavioural response to it.*

Every emotion comes with built-in action tendencies. Fear urges us to flee or avoid the perceived danger. Anger urges us to attack or assert ourselves against a threat. Sadness urges us to withdraw and conserve energy. Shame urges us to hide. Guilt urges us to repair. These action urges made evolutionary sense in ancestral environments where the threats and opportunities that triggered emotions were typically physical and immediate.

In modern life, however, our emotional systems often fire in response to situations where the evolutionarily programmed response is unhelpful. Social anxiety triggers avoidance urges that, if followed, prevent us from developing the social skills and connections that we need. Depression urges withdrawal that, if followed, deepens isolation and cuts us off from the activities that might lift our mood. Anger urges aggression that, in most contemporary contexts, damages relationships and creates more problems than it solves.

Opposite action means identifying the emotion's action urge and, when following that urge would be ineffective, deliberately doing the opposite. When anxiety urges avoidance, we approach. When depression urges withdrawal, we engage. When anger urges attack, we act with gentleness. When shame urges hiding, we share appropriately.

The key word is "when." Opposite action isn't about always overriding emotional urges. It's about choosing an alternative response when the urge does not fit the situation. As ACT reminds us, we always need to be mindful of the context that we are in.

Remember: primary emotions are our immediate reaction to a situation. If we are well attuned to our environment, then the primary emotion is often urging us to respond in a manner that improves the situation. In those cases, we respond (the secondary emotion) in a manner that addresses the need that the emotion is speaking to. But at other times, especially if we have a restricted window of tolerance, our primary emotion doesn't fit the situation. We feel anxious when there is no real threat. We feel anger when there's been no provocation. When the emotion doesn't fit the situation, that's where opposite action is useful.

From a flow perspective, opposite action is often what's needed to stay in the productive stretch zone rather than retreating to comfort or escalating to panic. The programmer facing a challenging bug might feel urged to give up or to bang away in escalating agitation. Opposite action might look like taking a deliberate break (opposite to frantic pushing) or returning to the challenge with fresh curiosity (opposite to avoidance). The athlete in a slump might feel the urge to over-train or to quit entirely, whereas opposite action might be measured, consistent practice with radical acceptance of current performance levels.

Opposite action works best when done *all the way*, with full commitment to the opposite behaviour. This includes your body language, facial expressions, and internal self-talk. Half-hearted opposite action tends to fail. If you're using opposite action for social anxiety by attending a party but then stand in the corner with closed-off body language, you're not fully engaging the technique. Approach means approach fully: open posture, engaged expression, genuine participation with the challenge in front of you.

Problem-Solving: When Change Is Warranted

When *check the facts* reveals that an emotional response fits the situation and there really is a problem that warrants concern, the appropriate response isn't acceptance of the emotion, but rather **problem-solving** of the situation. This is where the change side of DBT's dialectic comes in: some situations need to be changed, and effective action is the effective pathway forward.

DBT's problem-solving framework involves several steps:

1. Identify the problem clearly and specifically. Vague problems don't yield concrete solutions.
2. Check the facts about the problem to ensure you're solving the right thing.
3. Identify your goal. What outcome do you want?
4. Brainstorm possible solutions without judging any of them.
5. Evaluate the pros and cons of each possible solution.
6. Choose a solution and commit to implementing it.
7. Put the solution into action.
8. Evaluate the results and adjust as needed.

This systematic approach connects directly to the ARIA cycle of INVOLVE—Attending to the problem, Reflecting on possible responses, Informing the decision with analysis of options, and Acting on the chosen solution. Problem-solving is what ARIA looks like when applied to situations that need to change.

From a flow perspective, effective problem-solving often involves breaking large, overwhelming challenges into smaller, manageable sub-challenges. The panic zone activates when perceived challenge exceeds perceived skill. By dividing a massive problem into component parts, we transform one impossible-seeming challenge into multiple stretch-zone challenges that can be tackled sequentially. This is why the problem-solving mantra "one step at a time" has such power. It's not just folksy wisdom but a flow-facilitating strategy.

Distress Tolerance: The Emergency System

While emotion regulation skills help us manage our emotions to stay within our window of tolerance, there are times that life upsets us and we go into hyper or hypoarousal. Depending upon the size of our window, for those with a big window, it will take very intensive experiences to upset us, such as the unexpected death of a loved one, a severe medical diagnosis, a sudden job loss, or a relationship betrayal. For those with a small window, seemingly insignificant stressors upset us, such as missing the bus, an argument with a partner, or a stressful day at work. These acute crises can overwhelm even well-developed regulation skills.

For these moments, DBT offers **distress tolerance skills**: techniques designed to survive intense distress *without making things worse.* The goal of distress tolerance is to get through the crisis without doing anything that creates additional problems. This might mean surviving an intense urge without self-harming, getting through a devastating evening without drinking yourself into oblivion, or making it through a panic attack without fleeing a situation that you'll need to face again.

Distress tolerance doesn't make the pain go away. Its aim is to lessen the intensity of the emotional experience, bringing us back to the dysregulation zone or even into our window of tolerance, when coping strategies like those discussed above become possible.

From a flow perspective, distress tolerance skills are what prevent a panic-zone experience from becoming a catastrophe. When emotional intensity spikes far above our regulatory capacity, we're not going to find flow and that's not the goal. The goal is to avoid making decisions or taking actions from that dysregulated state that would create additional barriers to future flow experiences. Distress tolerance is about damage containment when regulation fails.

Think of it like the safety systems in a car. Seat belts, airbags, and crumple zones don't help you drive better; they protect you when driving goes wrong. Similarly, distress tolerance skills don't help you regulate emotions better, they protect you when emotions overwhelm regulation. Both types of systems are essential: we need good driving skills and safety systems, just as we need emotion regulation skills and distress tolerance skills.

TIPP: The Physiological Reset

When emotional intensity is extreme, cognitive techniques often fail because the prefrontal cortex, our thinking, planning brain, goes offline. DBT's **TIPP** skill works around this limitation by targeting the body directly, using physiological interventions to shift the nervous system out of crisis mode, lowering our levels of arousal to the point that we can use other strategies to get through the situation.

The **T** in TIPP stands for **Temperature change**. Specifically, TIPP recommends using the cold to snap you out of intense dysregulation. This might involve plunging your face into cold water, taking a cold shower, or applying an ice pack to your forehead or neck for at least 30 seconds. The most effective approach is to tilt your head forward and allow the cold water or ice to come in contact with your eyes and cheeks. This activates the mammalian dive reflex, an innate response that slows the heart rate and redirects blood flow away from extremities towards vital organs. This isn't a metaphor or a mindset trick. It's a hardwired physiological response that can dramatically reduce emotional intensity within a matter of seconds. The reduction in emotional intensity can be remarkable.

The **I** stands for **Intense exercise**. When we're in crisis, our bodies are flooded with stress hormones preparing us for physical action. This is the fight-or-flight response. Intense exercise provides an outlet for this physiological arousal, metabolising stress hormones and generating mood-improving neurochemicals like dopamine. Even a few minutes of vigorous activity such as running in place, jumping jacks (star jumps), dancing energetically, or fast walking can shift the body out of crisis mode. This isn't about getting fit; it's about matching the body's arousal with activity that makes biological sense of that arousal.

The first **P** stands for **Paced breathing**. When we are in crisis mode, our breathing becomes rapid and shallow, part of the fight-or-flight response. Purposefully slow, controlled breathing activates the parasympathetic nervous system, which is the rest-and-digest system that counterbalances the fight-or-flight response. This is most effective when you breathe out more slowly than you breathe in. But it also works if you slowly breathe in a controlled manner. One approach is to breathe in for five counts, then breathe out seven counts. Alternatively, try box breathing: breathe in for four counts, hold your breath for four counts, breathe out for four counts, hold your breath for four counts, and repeat. Do these breathing cycles for several minutes, focusing on making each exhale slow and complete.

The second **P** stands for **Paired muscle relaxation**. This involves briefly tensing, holding, and then releasing different muscle groups while pairing the release with slow exhales. The contrast between tension and relaxation heightens awareness of what relaxation feels like, while the pairing with breathing deepens the relaxation response. Start with your feet, then calves, upper legs, buttocks, stomach, fists, arms, shoulders, then face, progressively working through the body. Finally, tense your whole body, hold, and release. Be mindful of your own preferences and limitations, avoiding muscles that cause pain or discomfort.

These TIPP skills share a common feature: they work on the body to influence the mind. When emotional intensity is so high that thinking has gone offline, targeting the body directly can shift the system back towards a state where thinking and regulation become possible.

STOP: The Pause That Prevents Disaster

In crisis moments, our instincts often push us towards immediate action, and that action often makes things worse. We fire off the angry email, say the cutting thing, make the impulsive decision, reach for the numbing substance. DBT's **STOP skill** creates a pause that prevents crisis-driven action while creating space for more skilful responses.

S stands for **Stop**. Literally freeze, don't move, don't react. The moment you notice you're in crisis mode or have emotion-based urges, halt all action. Don't send the message, don't say the next word, don't reach for anything. Just stop. A mini freeze helps create space so you can respond rather than react to the situation.

T stands for **Take a step back**, physically if possible, mentally if not. Create space between yourself and the triggering situation. This might mean leaving the room, putting down the phone, or simply taking a few deep breaths and mentally zooming out. The goal is to interrupt the momentum of reactivity so that you can respond in a more effective manner. This separates you from judgements and helps you get a bit of perspective. Remind yourself that you are not your emotion.

O stands for **Observe your thoughts and feelings**. Notice what's happening, both around you and within you. What just happened? What are you feeling? What are your urges? What would you normally do here? Observation engages the thinking brain, which begins to come back online once the immediate reactive momentum is interrupted. Try not to jump to conclusions, make assumptions, or mind-read. Just collect data on what's happening in and around you.

P stands for **Proceed mindfully**. When you do respond, act with awareness rather than on autopilot. Consider: What is needed in this situation? What do I want to accomplish? What won't make the situation worse? What is going to be most helpful or effective? What is going to be better in the longer term? What are my options, and what will make the situation better? Then take that considered action.

The STOP skill connects directly to the Attending step of ARIA. It's the emergency version of mindful awareness, deployed when emotional intensity threatens to derail us. By creating a pause, STOP allows the prefrontal cortex to come back online and the full ARIA cycle to resume.

ACCEPTS: Strategic Distraction

Sometimes the best way to get through intense distress is to temporarily redirect attention away from the triggering situation. This isn't avoidance as a long-term strategy. It's strategic distraction as a bridge through acute crisis. It can help you tolerate an emotion until a later time, when it is safer to process the emotion or solve the problem. Distraction can easily be overused, so remember that it's a short-term solution to get through the triggering situation.

DBT's **ACCEPTS skill** provides pathways for this temporary attention redirection. It is to be used when emotion mind is overwhelming you, and when problems can't be solved immediately.

A is for **Activities**. Engage in activities that demand attention and can absorb your focus. This might be exercise, cleaning, playing a game, working on a puzzle, or any activity that requires enough attention to compete with the distressing thoughts and feelings. The activity doesn't have to be enjoyable in the moment; it just should occupy mental bandwidth.

The first **C** is for **Contributing**. Do something nice for someone else. Shifting attention from your own distress to another person's needs can provide both distraction and a sense of purpose. This might be helping a neighbour, volunteering, or simply doing something kind for someone you meet. Contribution reminds us that we have value to offer even in our most difficult moments.

The second **C** is for **Comparisons**. Compare your current situation to times when you dealt with worse, or to other people who are dealing with greater challenges. This isn't about minimising your pain or toxic positivity. It's about perspective, reminding yourself that you've survived difficult things before and that this too shall pass.

E is for **Emotions**. Generate different emotions than you are currently feeling. You might do this through movies, music, books, or other media. If you're drowning in sadness, a comedy might provide relief. If anxiety has you wired, calming music might help. The goal is to use external inputs to shift internal states.

P is for **Pushing away**. Mentally set aside the distressing situation for a specified time. Imagine putting the problem in a box on a shelf, promising yourself you'll return to it later but giving yourself permission to not think about it right now. This isn't denial; it's scheduled postponement that allows recovery, so you can face it when you have more emotional bandwidth.

T is for **Thoughts**. Occupy your mind with other thoughts. Say the alphabet backwards, recite song lyrics, do mental arithmetic, list state capitals. Any mental activity that occupies working memory reduces the bandwidth available for distressing rumination.

S is for **Sensations**. Use intense physical sensations to redirect attention. Hold ice cubes, take a cold shower, eat something with strong flavour, smell something pungent. Intense sensations demand attention and can break the grip of overwhelming emotion.

Distraction techniques generally do not lead to flow experiences. What they do is help you weather the emotional storm so that you do not make things worse. As you ride the emotional storm, it can bring you back into your window of tolerance, making future flow experiences possible.

IMPROVE: Making the Moment More Bearable

When distress is high but distraction isn't possible or is not working effectively, the **IMPROVE skills** offer ways to make the current moment more tolerable. Rather than escaping the situation, IMPROVE helps us change our relationship to it. Notably, the IMPROVE skills can help create conditions for flow to regularly occur.

I is for **Imagery**. Use mental images to create a sense of safety or remind yourself of previous flow experiences. Imagine yourself in a favourite place, visualise previous situations where you experienced flow, or picture your emotions as a wave that will crest and recede. Mental imagery can create felt experiences of safety even in unsafe-feeling moments.

M is for **Meaning**. Find or create a sense of meaning for a challenging situation. This might be asking what you can learn from this experience, how it connects to something you value, or how you might use this suffering to help you experience flow in the future. Meaning doesn't eliminate pain, but it can make pain more bearable as you skilfully navigate the challenges of everyday life.

P is for **Prayer**. This is broadly defined as connecting to something larger than yourself. This might be prayer to a God or Higher Power of your own understanding, meditation, communion with nature, or simply opening yourself to the universe. The specific form and who or what you pray to matters less than the shift in perspective from isolated suffering to connected presence.

R is for **Relaxation**. Engage in activities that soothe your nervous system. This might include progressive muscle relaxation, gentle stretching, a warm bath, or any activity that reduces physical tension. Relaxation doesn't solve the challenges that you are facing, but it creates a more manageable internal state from which to skilfully engage with those challenges.

O is for **One thing in the moment**. Focus entirely on the current moment rather than catastrophising about the future or ruminating about the past. Ask yourself: Right now, in this exact moment, what do I need to do? Just this one thing. Take one thing at a time, moving forward one step at a time. Breaking time into smaller units can make challenging situations more manageable.

V is for **Vacation**. Take a brief mental or physical vacation from the stressor. This might be watching an episode of a favourite show, taking a walk around the block, or simply giving yourself permission to not deal with the problem for a defined period. Brief respites allow recovery of resources for continued coping and flow experiences.

E is for **Encouragement**. Be your own cheerleader. Tell yourself: "Using my skills, I can get through this," "This challenge is hard but not impossible," "I've survived difficult things before through my skilful action." Self-encouragement isn't naive optimism if it is specific and sustains effort through challenging times.

From a flow perspective, the IMPROVE skills do more than make a challenging moment more bearable. Focusing on one thing in the moment trains the concentrated attention at the heart of flow. Finding meaning connects the challenge you are facing to your values, building the intrinsic motivation that makes absorbed engagement possible. Imagery lets you revisit previous flow experiences, reminding your mind and body what full engagement feels like. By improving the moment, you move back towards your window of tolerance, which is the zone where flow once again becomes possible.

ACT's Contribution: From Fighting Emotions to Living Values

The DBT skills we've covered in this chapter provide you with a powerful toolkit for managing your emotional and cognitive life. But ACT also contributes here. Where DBT asks "How can I manage this emotion effectively?" ACT asks a different question: "What if the real problem isn't the emotion itself, but the war I'm waging against it?"

Russ Harris, one of ACT's most accessible writers, offers a concept that captures this beautifully: **the Struggle Switch**. Imagine a switch at the back of your mind. When it's ON, you struggle against any pain that shows up and that struggling generates a whole layer of additional suffering. You feel anxious, and then you feel angry about feeling anxious, and then ashamed about being the kind of person who gets anxious. In contrast, when the Struggle Switch is OFF, emotions are free to rise and fall naturally without amplification.

This is where ACT offers a crucial insight for the REGULATE skill. The *control agenda* that we introduced in Chapter 2 applies to emotions as much as to values. Most of us operate under the assumption that we need to regulate our emotions before we can engage with what matters. We believe we need to feel calm before we can perform, confident before we can speak up, or relaxed before we can connect. ACT suggests that this belief is itself a major source of suffering. You can engage with what matters right now, with whatever emotions are present. The emotions can come along for the ride.

This does not mean that regulation skills are unnecessary. They are essential. But their purpose is not to eliminate difficult emotions associated with challenging tasks that you encounter in everyday life. Their purpose is to keep you within your window of tolerance so that you can engage with your values while difficult emotions are present. This is a subtle but important distinction. Regulation in service of the control agenda leads to more struggle. Regulation in service of values leads to freedom.

Think back to Marcus from our opening story. His anxiety before the presentation was a natural response to a genuinely challenging situation. But the voice in his head screaming "You shouldn't be feeling this way!" and the shame spiral that followed was an unnecessary struggle.

If you're thinking this sounds a lot like DBT's distinction between primary and secondary emotions, you're right. The two frameworks are saying something very similar in different ways. Both approaches agree that fighting your feelings often creates more suffering than the feelings themselves ever would.

ACT also offers its own rapid-deployment technique for emotional crises or challenging situations, one that sits nicely alongside the TIPP and STOP skills. Harris calls it **Dropping Anchor**, and uses the acronym **ACE**:

- **Acknowledge** whatever is showing up inside you ("Here's sadness," "Here's that familiar anxiety").
- **Come back** into your body by pushing your feet into the floor, stretching, or taking a few slow breaths.
- **Engage in** what you're doing by giving your full attention to the present moment through your senses.

The metaphor is simple and powerful: an anchor doesn't stop the storm, but it holds the boat steady so it doesn't get swept away. Notice the crucial first step. You acknowledge the emotion before grounding yourself in the body. Skip that step, and you're just using distraction, which, from an ACT perspective, is a control-based strategy rather than an acceptance-based one.

For those times when a difficult emotion lingers rather than surges, ACT offers the **Expansion or Opening Up technique**. Rather than trying to push the feeling away, you turn towards it with curiosity. Observe where you feel the emotion most strongly in your body. Notice its size, shape, and temperature. Breathe into that sensation. Make room around it, expanding your awareness so the feeling has space to be there without consuming you. Allow it to be present, like a guest you didn't invite, but you allow it to come along anyway. This isn't the same as liking the emotion or wanting it to stay. It's acknowledging that the feeling is already here, and that making room for it takes less energy than constant resistance. As we discussed in Chapter 6, this is what people with autotelic personalities often do.

So how do DBT and ACT fit together in your Values-Flow practice? Think of it this way. When faced with a challenging situation, sometimes you need to manage your emotions to get back into your *window of tolerance*. That's when you reach for your DBT skills like *TIPP* or *STOP*. At other times, the most effective thing you can do is to accept the emotion by turning off the *Struggle Switch*, *dropping anchor*, or *making room*. DBT's *Check the Facts* skill bridges beautifully to ACT: when your emotion doesn't fit the facts, use change strategies like *opposite action* or *problem-solving*. When your emotion does fit the facts, that's where *radical acceptance* and *willingness* come in. And throughout it all, your values guide when to use each one and how to balance challenges and skills in sustainable ways.

Using the Values-Flow Card to REGULATE

Here's how to use the REGULATE section with your Values-Flow Card. On the Practice side of your Card, under "REGULATE," rate the quality of your skill practice on a 0–6 scale (Table 8.2).

The practical integration looks like this: When you notice dysregulation, first check whether you're dealing with a crisis (requiring distress tolerance

Table 8.2 Rating Scale for Your REGULATE Practice

Score	*Meaning*
0	Did not try to engage with any emotion regulation or distress tolerance skills.
1	Noticed my emotional reactions but could not identify what emotion I felt.
2	Noticed my emotional reactions but did not try to regulate them.
3	Tried to regulate my emotions but got bored or half-checked out.
4	Tried to regulate my emotions but felt overwhelmed or anxious.
5	Tried to regulate my emotions and felt some benefit.
6	Fully regulated my emotions, effectively staying within or returning to my window of tolerance.

skills) or a regulation challenge (requiring emotion regulation skills). For crises, deploy TIPP, STOP, ACCEPTS, or IMPROVE to get through the acute moment. For regulation challenges, check the facts, consider whether opposite action is warranted, ensure PLEASE foundations are in place, cope ahead, and accumulate positive emotions.

How does emotion regulation fit within the broader Values-Flow framework? We can think of regulation skills as the infrastructure that makes the other elements possible. VIRTUE requires enough emotional stability to identify and live according to our values rather than being blown about by momentary feelings associated with the challenges that we face. INVOLVE requires enough regulation to work through the Attending, Reflecting, Informing, and Acting cycle rather than getting stuck in reactive patterns. VITAL requires enough baseline regulation for the autotelic personality and serious play to occur. ACCEPT aligns with the radical acceptance of emotion regulation and the ACT strategies supporting values-based and flow-informed living.

Flow Nudges: REGULATE in Action

1 **The Morning PLEASE Check**: Each morning, briefly make an inventory of your vulnerability factors. How did you sleep? Have you eaten? Is there physical discomfort that needs attention? Have you moved your body? This quick check helps you calibrate your day's challenges to your current regulatory capacity. On a low-resource day, choose gentler challenges; on a well-resourced day, you can push into more demanding territory.

2 **The Emotion Check-In**: Several times during the day, pause to notice your emotional state. Name what you're feeling without judging it. Ask: Is this emotion fitting the facts of my situation? Is its intensity proportional? Is its action urge helpful right now? This simple check-in catches dysregulation early before it escalates to crisis levels.

3 **The Opposite Action Experiment**: Choose one area where an emotional urge regularly pulls you away from your values. For one week, practise *opposite action* in that domain, approaching what anxiety urges you to avoid, activating when depression urges withdrawal, being gentle when anger urge aggression, engaging in self-care when the self-harm urge soars. Notice what happens when you act opposite to the urge. Track the results on your Values-Flow Card.

4 **The TIPP and STOP Emergency Kit**: Create a physical emergency kit for emotional crises. Write out the TIPP and STOP skills on note cards. Add items for temperature change (perhaps a cold pack you can keep in the freezer), items for intense sensation (strong mints, ice, sour sweet, a strongly scented oil), and written reminders of your TIPP and STOP protocols. Having the kit prepared means you don't have to think clearly in crisis; you just grab the kit and follow the steps.

5 **The Positive and Flow Experience Schedule**: Don't leave positive and flow experiences to chance. Each week, schedule at least one short-term

pleasant activity daily and make progress on one long-term values-aligned or flow-based goal. Treat these scheduled experiences with the same seriousness you treat other appointments. They're not optional extras; they're regulation infrastructure.

Sound Bite Summary

1. **Emotion regulation** is the infrastructure that makes flow possible. You can't engage meaningfully when emotional intensity pushes you outside your window of tolerance.
2. The **window of tolerance** is your personal flow zone. Regulation skills are what keep you within your window and what help you return when pushed out.
3. The core dialectic of emotions and flow is that we need to feel enough to be engaged while staying regulated enough to function.
4. **PLEASE skills** address baseline vulnerabilities. Sleep, food, exercise, health, and avoiding mood-altering substances create the foundation for regulation.
5. **Cope ahead** can help you prepare for, tolerate, and recover from stressful experiences.
6. **Check the facts** before acting. Much emotional intensity comes from our interpretations rather than reality.
7. **Opposite action** is a powerful intervention when emotional urges would move you away from your values. Approach when anxiety urges avoidance, activate when depression urges withdrawal.
8. **Building positive experiences** is a regulation strategy, not an optional extra. Emotional deposits make withdrawals more manageable.
9. **Distress tolerance skills** (TIPP, STOP, ACCEPTS, IMPROVE) are for crises. They don't solve problems but prevent you from making things worse.
10. You can accept and tolerate emotions associated with challenges that you are facing by **dropping anchor** or through the **Expansion or Opening Up technique** in ACT.
11. **Track your REGULATE practice** daily on the Values-Flow Card, noticing patterns between regulation and your capacity for meaningful engagement.

Final Word

Remember Marcus from our opening story, the talented developer whose emotional thermostat kept knocking him out of the flow zone? After months of working with emotion regulation skills, his experience of work transformed. He still felt anxiety before code reviews and frustration when bugs proved stubborn. But now these emotions were signals rather than emotional hijackers, information about his engagement rather than forces that controlled his behaviour.

He learned to check his PLEASE foundations before demanding projects, ensuring he started with adequate resources. He practised checking the facts when criticism triggered shame spirals, usually discovering that the feedback was about one small thing rather than his entire worth. He used opposite action when avoidance urges arose, approaching difficult conversations rather than putting them off indefinitely. And when true crises hit, such as a major system failure or a family emergency, he deployed TIPP and STOP to get through without making impulsive decisions he'd regret.

Most importantly, Marcus came to understand that emotion regulation wasn't about eliminating feelings or achieving permanent calm. It was about creating enough stability that he could show up skilfully for the challenges that mattered to him. His emotions became weather to be navigated rather than storms that blew him off course. And in that stability, flow found him more and more often, with hours of absorbed coding, the satisfaction of elegant solutions, the deep engagement with work that expressed his values.

The reason that Marcus needed regulation skills was not that his emotions were broken. It was that he cared deeply about his work, and that caring made him vulnerable to the emotional intensity that comes with investment. His emotional dysregulation was, in a real sense, evidence of his values. The anxiety before code reviews reflected how much he valued competence. The frustration with bugs reflected how much he valued excellence. The shame spirals reflected how much he valued the respect of his colleagues. Regulation skills did not replace these values. They gave Marcus the capacity to carry those values without being overwhelmed by the emotional weight they brought. The REGULATE skills serve VIRTUE. The skills in this chapter exist to help you hold what you care about without being crushed by the intensity of caring.

Today, when you look at the **REGULATE** row on your Values-Flow Card, remember that optimal regulation isn't about perfect emotional control. It's about maintaining enough stability that you can engage with what matters. That willingness, combined with increasing REGULATE skills, is what makes a life of Values-Flow possible.

Keep calibrating your thermostat. Keep building your capacity. Keep showing up for the challenges that matter. In the dialectical dance of emotions and flow, you're learning to be a better partner, responsive to the music, stable on your feet, and ready to engage with whatever the dance brings next.

9 RELATE

Optimal Interpersonal and Environmental Relationships

Chapter Overview

This chapter describes the sixth Values-Flow skill: RELATE, which helps you navigate your interpersonal relationships and the environments that you are a part of. DBT's interpersonal effectiveness module offers a sophisticated toolkit for navigating relationships skilfully, depending upon your goals in the relationship, including meeting a specific objective, maintaining the relationship, and maintaining self-respect. In Values-Flow, we add the recognition that relationships themselves can become flow channels. Relationships are cultivated through repeated positive interactions, ongoing investment, and prompt repair of ruptures. The environment we are in also impacts our experiences of life. Toxic environments make thriving unlikely, and when we are in the position of power over others, we ought to create environments where others can thrive.

The Dance Partners

Vienna had always thought of herself as a good communicator. As a project manager at a tech startup, she prided herself on her clarity, her efficiency, and her ability to get things done. But lately, something had shifted. Her team meetings felt like navigating through fog. Her conversations with her partner at home had become a series of disconnected exchanges. Even calling her mother had started to feel like a chore.

The breaking point came during a quarterly review when her most talented team member resigned, citing a "lack of genuine connection" with leadership. Vienna was stunned. She had thought she was being clear, direct, and efficient. What she hadn't realised was that she had been so focused on the transaction of communication—getting information from A to B—that she had forgotten the relationship in which that communication lived.

Her coach introduced her to a different way of thinking about relationships. "Think of every conversation as a dance," she said. "You're not just moving through steps. You're responding to your partner, adjusting to the rhythm, creating something together that neither of you could create alone."

DOI: 10.4324/9781003771173-11

Vienna realised she had been treating her relationships like solo performances, forgetting that the beauty of dance lies precisely in the attunement between partners.

Over the following months, Vienna learned to approach her relationships as she approached her best work projects: with full attention, with appropriate challenge, with genuine skill, and with openness to the unexpected moments of feedback that emerge when two people genuinely meet one another in conversation. She discovered that actively enabling effective relationships could create a sense of flow, both for her and those that she interacted with.

This chapter explores those skills. Chapter 8 gave you the emotional regulation tools to stay balanced within yourself. This chapter extends that stability outward into the intricate, challenging, deeply rewarding territory of connection to other human beings and to the environments in which we reside.

Interpersonal Effectiveness in Values-Flow

In the Values-Flow framework, optimal interpersonal relating represents the natural extension of self-regulation into the social world. Emotional regulation keeps your internal weather systems stable enough for flow to occur, while interpersonal effectiveness ensures that your relationships—the ecosystems in which much of life's meaning emerges—support your capacity for optimal engagement.

DBT's interpersonal effectiveness module provides solid relational skills. Values-Flow adds recognition that relationships themselves can be channels for flow to occur. When you engage in a conversation with full presence, appropriate skill, genuine challenge, and clear feedback, you create the conditions for **interpersonal flow**. These are moments of deep connection where time seems to slow down, where you feel simultaneously yourself and in genuine contact with the other person.

Think back to our garden metaphor in Chapter 2. Your emotional life is like the internal health of a plant, such as the roots, the cellular processes, and the internal vitality. Your interpersonal life is the garden itself, the ecosystem of relationships in which you are embedded. The health of the garden affects every plant within it, and each plant contributes to or detracts from the garden's overall vitality. Optimal interpersonal relating is the skill of tending to your relational garden so that both you and those around you can thrive.

The Three Priorities of Interpersonal Effectiveness

DBT identifies three fundamental priorities that we might pursue in our interpersonal interactions: **objective effectiveness** (getting your needs or objectives met), **relationship effectiveness** (maintaining a strong relationship with the other person), and **self-respect effectiveness** (building self-respect and confidence). Strong interpersonal relationships arise from being clear on which priority is most important to you at the time and using specific skills to achieve that priority. Values-Flow suggests that relational flow is most likely to arise when the three goals are skilfully attended to simultaneously.

DBT also identifies specific skills that help you achieve each of the three priorities. The skills can be used individually (when a single priority is most important to you) or simultaneously (when multiple priorities are important to you).

The dialectical challenge is that these three goals can pull in different directions. Being maximally assertive might achieve your objective but damage the relationship. Prioritising relationship harmony might preserve connection at the cost of self-respect. Maintaining rigid boundaries might protect your integrity while isolating you from meaningful connection. Optimal interpersonal relating requires holding all three goals simultaneously, identifying which priority is most important in any given conversation, and finding the synthesis that supports thriving for you and others.

Objective Effectiveness: Getting What You Need

The first priority is to achieve your immediate objectives or needs in the interaction. You might want to ask for a raise, decline an invitation, resolve a conflict about household responsibilities, or negotiate a deadline at work. Here we need to be clear on what we want to get out of the social interaction. It is transactional in nature. You want something, and so you are going to assertively advocate for what you need, in ways that produce desirable results.

You might struggle with **objective effectiveness** either because you are not clear on what you want, or because you lack the skills to ask for it effectively. In the first case, it is helpful to take some time for mindful reflection on what your needs or objectives are. Being as specific as possible is helpful here.

In the latter case, you might not assertively communicate your needs. You hint rather than state. You apologise before you've even made a request. You undermine your own position with qualifiers and hedges. Or conversely, you demand rather than request, creating resistance rather than cooperation. Objective effectiveness means developing the skill to make clear, direct, respectful requests and to say "no" when necessary, without guilt or aggression.

Assertive communication is the most effective way of communicating your needs and wants. With assertive communication, you are respectful of both yourself and others. Actions and expressions align with the words spoken. You are warm and welcoming, friendly, with appropriate gestures.

From a flow perspective, objective effectiveness allows your interpersonal interactions to be genuine opportunities to pursue what matters to you, rather than being frustrating exercises in miscommunication. When you know and can articulate your needs clearly and respond to others' responses adaptively, conversations become more like the fluid motion of two dancers moving to the music than like two ships passing in the darkness.

DBT offers an acronym for objective effectiveness: **DEAR WOMAN**. This skill provides a structured approach to making requests or saying no in ways that maximise your chances of achieving your goals while remaining respectful and clear. The first four letters (DEAR) refer to what you wish to say. The other letters (WOMAN) refer to how you say what you say.

D is for **Describe**. Begin by describing the situation factually, without judgement or interpretation. For instance, "we agreed that you would handle the dishes on weekdays" rather than "you never do your fair share." This might seem simple, but it's surprisingly difficult when emotions are running high. Describing requires the attending skills from your INVOLVE practice, really observing what happened rather than filtering it through your assumptions and reactions.

E is for **Express**. Share your feelings and opinions about the situation using "I" statements. For instance, "I feel frustrated when the dishes pile up" rather than "You're so inconsiderate." Expressing connects to ACCEPT and REGULATE skills. You first need to be aware of and accepting of your own emotional experience before you can communicate it effectively to others.

A is for **Assert**. Make your request or say no clearly and directly. For instance, "I need you to do the dishes tonight" or "I can't take on that extra project." Many people skip this step, hoping the other person will somehow guess what they need from the description and expression alone. But clear assertion respects both yourself and the other person by making your needs explicit.

R is for **Reinforce**. State the positive consequences that will arise from the other person giving you what you need, or the negative consequences of not doing so. This isn't manipulation. It's helping the other person understand why your request matters. For instance, "If we can stay on top of the dishes, I'll feel less stressed and we'll have more quality time together." Reinforcing connects your request to shared values and provides the opportunity for mutual benefit.

W is for **Willingness**. Be willing to handle not getting what you want. Keep an open mind to the outcome and have strategies to exit the conversation gracefully if it goes astray. This is part of the ACCEPT skill in Values-Flow. By accepting and moving forward gracefully when you meet too much resistance, you are better able to maintain self-respect and continue on the pathway towards healthy social relationships.

O is for **Openness**. Be open to what might come out of the conversation. This allows you to adapt your response to the situation, rather than forcing the conversation along your pre-conceived notions of how the conversation should go. This is the dance of conversation and interpersonal flow, expressing your needs but being open to shifts in perspective as needed.

M is for **Mindful**. Stay focused on your objective, not getting derailed by tangents, counterattacks, or attempts to change the subject. This is where your mindfulness practice is beneficial. When the other person brings up that thing you did three months ago and you notice the pull to defend yourself, you gently return to the current conversation. For instance, "I'm happy to discuss that another time. Right now, I'm focused on the dishes."

A is for **Appear confident**. Use your body language and tone of voice to convey confidence, even if you don't feel it internally. Make eye contact. Speak clearly at a moderate pace. Avoid excessive apologising. This isn't about faking or performing. It's about aligning your external presentation with the legitimacy of your request. Your needs are valid, and your body language should reflect that. Planning what you want to say in advance can help you portray a sense of confidence.

N is for **Negotiate**. Be willing to give to get. For instance, "If you do the dishes tonight, I'll handle them for the rest of the week." Or, "I can't take on the whole project, but I could contribute to one section." Negotiating keeps you from the all-or-nothing thinking that derails many interpersonal interactions. It acknowledges that the other person also has needs and constraints, and it models collaborative problem-solving that strengthens relationships.

From a Values-Flow perspective, DEAR WOMAN creates the clear goals, immediate feedback, and balance of challenge and skill that flow requires. You know exactly what you're asking for. You can observe the other person's response in real time. And you have a structured framework for adjusting your approach based on that feedback. You stay mindful, are willing and open to what the conversation holds, you negotiate, and you reinforce. The challenge of effective advocacy meets the skills of clear communication, creating conditions where interpersonal flow becomes possible.

Relationship Effectiveness: Nurturing Connection

The second priority recognises that our interactions don't occur in a vacuum; they occur within ongoing relationships that we often want to maintain or strengthen. You might get exactly what you asked for in a conversation while simultaneously damaging the relationship. **Relationship effectiveness** means pursuing your objectives in ways that preserve and ideally enhance the connection with the other person. You consider how you want the other person to come out of the conversation, and care that the emotional needs of the other person are being met.

Think of relationships like having an emotional bank account. Every interaction makes a deposit or a withdrawal. Relationship effectiveness involves being mindful of the account balance and ensuring that even difficult conversations such as conflicts, requests, or boundary-setting are conducted in ways that don't bankrupt the relationship. Sometimes this means softening your approach. Sometimes it means timing your conversation for when the other person can really hear you. Sometimes it means acknowledging the relationship explicitly: "I value our friendship, which is why I need to be honest with you about this."

From a Values-Flow perspective, relationships aren't just instrumental means to getting what you want. They are also ends in themselves, sources of meaning and connection that contribute to a thriving life. Relationship effectiveness honours this by treating each interaction as an opportunity to strengthen the web of connection in which our lives are embedded.

In DBT, the **GIVE** skill addresses how you go about a conversation in a manner that preserves and strengthens the relationship. This skill reminds you that objective effectiveness achieved at the cost of relationship effectiveness is often a hollow victory.

G is for **Gentle**. Approach the interaction without attacks, threats, or judgements. Avoid sarcasm that masks hostility. Don't issue ultimatums unless you genuinely mean them and are prepared for the consequences. Gentleness doesn't mean weakness. It means approaching the other person with the kind of respectful care that keeps their defences from going up unnecessarily. Think of how a skilled gardener handles a plant: with firmness when needed, but never with violence.

I is for **Interested**. Show genuine curiosity about the other person's perspective, needs, and constraints. Listen to their responses rather than just waiting for your turn to speak. Ask questions that demonstrate you're trying to understand rather than simply trying to win an argument. Interest transforms a negotiation into a dialogue, creating space for solutions neither of you might have imagined alone.

V is for **Validate**. Acknowledge the other person's feelings, wants, and difficulties, even when you disagree with their position. For instance, "I can see this deadline puts you in a difficult position" or "It makes sense that you'd feel frustrated about this." Validation doesn't mean agreement. It means communicating that you understand and take the other person's experience seriously. This is often the single most powerful thing you can do to keep a difficult conversation productive.

E is for **Easy manner**. Approach the conversation with lightness where possible. If appropriate, incorporate kind humour. Smile. Avoid unnecessary intensity. An easy manner signals that this conversation, however serious in its content, doesn't need to be a battle. It invites collaboration rather than combat. Of course, this needs to be calibrated. Some conversations are genuinely grave and don't call for levity. But many difficult conversations go better when approached with a certain spaciousness rather than grim determination.

The GIVE skills provide a sense of moving together with another person rather than struggling against them. When you approach someone with gentleness, genuine interest, validation, and an easy manner, you create conditions where they can be present with you rather than defending against you. The dance metaphor becomes literal: you're creating the conditions for a genuine meeting and interpersonal flow.

Self-Respect Effectiveness: Maintaining Integrity

The third priority involves thinking about how you want to feel coming out of the interaction, with your needs met and having a sense of self-respect and confidence. You might achieve your objective and preserve the relationship while simultaneously violating your own values, compromising your integrity, or feeling diminished in the process. **Self-respect effectiveness** means advocating for yourself in ways that leave you feeling good about how skilfully you showed up in the conversation.

This priority is especially important for people who tend towards people-pleasing or who tend to sacrifice their own needs for the comfort of others. Getting what you want by begging, threatening, or manipulating might "work" in the narrow sense of achieving your objective, but it often costs you something precious: your sense of yourself as someone who acts with dignity and integrity. Self-respect effectiveness ensures that the way you pursue your goals aligns with your values, supporting the VIRTUE part of Values-Flow.

The **FAST** skill from DBT ensures that however an interaction turns out, you walk away with your self-respect intact. You act in alignment with your values even when it's difficult.

F is for **Fair**. Be fair to both yourself and the other person. Don't fall into the trap of making yourself a martyr or treating your needs as less important than others. Equally, don't swing to the other extreme of prioritising yourself at others' expense. Fairness requires the *Wise Mind* balance, holding your perspective and the other person's simultaneously, finding solutions that honour both.

A is for **Apologies**. Make no unnecessary apologies. Apologise when you've done something wrong, but don't apologise for having needs, for existing, or for taking up space. Excessive apologising undermines your position and communicates that your needs aren't legitimate. "Sorry to bother you, but..." already frames your request as an imposition. Simply make the request.

S is for **Stick to your values**. Don't compromise your fundamental values to get what you want or to avoid conflict. If honesty is a core value, don't manipulate. If respect is important to you, don't demean. If integrity matters, don't make promises you can't keep. This doesn't mean being rigid, as values can be expressed in many ways, but it means not abandoning what you stand for in the heat of the moment.

T is for **Truthful**. Don't lie, exaggerate, or act helpless when you're not. Deception might achieve short-term objectives, but it corrodes both relationships and self-respect over time. Truthfulness also means being honest about your own feelings and needs rather than masking them or expecting others to guess what you feel. Authentic communication builds the kind of trust that makes relationships genuinely nourishing.

FAST skills ensure that your interpersonal interactions serve your long-term functioning rather than just your immediate goals. Even if a particular conversation doesn't go the way you hoped, you can walk away knowing that you showed up with integrity. This connects to the deeper purpose of Values-Flow: not just achieving outcomes, but living a life where you live according to your values, both individually and in relationship with others in your life.

Building Relationships: The Long Game

Beyond offering the skills of DEAR WOMAN, GIVE, and FAST for navigating specific interactions, DBT offers wisdom about building and maintaining relationships over time. These insights align beautifully with the Values-Flow emphasis on optimal engagement—the sustained, meaningful involvement with activities and relationships that creates a rich and flow-filled life.

Building relationships requires intentional effort. Unlike the movies where meaningful connections seem to happen spontaneously, real relationships are cultivated through repeated positive interactions with a person over time. DBT encourages actively seeking out and joining groups where you might meet like-minded people, practising conversation skills even when it feels awkward, and being willing to extend invitations and accept rejections gracefully.

Maintaining relationships requires ongoing investment. Show interest in others' lives. Remember what matters to them. Follow up on things they've shared. Repair ruptures promptly. Don't let small grievances fester into relationship-ending resentments. Express appreciation regularly. These aren't grand gestures but daily practices that compound over time into deep connection. Just as accumulating positive emotions builds your emotional bank account (as described in Chapter 8), small acts that honour the relationship build your relational bank account.

From a flow perspective, relationships are challenges that grow with us. A new friendship might offer the challenge of vulnerability and the skill development of learning to trust. A long-term partnership offers the challenge of maintaining novelty and the skill development of navigating conflict constructively. Parenting offers challenges that evolve from moment to moment and year to year, requiring constant skill adaptation. Relationships never become "solved." They remain ongoing opportunities for growth, engagement, and optimal relating.

Walking the Middle Path: Dialectical Balance in Relationships

DBT introduces the concept of **walking the middle path**. We can be prone to thinking of things in black-and-white terms, all-or-nothing thinking, and right or wrong actions. Walking the middle path finds a sense of harmony between extremes, the many shades of grey that exist. Walking the middle path is especially relevant within the interpersonal relationships that we have. Relationships constantly present us with dialectical tensions:

Acceptance AND Change: You can accept your partner exactly as they are while also supporting their growth. You can accept yourself completely while also working to develop new skills. These aren't contradictions; they are dialectical syntheses. Acceptance creates the safety that makes change possible, and change creates the growth that keeps acceptance from becoming stagnation.

Closeness AND Independence: Healthy relationships involve both deep connection and preserved autonomy. Too much closeness can become co-dependency; too much independence can become isolation. The middle path involves being fully yourself while also being genuinely in relationship, neither losing yourself in the other nor walling yourself off from genuine intimacy.

Your Needs AND Others' Needs: Self-sacrifice isn't always virtuous. When taken to the extreme, it breeds resentment, exhaustion, and burnout. But pure selfishness corrodes relationships. The middle path involves honouring your needs while also genuinely caring about others' wellbeing, finding solutions that serve both of you rather than one person benefitting at the other person's expense.

Consistency AND Flexibility: Relationships need reliability, the trust that comes from knowing what to expect from each other. But they also need adaptability, the capacity to grow and change as circumstances evolve and as people evolve. The middle path involves being consistent in your core values and commitments while remaining flexible in how they're expressed.

Walking the middle path requires ongoing calibration. Like a surfer reading the waves, you're constantly adjusting your balance based on the feedback the relationship provides. These create the conditions for interpersonal flow to occur: full engagement with the ever-changing dynamics of connection, responsive adjustment based on real-time feedback, and the challenge of balance met with growing skill.

Interpersonal Flow: When Connection Becomes Absorption

You've likely experienced moments of **interpersonal flow** without naming them as such. Think of a conversation where time seemed to stop. Or a collaboration where ideas built on each other effortlessly. Or a shared activity where you and another person seemed to move as one. These experiences have the hallmarks of flow: deep absorption, the merging of action and awareness, the loss of self-consciousness, and intrinsic reward. These are flow experiences that co-occur with another person and within the context of relating with one another.

Interpersonal flow requires appropriate challenge (the conversation or activity must engage your skills), clear goals (you know what you're trying to create together), immediate feedback (you can see and feel the other person's responses), and having the skills to meet the moment. But it adds something unique: two people, interacting with one another. Interpersonal flow is co-created. It emerges in the space between people when conditions are right for both persons.

The DEAR WOMAN, GIVE, and FAST skills don't directly create interpersonal flow, but they create the conditions in which interpersonal flow becomes possible. They clear the obstacles such as misunderstandings, defensiveness, and unspoken resentment that prevent genuine connection.

They build the relational foundation on which moments of deep relationship can arise.

This is why interpersonal effectiveness matters even for people who are "good at relationships." Vienna, from our opening story, wasn't bad at connecting. She was missing the skills that would allow connection to deepen into flow. The DBT skills gave her the tools to clear the ground, and flow emerged naturally once the obstacles were removed.

RELATE in Context: Environmental Effectiveness

Our experiences of life and our connections with other people all exist within the environments in which we reside. Thriving in life, optimal functioning, and flow experiences do not occur in a vacuum. We need to create conditions that are supportive. This begins with accepting the realities in which we reside, identifying what needs to change and what needs to be accepted, and taking action accordingly (which at times means taking action off the table, as described in Chapter 5).

Some environments are conducive to thriving, whereas other environments push us towards the basement of the House of Functioning. The environment involves the ecological context in which we live, the communities that we are (or would like to) be a part of, the social norms that govern appropriate behaviour, the political landscape in which we reside, and the social environments that transpire throughout the different parts of our life. This includes home, the workplace, the local neighbourhood, the city in which we reside, our nationality, and policies that govern our rights and responsibilities.

Everyone ought to have the right to experience wellbeing and even to thrive in life, but unfortunately that is not the case. Stereotypes and prejudice exist, power corrupts, and those who are in charge often make decisions from a limited viewpoint, which compromises the needs of those for whom those decisions are made. For instance, if you work in a toxic workplace, it doesn't matter how many wellbeing exercises you do. Your window of tolerance will decrease, and it will be hard to thrive. Not impossible, but certainly very hard to do. If you are in a very toxic environment, often the most effective action is to leave, even if that means changing jobs or moving to a new location.

However, there are often times when we cannot escape toxic environments. We often spend a lot of time trying to control what is out of our control, and very little time focusing on what is within our control. It can be helpful to map out what in your environment is unhealthy, what aspects you can control on your own, what aspects you can control with the help of others (e.g., a supervisor, your partner), and what is beyond your control. You have the most control over your thoughts, emotions, and behaviours, and less control over other people that you interact with. You can choose to be bitter and resentful towards your situation, or you can choose to be grateful for what you do have. Other people often can provide a different perspective and give you ideas on how to improve your environment. For things that are beyond your control, you can choose to accept the reality that you are in (remember the ACCEPT skills in Chapter 7!), while not approving of and even actively working to change that reality.

Environmental factors are critical for flow experiences. You can have the perfect challenge-skill match, high levels of intrinsic motivation, and work all your other skills, but if you are in a distracting environment, flow is unlikely to occur. Those who experience flow often spend significant time setting up the environment to promote focused attention. This might mean turning off your smartphone, scheduling a time to do a flow-conducive activity, and removing distracting stimuli.

The idea that the environment matters as much as individual skills has deep roots in DBT and ACT. DBT's biosocial theory places the environment right at the centre of emotional life. Linehan stated that emotional vulnerability plus an invalidating environment equals pervasive emotion dysregulation. This reminds us that you can have all the regulation skills in the world, but if the people around you consistently dismiss, criticise, or punish your emotional experiences, those skills will be fighting an uphill battle. The invalidating environment is any context where you don't fit. This can extend well beyond family to workplaces, social groups, and institutions that systematically ignore or undermine the needs of certain people.

DBT is also quite clear about where to start when you're dealing with a problem: change the situation first, and only then turn inward. The problem-solving hierarchy puts environmental change at the top. Leave or modify the situation if you can. Only when you can't change the environment do you shift to regulating your feelings about it, and only when that isn't enough do you move to acceptance. This isn't a throwaway suggestion. It's the preferred first response. If your office is noisy and it's destroying your concentration, the most effective intervention isn't deep breathing, it's closing the door or finding a quieter space.

ACT takes this a step further through its philosophical roots in *functional contextualism*—the idea that behaviour can only be understood in context. When ACT encourages committed action in the service of values, that naturally includes changing your circumstances when they aren't workable. ACT's *Choice Point model* explicitly treats changing or leaving the situation as a legitimate 'towards move'. Sometimes the most values-aligned action is to re-engineer the environment and the challenges that you face to better serve the life you want to live and create opportunities for flow experiences to occur.

Anthony Biglan, working within the broader ACT tradition, identified four features that define what he calls ***nurturing environments***:

1 They minimise toxic conditions such as coercion, chronic stress, and adversity.
2 They richly reinforce prosocial behaviours.
3 They limit opportunities for problem behaviours.
4 They foster psychological flexibility, supporting people to act on their values even under pressure.

Notice that last feature: a truly nurturing environment doesn't just remove what's harmful, it actively cultivates the capacity that sits at the heart of ACT. Whether you're designing a household, a classroom, a team, a workplace, or a community, those four principles offer a practical checklist for environmental effectiveness.

Similarly, Csikszentmihalyi identified specific environmental conditions that make flow experiences more likely: clear goals and opportunities for action that give you structure, immediate feedback so you know how you're going, a well-calibrated match between the challenge and your skill level, the opportunity for deep concentration without distraction, and a sense of control or agency over your situation. These aren't just internal states. They're features of how an environment is designed.

When we bring the DBT, ACT, and flow perspectives together, a coherent picture emerges in Values-Flow. The most effective approach isn't just building internal skills to cope with whatever life throws at you, but also actively shaping the environments where you live, work, and relate to others so that they support rather than undermine your capacity to thrive.

Importantly, we also must do what we can to shape the environments of others. If you are in a position of responsibility, whether at work or at home, you play a key role in creating an environment for those that you lead or influence. Do your house or workplace rules promote respect for all people, kindness of talk and behaviour, taking responsibility, and a sense of psychological safety? Do you give people time to practise strategies that support their emotional regulation (see Chapter 8)? Are you kind and understanding with your subordinates or children? Do you have effective boundaries in place? As we make effective environments for others, it feeds back to us, creating an environment that is supportive of our own thriving.

Using the Values-Flow Card: RELATE in Interpersonal and Environmental Contexts

Here's how to use the RELATE section with your Values-Flow Card. On the Practice side of your Card under "RELATE," rate the quality of your skill practice on a 0–6 scale (Table 9.1).

As you track your practice this week, pay particular attention to which priorities you focused on at different times (objective, relational, self-respect effectiveness, or environmental) and moments when you applied DEAR WOMAN, GIVE, or FAST skills. Notice how they connect to your overall sense of regulated engagement.

Begin noticing your interpersonal interactions with fresh eyes. Where do you tend to prioritise objective effectiveness at the cost of relationships or self-respect? Where do you sacrifice your needs for connection, or connection for self-protection? What would it look like to hold all three goals simultaneously, finding the synthesis that serves your overall thriving?

Table 9.1 Rating Scale for Your RELATE Practice

Score	*Meaning*
0	Didn't think about using interpersonal relationship skills and ignored environmental influences.
1	Identified a relational goal or noticed my environment but did not use any skills to address these.
2	Tried to practise a relational or environmental skill, but all felt effortful.
3	Tried to practise a relational or environmental skill, but got bored or half-checked out.
4	Tried to practise a relational or environmental skill, but felt overwhelmed or anxious.
5	Practised a relational or environmental skill and felt some benefit. It was enjoyable, but I didn't experience flow.
6	Completely practised relational and environmental skills. I experienced a sense of flow or deep involvement.

Also notice the environmental factors that influence your functioning. What environments support your wellbeing and which ones cause distress? What are the social norms in your environment and how well do you follow those? What parts of your community or culture are you proud of and what would you like to see change? Do you create a healthy environment for those whom you have an influence upon?

Flow Nudges: RELATE in Action

Here are practical ways to develop your interpersonal and environmental effectiveness skills this week:

1 **The Three Goals Check**: Before entering a significant interpersonal situation, ask yourself: What do I need from this interaction (objective effectiveness)? How can I pursue this in a way that strengthens rather than damages the relationship (relationship effectiveness)? How do I want to feel about myself afterwards (self-respect effectiveness)? Holding all three questions creates the dialectical awareness that enables harmonised navigation.

2 **The DEAR WOMAN Rehearsal**: Before a conversation where you need to make a request or set a boundary, write out each component of DEAR WOMAN. Describe the situation factually. Express your feelings. Assert your specific request. Note the reinforcement you'll offer. Remind yourself to stay Willing, Open, Mindful, Appear confident, and be willing to Negotiate. Even if you don't use the script word-for-word, the preparation builds skill and confidence that makes it more likely that your need will be met.

3 **The GIVE Experiment**: In your next challenging conversation, consciously apply the GIVE skill. Begin with Gentleness in your opening. Show genuine Interest by asking at least one curious question. Offer Validation of the other person's perspective before sharing your own. Maintain an Easy

manner throughout, especially if things get tense. Afterwards, reflect on whether the conversation felt different from your usual approach.

4 **The FAST Audit**: At the end of each day this week, review your significant interpersonal interactions through the FAST lens. Were you Fair to both yourself and others? Did you offer unnecessary Apologies that undermined your position? Did you Stick to your values even when it was difficult? Were you Truthful in your communications? This reflection builds awareness of patterns that might be undermining or supporting your self-respect.
5 **The Relationship Investment**: Choose one relationship you want to strengthen. This week, make three intentional deposits into the relationship bank account. Reach out to show interest, express appreciation for something specific, or offer support without being asked. Notice how these small investments shift the tone of the relationship over time.
6 **Choose Environments Supportive of Wellbeing**: Identify which of the environments that you interact with are supportive and hindering of your wellbeing. Arrange your schedule so that you spend more time in the supportive environments. See how this affects your wellbeing.
7 **Create Healthy Environments**: Even as the environment has an impact on your functioning, you also shape that environment. Consider what you can do to make it a healthier environment for yourself and others whom you interact with.

Sound Bite Summary

1 **Three Interpersonal Goals**: Social interactions provide opportunities for **objective effectiveness** (getting what you need), **relationship effectiveness** (maintaining connection), and/or **self-respect effectiveness** (preserving integrity). At different times, different goals will be your priority. Optimal relating balances all three.
2 **DEAR WOMAN for Objectives**: Describe, Express, Assert, Reinforce, be Willing and Open, stay Mindful, Appear confident, Negotiate. These skills create the clear goals and feedback loops that make interpersonal flow possible.
3 **GIVE for Relationships**: Gentle, Interested, Validate, Easy manner. These skills preserve and strengthen connection even during challenging conversations.
4 **FAST for Self-Respect**: Fair, no unnecessary Apologies, Stick to values, Truthful. These skills ensure you walk away from interactions with your integrity intact.
5 **Walk the Middle Path**: Relationships require dialectical balance—acceptance AND change, closeness AND independence, your needs AND others' needs.
6 **Interpersonal Flow**: When interpersonal skills meet relational challenges, moments of deep connection become possible. These can become co-created flow experiences that simultaneously enrich both people.

7 **Building for the Long Term**: Relationships are cultivated through repeated positive interactions, ongoing investment, and prompt repair of ruptures.
8 **Create Healthy Environments**: Identify what in your environment you can control. Accept the things that you cannot change and take action towards changing the things that you can.
9 **Track Your Progress**: Use the RELATE row on your Values-Flow Card to monitor interpersonal and environmental effectiveness, building awareness of patterns and areas for growth.

Final Word

Vienna from our opening story discovered that relationships are not just contexts in which we pursue goals. They are themselves arenas for flow, sources of meaning, and essential components of the life well lived. The skills in this chapter won't make relationships or existing in the world, free of challenges. But they will make interpersonal relationships and environmental experiences more manageable, and in that negotiation lies the possibility of genuine connection and growth.

Today as you look at the RELATE row on your Values-Flow Card, remember that it holds two dimensions: the interpersonal effectiveness that allows you to connect effectively with others and environmental effectiveness that actively creates environments where you and others can thrive. Both are essential. Both require practice. And both, when developed, create the conditions for the deep, engaged, meaningful life that Values-Flow is designed to support.

Step onto the dance floor. Your partners are waiting.

Part 3

From Skill Knowledge to Practical Application

10 From Burning in Hell to Values-Flow

A Personal Story

Chapter Overview

This chapter describes Peggy's personal story, which includes struggles with severe mental illness (burning in the basement), times of surviving life (the lower floor), thriving in life (the upper floor), and visits to the attic (recurrent flow experiences). The transition from severe behavioural dysregulation to freedom and contentedness is a long, slow, and painful journey, but illustrates what is possible when ongoing effort, appropriate clinical supports, and the Values-Flow process come together. We describe the Values-Flow skills that Peggy drew on, and the process of growth and change that resulted, even as that process continues to unfold. This chapter offers hope of what is possible for those who are struggling on the lower floors of the House of Functioning.

Transitioning to Application

In Chapter 1, we introduced the House of Functioning. Then, over the past eight chapters, we described the Values-Flow framework and skills. Throughout the chapters, we've provided case study examples of everyday people learning how to put these skills into practice. Although these reflect people that we have worked with over the years, they are hypothetical in nature, included to illustrate the ideas of the chapter.

This leaves a valid question: do the Values-Flow skills work in the real world? What does it practically look like to be at, and to inhabit, the different floors of the House of Functioning and to inhabit the different floors? How do you practically put the skills together into a coherent approach to therapy, teaching, managing, or coaching?

In this third section of this book, we describe what Values-Flow looks like in four different scenarios: an individual struggling with mental illness, counsellors and therapists working with clients, educators working with students, and coaches and managers working with employees. This is not a treatment manual or a lesson plan. Rather, it's an illustration of what is possible when the Values-Flow skills are applied, be it an individual who desires to find the life well lived, or someone who creates the conditions that allow others to thrive.

DOI: 10.4324/9781003771173-13

We begin with the individual sojourner who might want to use the skills described in the past six chapters in their own life. Rather than using a hypothetical person, which may come across as a nice but unrealistic story that doesn't apply to you, we describe Peggy's personal story, providing a real-world example of what it looks like to put the Values-Flow skills into action. Despite working in the wellbeing industry, Peggy has experienced severe mental illness, with extended periods of time living in the basement of the House. The battle has been real, but so has the healing journey. We illustrate what is possible when ongoing effort, appropriate clinical supports, and the Values-Flow process come together.

An important trigger warning. This chapter mentions trauma, sexual assault, eating disorders, substance abuse, self-harm, and suicidality. These are important issues, which often carry a lot of stigma. We believe that Peggy's story can provide hope of what is possible regardless of where you are in the House. However, if these are triggering topics for you, then you might want to skip this chapter or go through it with the support of a professional.

Background: The Struggle to Belong

Peggy was born in the U.S. into a White, middle-class family. She had an older sister, a younger brother, and two parents. In many ways, she had a privileged upbringing. The family had food on the table each night, access to good healthcare and decent schools, and relative peace in the family.

Despite coming from a loving home, Peggy often felt like she didn't fit anywhere. In a family that valued intellect, she was a sensitive, emotional child. She felt distressed at times but subconsciously got the message that physical pain was acceptable but emotional pain was not. Wanting the approval of her parents, she learned to bury her emotions and act as a happy child.

This act was particularly challenging due to pressures at church and school. She longed to fit in and have friends but felt overwhelmed by how noisy and disruptive the other kids were, and other kids often made fun of her because she was different. She tried to understand and follow the social cues but found the behaviours of other kids to be confusing. She was athletic and enjoyed playing sports with the boys, but then other girls would make fun of her and call her selfish for not playing with them.

The one place she thrived was in academics. She was a straight A student and considered by other kids to be a teacher's pet. She was put into the Gifted and Talented Education (GATE) programme, which was the one place she felt like she did belong. The periods she spent out of the classroom were intellectually stimulating and exciting. But other kids did not appreciate her intellect, making fun of her for being in the GATE program.

Still, she lived a protected childhood, and home was a safe place, where she allowed her imagination to come alive. She loved being outdoors, hiking, playing softball, or running around the home-made playground.

This all changed when she entered middle school. She attended a low socioeconomic school, and struggled with seeing the contrast between her own upbringing and the struggles of those around her. She rode the city bus to school and was introduced to people from different backgrounds and socioeconomic classes. She was a kind-hearted child and endeared herself to others on the bus. On the one hand, she showed care to several mentally challenged individuals. But on the other hand, she saw the ugly side of what life can bring and how people can treat you.

Vulnerabilities: The Lasting Impact of Trauma

In Chapter 8, we talked about *vulnerabilities*. DBT further introduces the concept of the **stress-vulnerability bucket** (see Figure 10.1). We each have a bucket, which represents our ability to function effectively in everyday life. Some people have very big buckets (they are well resourced in their mental health), whereas other people have small buckets (they have low levels of tolerance). Different things fill up parts of the bucket, and when our bucket overflows, that's when we experience mental breakdown. Vulnerabilities are things that permanently fill part of our bucket, such as genetics, personality, experiences in life, and trauma. Everyday stressors fill more of our bucket and, if they become bigger than the bucket, the bucket overflows and dysfunction occurs, pushing us into *hyperarousal* or *hypoarousal*. While we can't do anything about the vulnerabilities that we have or the size of our bucket, we can manage the stressors by poking holes in the bucket, so that it doesn't overflow.

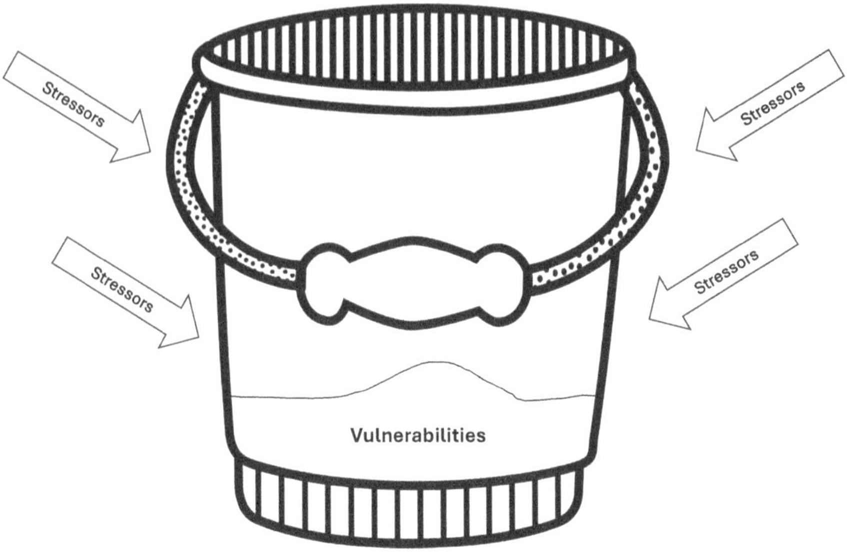

Figure 10.1 The Stress-Vulnerability Bucket.

This book is full of strategies to manage our buckets so that we don't become overwhelmed.

A major vulnerability factor that determines both the size of our bucket and fills up part of the bucket is **traumatic experiences**. Trauma can take two forms. **Big T trauma** refers to single events that have a major, lasting negative impact, such as natural disasters, sexual or physical assault, witnessing crime, or war. Such trauma can lead to *post-traumatic stress disorder* (PTSD). **Little t trauma** refers to small stresses that accumulate to have a negative and lasting impact on a person. Both types of trauma dysregulate the person's physiological system, reducing the size of the person's *window of tolerance*, and making them more susceptible to *hyperaousal* or hypoarousal.

Growing up, Peggy experienced both types of traumas, filling up part of her bucket. The lack of belonging and bullying by other kids, along with feeling rejected by her father, were traumas that ate away at her self-esteem, personal relationships, and sense of competence. She became a people pleaser, sacrificing her own needs for those of others. She also experienced unwanted sexual attention on the bus, which made her feel ashamed of herself. She struggled with anxiety and depression throughout her adolescence, and at age 20 became suicidal, her first visit to the basement of the House. Through a friend's pleading, she saw a counsellor and got some limited help, which stopped her from ending her life and carried her back to the lower floor, but did little for the constant anxiety and depression that she felt.

Later that year she went on a study abroad experience in a developing country in South America, to help her learn to understand and speak Spanish. She felt very isolated, and over the subsequent four months experienced a range of traumatic experiences, ranging from robberies to sexual assault. She picked up a parasite while she was there, and returned to the U.S. physically ill and suffering from PTSD. The extent of her trauma was not acknowledged. The experience completely overfilled her bucket, landing her back in the basement. She self-injured several times, but others noticed the cuts; she felt embarrassed and stopped cutting. She lost a significant amount of weight and struggled with an eating disorder for the subsequent two decades. She was living in the basement, seemingly with no way out.

She was placed on antidepressants and had a number of psychiatric sessions based on Cognitive Behavioural Therapy, which stabilised her mental health for a period, but never dealt with the deeper traumas that she had experienced. She was a resilient individual, and the therapy and medications, along with moving to a different state for graduate school, pulled her back to the lower floor of the House. She threw herself into academics, athletics, and people-pleasing.

During that period, she was successful in her career and athletics, living on the upper floor in terms of her accomplishments. She even had visits to the attic as she experienced the runner's high on her long runs. However, she experienced recurring bouts of severe depression, burnout, and ongoing generalised anxiety, such that in other areas of life she resided in the basement or lower floor of the House. She experienced additional traumas, including workplace bullying and harassment. She dealt with things through controlling the food that she ate, excessively exercising, drinking alcohol, and being a workaholic. At times, as she burned in hell, she engaged with therapy to manage the symptoms of mental illness that she experienced, but as a whole, she got through life by pushing herself physically and mentally. She was always an overachiever. Indeed, she prided herself on being able to keep going despite living on the lower floors of the House.

The Tipping Point

Peggy successfully functioned in her life and career for decades after her traumas occurred. Although she had ongoing struggles with anxiety, depression, an eating disorder, and workaholism, she existed on the lower floor of quiet desperation. The tipping point came with the Covid 19 pandemic. As an academic, she worked hard to shift her teaching from face-to-face to online learning. She gave presentations on how to maintain wellbeing through the stress of the pandemic. She was a productive researcher. She worked 70+ hours a week, volunteered for the local church, and prided herself on being everything to everyone.

Then lockdown occurred. In Melbourne, Australia, lockdowns were extensive. You were only allowed outside for one hour a day. Social activities were shut down, such that the only contact Peggy had with the outside world was through Zoom. Peggy's coping mechanisms broke down. The lockdown retriggered her PTSD, the excessive work exhausted her, she started drinking excessively, and her functioning significantly deteriorated. She had overfilled her bucket, and this time it would remain overfilled. She became suicidal and started self-harming. She tried to deal with her worsening mental health by working harder, but that only pushed her further into despair. She fell into the basement, and there she would stay for the next several years.

The Stabilisation Process: Engaging with ACT and DBT

Through the urging of friends, Peggy sought psychological and psychiatric support. She started seeing an ACT-based therapist and completed an outpatient DBT-based programme. With her therapist, she shared the traumatic experiences that she had never told anyone about. She learned the various ACT and DBT skills that we have covered in this book. Still, her functioning declined. She abused substances to a greater degree, her self-harm behaviour became more constant and extreme, she struggled with suicidality, and had countless visits to the emergency department, rehab, and inpatient admissions at a local mental health facility. While she was given skills to use, the skills were inaccessible to her. She was stuck in the basement, and care remained focused on reducing life-threatening behaviours and keeping her alive.

Ultimately, she had to quit working because her functioning was so poor. But work was an important part of her identity, so that drove her deeper into her substance abuse and self-harm. All care was focused on safety and stabilisation, and there was seemingly no forward progress, as her care team struggled to keep her alive. She couldn't access skills. When she felt overwhelmed, she would self-harm and end up in the emergency department, wanting to give up on life. Her stress bucket was constantly overflowing, her physiological system was constantly overwhelmed, and ACT and DBT skills remained useless tools lying at her feet.

The Turning Point: Values-Flow in Action

While there was no progress on the surface, like seeds germinating in the winter, Peggy had learned the various ACT and DBT concepts and skills described in this book, and she developed a toolkit that would prove to be useful for recovery once she was able to access the skills. The turning point was when she stopped trying to fight and control life (the *control agenda* that ACT describes, see Chapter 2), and instead started accepting herself as a valued human being, treated herself with self-compassion, and started to use the Values-Flow framework. As part of that process, she activated *Wise Mind*, finding an integration between Emotion and Reasonable mind. Wise mind allowed her to access the many tools that she had learned that were previously inaccessible to her while she was wasting away in the basement.

She began by learning to understand the roots of her problems. While she presented as a patient struggling with self-harm, substance abuse, suicidality, and disordered eating, she came to understand these as symptoms of a dysregulated system, rather than the underlying cause. The traumas that she had experienced in both childhood and as an adult meant that she had a small window of tolerance and easily became dysregulated. She was diagnosed with Autism Spectrum Disorder, which meant that at a physiological level, she was constantly dysregulated due to masking and trying to fit into a neurotypical world. Drinking, self-harming, and controlling food were ways that she tried to make life more predictable and controlled—core needs of an Autistic individual.

Peggy began to have a sense of identity as she learned about her neurodiversity, along with intrapersonal (regulation difficulties, Chapter 8), interpersonal (relational difficulties, Chapter 9), and environmental factors (environmental difficulties, Chapter 9) that dysregulated her system. She recognised that her *struggle switch* was turned on, such that she caused a lot more suffering through not accepting the pain of the traumas that she had experienced and who she was as a person. She *radically accepted* her neurodiversity and began to honour the unique traits that defined her, rather than feeling inferior because she was different from those around her. She also radically accepted her alcoholism, workaholism, and tendency to overachieve at everything. It was humbling yet freeing to let go of the *control agenda* and move into *willingness*.

With a better understanding of her identity, she could practise the VIRTUE skills (Chapter 4). She identified her *core values* and *strengths*, and then started to act in ways that honoured these. For instance, she valued connection with others, but realised that group situations were overwhelming from a sensory perspective due to her autism. Rather than going to big group gatherings, she set up one-on-one meet-ups with friends and started to wear earplugs that allowed the conversation in while blocking out peripheral noise that made it hard to concentrate. She valued nature, so she started spending purposeful time outdoors.

She realised that her strengths included attention to detail, perseverance, creativity, and systems thinking. These skills made her a good researcher. Working with her employer, she crafted her work tasks so that she could use her strengths in her job, which made the work more fulfilling and flow-inducing. By using her strengths, she had flow experiences while working, which made the work enjoyable, rather than being a drain on her system that pushed her towards hyperarousal or hypoarousal.

As she went through each day, she engaged with the *ARIA* skills (Chapter 5) to effectively respond to self-destructive urges. For example, when she had the urge to self-injure, she identified what was going on in and around her that was dysregulating her (*Attend*) along with the thoughts ("I am worthless, I can't do this"), feelings ("I feel really overwhelmed right now") and physiological sensations ("my skin is crawling, making me want to self-injure") that she was experiencing (*Reflect*). Rather than reacting to the urge, she determined specific skills (such as the *TIPP*, *STOP*, and *opposite action* skills) that slowed down the immediate reaction of self-injuring so that she could respond effectively (*Inform*), and then engaged in those behaviours (practising self-care rather than self-harm; *Act*).

She found that slowing down her life created a better rhythm, where she actually accomplished more than when she was constantly in panic mode, reflecting Wilson's *Slow is Fast* principle (Chapter 5). As part of slowing down, she started to regularly practise *mindfulness* (Chapter 5) in a manner that worked for her. She found that guided meditations that focused on bodily sensations or visualisation did not work for her, often causing flashbacks and nightmares. Instead, more active mindful exercises, such as mindful walking, breath work, and sensory-based meditations, allowed her to be mindful while not triggering traumatic memories.

She began applying the *emotion regulation* and *distress tolerance* skills (Chapter 8) that she had learned through her ACT and DBT training. She recognised that a combination of the trauma that she had experienced as both a child and adult, combined with her neurodiversity, meant that she had a small window of tolerance. She began to monitor her levels of arousal, identifying when it was heading towards hyperarousal resulting in meltdown, or hypoarousal resulting in shutdown, and applying the emotion regulation and distress tolerance skills when she was in the *dysregulation* zone, helping her to regulate herself before entering panic or dissociation.

When she did go into *hyperarousal*, she felt panicky – she had trouble breathing, felt nauseous, and the world spun around her. Her skin began to crawl and she had strong urges to self-injure. But instead of engaging in the harmful behaviour, she used the *STOP* skill, literally stopping herself from the self-harm action. She placed an ice pack on her face and neck and purposefully took deep, long breaths, drawing on the *TIPP* skill. These two skills took her from panic to a place where thoughts could come back online. She was then able to identify negative consequences that would occur if she self-injured (e.g., having to go to the hospital for stitches), and positive benefits of staying safe (e.g., her family would be proud of her for not self-harming and she'd be able to spend time with her dog), which helped her respond from a place of safety rather than react from a place of dysregulation.

At other times she would drop into *hypoarousal*, where it felt impossible to do anything. She felt depressed, isolated, detached, and dissociated from her body. Life felt impossible, and it brought the urge to give up on life. Using her *emotion regulation* skills, she engaged in *opposite action*, making herself go out on a walk. She texted a few friends to create connection. She took a hot shower and played with her dog, creating movement and action.

As time went on, she found it helpful to *cope ahead* for activities that she knew would dysregulate her. She realised that even enjoyable activities often involved a lot of sensory stimulation, which was overwhelming. She started to monitor what activities might overwhelm her, and be more purposeful about which activities she said yes to, and which she skipped. If she did go to an event, she spent time relaxing before the activity, went to the activity for a set period of time, and then came home and engaged in actions that soothed her senses, such as diffusing essential oils in her home, listening to calming music, and spending time with her dog.

By using the REGULATE skills, she was able to more consistently stay within her *window of tolerance* (Chapter 8). Rather than life constantly feeling like it was too hard (resulting in anxiety), she cultivated the conditions for flow experiences to occur (Chapter 2). She crafted some of her work and life tasks so that there were clear goals (such as writing this book), immediate feedback, and challenge–skill balance, key conditions for flow experiences. Activities became intrinsically motivating to her, her concentration improved, and at times she lost herself in the tasks she engaged in, having flow experiences. The sense of engagement that she felt was rewarding in and of itself, such that it pulled her into living more aligned with her values and away from self-harming behaviours.

As she used her skills effectively, she began engaging in life with the *VITAL* skills (Chapter 6). Rather than engaging in activities to try and make other people happy, she explored what activities she enjoyed doing and spent time doing those activities. At work, she spent more time focusing on the things that she enjoyed doing, such as deep-level thinking, writing, and collaborating on various projects. Cultivating the *autotelic personality*, she rediscovered the curiosity and interest that had driven her as a child. Writing this book was one of the activities that she was *intrinsically motivated* to do. She also engaged in *serious play*. She explored different ways of doing her work, finding approaches that were meaningful and engaging.

As part of ACCEPT (Chapter 7), she practised *willingness*. She became willing to change the way that she worked and approached life, so that it would be more personally fulfilling and result in meaningful engagement. She learned to accept the traumas that had happened in her life, choosing to appreciate what they taught her and how they formed her. She wasn't grateful for the traumas themselves, but she was grateful for the person that she had become because of the pain and suffering that she had gone through at various times in her life. She learned to accept that she was prone to cope with stress in unhealthy ways, such as drinking and self-injuring, and then took steps to better manage the stress in her life through the DBT and ACT skills described in this book.

She became more effective in her *interpersonal relationships* (Chapter 9). Rather than being a people pleaser, she learned to value and express her own needs, using the *DEAR WOMAN* skill. She was no longer there for everyone, compromising her own needs for others, but she was there for those that mattered. She also learned to reach out to others for support when she was struggling, rather than trying to do everything herself.

She identified *environmental factors* (Chapter 9) that undermined her well-being. For instance, due to her sensory sensitivities, loud and busy environments were very stressful for her. She used noise-cancelling headphones and spent time after being in an overstimulating environment to engage in self-care and silent reflection. She found that she could create a supportive environment by limiting visual and audio stimuli, using a diffuser to create nice smells, and playing a nature track in the background to create a calming environment.

Finally, she *tracked her journey* across days and months. Each day she spent time identifying where she was in terms of what was planned for the day, her physical and emotional pain and stress levels, and what resources were available to meet the demands of the day. While she did not use the *Values-Flow Card* (Chapter 3), she informally tracked her use of the skills described in this book, her levels of arousal, and the results of the day.

Inhabiting the Upper Floors

Through the use of these skills, Peggy moved from burning in hell (the basement) to regularly inhabiting the upper floors of the House. Importantly, this movement through the House did not occur overnight. The use of these skills occurred over a period of several years. She had a lot of relapses resulting in hospitalisations. But over time, the days with no drinking or self-harming increased, her eating disorder faded, and she has come to find a contentment with life.

Which skill made the difference? There's no clear answer, nor is there a need for an answer. This is why trying out the different skills in this book matters. Some will resonate with you, others will not. The key is that you're willing to give things a go, be patient with the journey, be gentle with yourself over time, take things one day (or sometimes one hour) at a time, and stick with things until the miracle happens.

The story has a happy ending…for today. She still has a lot of growth and change needed to live well, but through the skills described in this book, she is well on her way in her journey up through the House. Will Peggy stay on the upper floors of the House? Perhaps she will, perhaps not. Life happens. Things get busy, relationships break down, others criticise you, overwhelm happens. There may still be visits to the basement. But the key is that Peggy is willing to keep trying, keep growing, and prioritise living life for what it is, through the highs and lows that life inevitably brings.

Flow Nudges

1 **Revisiting the House of Functioning**: Go back to the House of Functioning. Consider different domains of your life, such as work, relationships, health, creativity, or spirituality. For each one, consider: where am I in the House? What are the wellbeing implications for me and others in my sphere of influence?
2 **Share with Others**: Take some time to describe the House of Functioning to a trusted friend or partner. Share where you are honestly at, and how that affects your functioning. Ask for support to move towards or to continue to inhabit the upper floors of the House.
3 **Review the Values-Flow Skills**: In Chapters 4 through 9, we described the various Values-Flow skills, with strategies for implementing these in your life. Spend some time reviewing the skills. Which ones do you connect with? Which have you tried or are interested in trying? Which ones stick?
4 **Find your Skills Recipe**: Take out a sheet of paper and write down the Values-Flow skills that resonate with you. Consider how often each one might be applied, under what conditions, and for what purpose. Try things out over the week, using the Values-Flow Card to track your progress. Note what works and what doesn't work and tweak your recipe accordingly, being mindful of the everyday challenges that you experience.
5 **Regularly Use Your Recipe**: Once you are happy with the combination of Values-Flow skills that are right for you, take the time each day to practise the skills. Track your progress using the Values-Flow Card. Observe the effects this has on your functioning over time.

Sound Bite Summary

1 **Our capacity to withstand challenges is like a bucket**. Vulnerabilities and stress fill up our bucket, and if the bucket overflows, we tip into overwhelm. The Values-Flow skills punch holes in the bucket, enabling us to handle the challenges that life throws at us in skilful ways, without being overwhelmed by them.
2 **Trauma** makes us vulnerable to overwhelm or shutdown and often pushes us down to the lower floors of the House. Acknowledging and accepting traumatic experiences is the first step towards healing the wounds that have occurred.

3 **The House of Functioning is fluid**. At different times in life, you might be in the basement, on the lower or upper floors, or up in the attic. You don't have to stay where you are. Through consistent effort and willingness, you can move towards the upper floors.
4 **Multiple Values-Flow Skills** are needed. We are complex human beings. There's no silver bullet, quick-fix approach to improving functioning. It takes consistent effort and the use of multiple skills.

Final Word

Peggy's story demonstrates what is possible when you put the skills in this book into practice. Practice is the key word here. The skills are not just something to read about and then forget. Pick them up, try them out, record what happens using the Values-Flow Card. Follow the ARIA process to identify what works and what doesn't work. The goal is not to practise the skills perfectly. The goal is progress, not perfection. The key is that you start somewhere and keep going.

This chapter demonstrates the Values-Flow process from the individual's perspective. What if you are in a position where you support the wellbeing of others? In the next chapter, we look at how therapists and clinicians can apply the process with clients.

11 Values-Flow in the Therapy Room

Chapter Overview

This chapter describes strategies for counsellors and psychologists to apply Values-Flow in the therapy room. Chain analysis is a core tool in clinical care, and the same structural framework (vulnerability factors, prompting event, links, target experience, consequences) that reveals how problem behaviours happen can reveal how flow experiences happen. We describe problem chains, flow chains, and blocked chains, and emphasise the value of comparing chains. We describe the steps involved in conducting a flow chain analysis and provide clinical considerations.

The Therapist Who Forgot to Look Up

Meet Anika. She's a clinical psychologist in her mid-forties, experienced and well-trained. She's completed advanced training in both ACT and DBT, supervises junior clinicians, and genuinely cares about her clients. She's good at what she does. Her caseload includes people on every floor of the House of Functioning, including clients burning in the basement with self-harm and suicidal crises, clients on the ground floor managing chronic depression and anxiety, and a handful of clients on the upper floor who are doing reasonably well but feel like they want something more.

Anika is skilled at helping people move out of the basement. She knows how to assess problem behaviours, use distress tolerance skills when clients are in crisis, and deploy emotion regulation strategies when dysregulation threatens to overwhelm. She's saved lives with these skills. She's proud of that, and she should be.

But here's what Anika noticed. She spent most of her therapeutic energy *looking down*. Down into the basement, down into problems, down into what went wrong. When a client arrived for a session, Anika's instinct was to pull out the DBT diary card, identify the most severe problem behaviour from the past week, and work with the client to analyse what went wrong. What happened? What were the vulnerability factors? What was the prompting event? What thoughts, emotions, and actions linked the prompting event to the problem

DOI: 10.4324/9781003771173-14

behaviour? What consequences reinforced it? How do we stop it from happening again?

This is excellent therapy. It is evidence-based, rigorous, and often lifesaving. But Anika began to realise that she had no equivalent process for *looking up*. When a client reported a genuinely good week, such as a morning where they felt absorbed in a meaningful project, an afternoon where they lost track of time playing music, a conversation that left them feeling deeply connected, Anika would smile, validate the experience, and then move on. She had no structured way of understanding *what had gone right*. There was no examination of what conditions, skills, and choices had created the experience of engaged, values-aligned living. She had a sophisticated toolkit for understanding the basement and lower floor, but only vague encouragement for the upper floor and the attic.

One day, after a particularly good session where a client described an unexpectedly powerful experience of creative absorption, Anika found herself thinking: *What if I analysed that the way I'd analyse a crisis? What if I traced the events that led to flow with the same rigour I use to trace the events that lead to self-harm?*

That question changed her practice.

The Surprising Crossover: Problem Chains and Flow Chains

In Chapter 10, we saw how Peggy's journey from the basement to the upper floor required the integration of multiple Values-Flow skills over time. In this chapter, we turn to the therapist's perspective: how can clinicians systematically help clients not only reduce suffering but also understand, cultivate, and sustain the experiences of engaged living that characterise the upper floor and the attic?

The tool we propose is one that most clinicians already know; they just haven't been using it in this direction. It's called **chain analysis**, and it's a centrepiece of assessment and intervention in DBT.

Charles Swenson, one of Linehan's closest collaborators, describes chain analysis as the primary means of determining the controlling variables of target behaviours. It is the initial step in problem-solving and the organising framework of therapy sessions. As a therapeutic tool, it is built for one purpose: to understand *how* a behaviour happened by tracing the chain of events in enough detail that you can see the patterns and intervene.

Here is the insight at the heart of this chapter: *the same structural framework that reveals how problem behaviours happen can reveal how flow experiences happen*. As illustrated in Figure 11.1, the architecture is identical. The process is the same. The clinical skills transfer directly. What changes is the direction of the practitioner's gaze.

In a traditional problem behaviour chain, the therapist and client trace the path from vulnerability to crisis. They work from the prompting event through escalating emotional intensity that lead to the problem behaviour (e.g.,

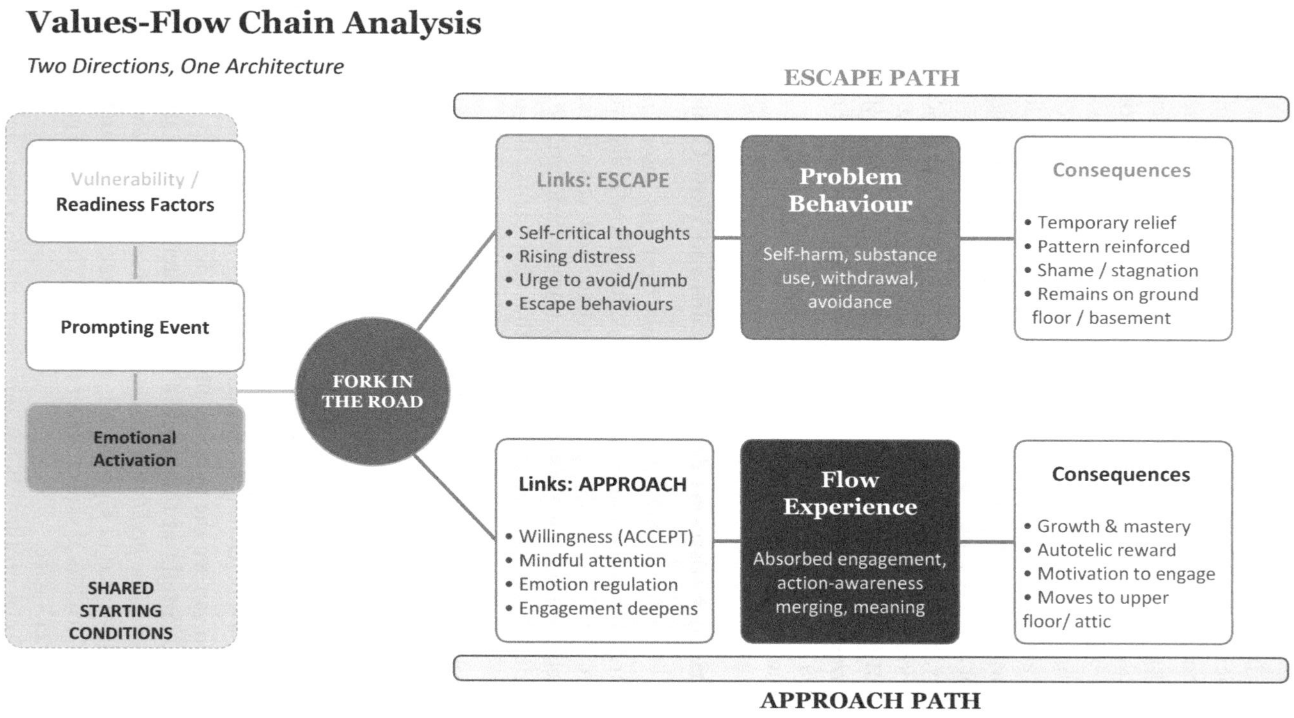

Figure 11.1 Chain Analysis in Both Directions: The Same Architecture, Different Outcomes.

self-harm, substance use, withdrawal) that temporarily reduces the unbearable feeling.

In a **Values-Flow chain**, the therapist and client trace the path from readiness to engagement. They work from the prompting event through the challenge–skill balance to the experience of absorbed, values-aligned action.

The difference between a problem chain and a Values-Flow chain is in whether the person, at the critical moment, *avoided* the difficult emotion through ineffective behaviours or *approached* it with willingness and skill. This is not a superficial analogy. The crossover runs deep, and it has important implications for how therapists work with clients across every floor of the House.

The Five Elements of a Values-Flow Chain

A DBT behavioural chain typically consists of five consecutive elements, visualised from left to right: vulnerability factors, prompting event, links in the chain (thoughts, emotions, actions, environmental events), the target behaviour, and consequences. As illustrated in Figure 11.1, each of these elements has a direct parallel in the analysis of a flow experience.

Readiness Factors (Vulnerability Factors)

In a problem chain, **vulnerability factors** are the conditions that make the person more susceptible to emotional dysregulation on any given day, such as poor sleep, accumulated stress, interpersonal conflict, or physical illness. These fill up the *stress-vulnerability bucket* (Chapter 10) and narrow the *window of tolerance* (Chapter 8). For instance, in Peggy's story (Chapter 10), factors such as sleep deprivation, missed medications, and visually or auditorily stimulating environments made her more susceptible to becoming dysregulated. The main question that we ask is: what are the factors that make the person *vulnerable* to emotional dysregulation?

In a flow chain, the same question applies, but we ask it in the approach direction. What made the person *ready* for flow? This might be factors such as a good night's rest, their PLEASE skills (Chapter 8) are in good order, they had accumulated positive emotions (Chapter 8), and worked out interpersonal problems (Chapter 9). For Peggy, the REGULATE (Chapter 8) and RELATE (Chapter 9) skills were important for reducing vulnerabilities and making her ready to have clear goals, be able to skilfully negotiate challenges as they arose, and use immediate feedback. Together, these created the conditions to make flow experiences possible.

The readiness factors for flow are often the *inverse* of the vulnerability factors for crises. This is therapeutically powerful, because it means that every intervention a therapist uses to reduce vulnerability, such as improving sleep hygiene, reducing substance use, building positive experiences, and managing interpersonal stressors, is simultaneously building the foundation for flow.

The REGULATE and RELATE skills are not just for crisis prevention; they have the potential of be flow infrastructure.

The Prompting Event (The Invitation to Engage)

In a problem chain, the **prompting event** is the stimulus or challenge that sets off the chain towards the problem behaviour. For instance, when Peggy was overstimulated by a sudden loud noise or plans suddenly changed, it caused feelings of overwhelm, sending her into hyperarousal and self-harm behaviours. The main question that we ask is what event or stressor set off the negative process?

In a flow chain, the prompting event is the moment something *invited engagement*—the moment a challenge appeared that matched the person's skills, values, and interests. The prompting event in the flow chain might be a work task that requires creative problem-solving, a conversation that demands genuine presence, a physical activity that stretches existing ability, or an artistic endeavour that calls for full attention. For Peggy, this occurred when she was taught the DBT skills through a neurodiverse lens. She felt overwhelmed at times, but now she had the skills ready to meet such challenges. The main question that we ask is what event or circumstance set off the flow process?

Crucially, the prompting event often involves *the same discomfort that triggers problem behaviour chains.* The challenge feels uncomfortable. There is uncertainty about whether you can manage it. Anxiety, self-doubt, and even fear may be present. The divergence happens in what comes next in the links between the prompting event and the target experience.

The Links: Where Avoidance and Approach Diverge

The links are where the crossover between problem chains and flow chains occurs. In both chains, the links consist of thoughts, emotions, actions, physiological sensations, and environmental events that unfold in sequence after the prompting event. In both chains, *difficult internal experiences are present.* The question is what the person does with them.

In a **problem behaviour chain**, the links typically follow a classical conditioning pattern that Swenson describes as *cue → emotion → avoidance.* A present-day cue triggers an intense emotional response such as panic, shame, anger, or despair. The person then engages in an avoidance behaviour to eliminate or reduce the unbearable feeling. The avoidance might be action-based (self-harm, substance use), cognitive (dissociation, rumination, distraction), or emotional (shifting from a primary emotion like shame to a secondary emotion like anger) in nature. The escape works in the short term as the emotion temporarily recedes, which reinforces the pattern. For Peggy, the feelings of overwhelm made her panic (*hyperarousal*), which would then lead to substance abuse or self-harm. The substance use or self-harm reduced the feeling of overwhelm, which reinforced using substances or self-harm to deal with overwhelming feelings and situations.

In a **flow chain**, the links follow the pattern: *cue → emotion → approach*. The challenge triggers emotional activation, such as anxiety about difficulty, excitement about possibility, boredom, or vulnerability about caring. However, instead of avoiding the challenge, the person *approaches* the challenge with willingness and skill. They stay with the discomfort long enough for something to shift. Attention narrows. Self-consciousness recedes. Action and awareness begin to merge. The ACCEPT skills (Chapter 7), including *willingness*, *radical acceptance*, and the courage to stay present, are what make this approach possible. The REGULATE skills (Chapter 8) keep arousal within the *window of tolerance* while the person engages. For Peggy, she *radically accepted* that she felt overwhelmed and engaged in *opposite action*, practising self-care rather than turning to self-harm.

Here is the dialectic at the heart of this chapter: **flow and crisis share the same starting conditions**. Both begin with emotional activation in response to a challenge. Both involve the presence of difficult thoughts and feelings. Both reach a fork in the road. As illustrated in Figure 11.2, the difference is which direction the person takes when they reach that fork—do they avoid or approach? The skills that prevent avoidance, such as *distress tolerance*, *emotion regulation*, *mindfulness*, and *willingness*, are the *same skills* that enable the approach. The therapist who has been building these skills to keep a client out of the basement has simultaneously been equipping them for the attic.

The Target Experience: Flow Instead of Crisis

In a problem chain, the **target behaviour** is what the therapist is trying to reduce, such as self-harm, bingeing and purging, angry outbursts, and avoidance. For instance, Peggy's psychologist and psychiatrist tried to reduce how often Peggy restricted food, drank excessively, self-harmed, and struggled with suicidal thoughts. Describing the target experience includes questions such as: What were you doing when you went into self-harm mode? What was happening in your body? What were you thinking or not thinking? What did you feel? The therapist guides the client to inhabit the experience in the present tense, bringing the experience alive within the session.

In a flow chain, the **target experience** is what the therapist is trying to understand and cultivate, including the absorbed engagement, the sense of action and awareness merging, the experience of being carried by a current of meaningful activity. For instance, for Peggy, it was important to delay and distract herself from the negative urges and create a calming environment, by using essential oils, focusing her attention on visually calming stimuli, and holding a weighted bear. This allowed her to be able to connect with her values and skills, which then made it possible to approach rather than avoid the challenges that were before her.

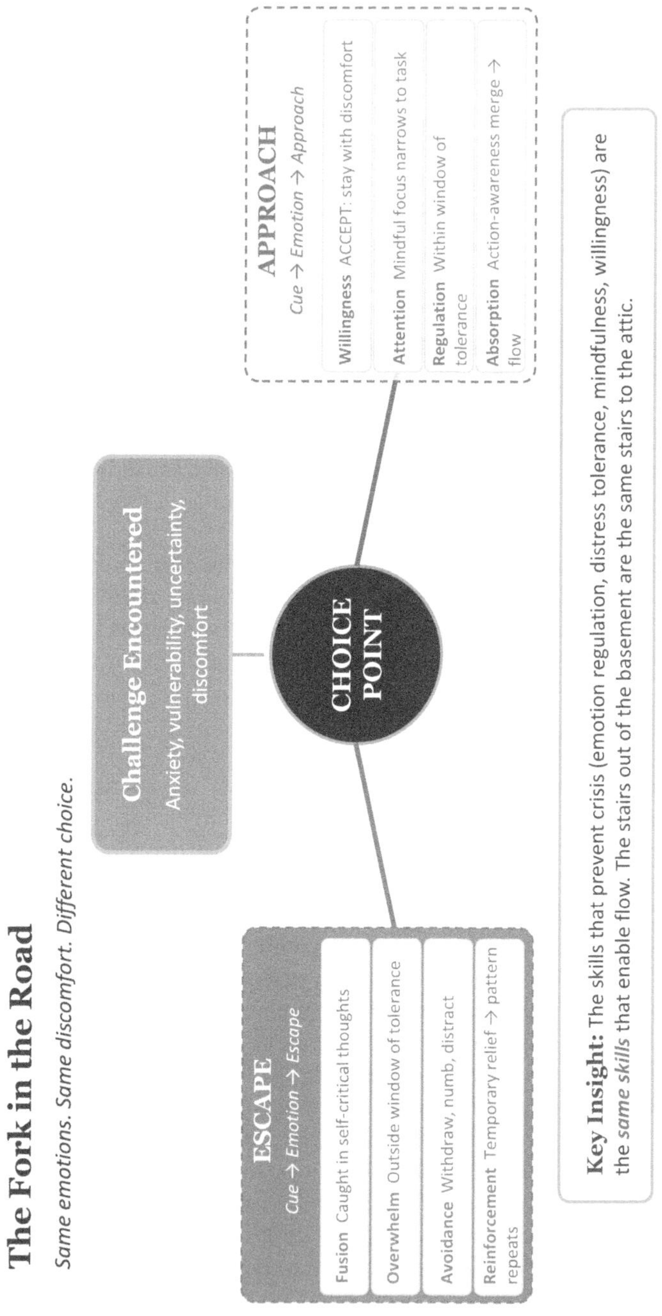

Figure 11.2 The Fork in the Road: Where Escape and Approach Diverge.

Describing the target experience includes questions such as: What exactly did the experience feel like? What were you doing? What was happening in your body? What were you thinking or not thinking? How did time seem to pass? The therapist invites the client to inhabit the experience in the present tense: *"OK, you're at your desk now, and you've just started working on the design. What are you noticing? What's happening with your attention? What's the quality of your engagement?"* This detailed recounting serves the same function as it does in a problem chain. It brings the experience alive in session, activates the associated emotions, and creates the conditions for learning.

Consequences: What Flow Reinforces

In a problem chain, the therapist pays particular attention to the **consequences that reinforce** the problem behaviour, such as the relief that follows avoidance, the numbness that replaces pain, the sense of release that cutting provides. For instance, when Peggy drank alcohol, the anxiety that she felt would temporarily be reduced. When she self-harmed, she would feel a release from the tension and overwhelm that she felt, receive care at the emergency department, which filled a need for social connection with others, and pacified feelings of self-loathing that she felt. Understanding these reinforcers is essential for changing the pattern. The question to ask is: what happens when you engage in the problem behaviour that makes you want to do it again?

In a flow chain, the **consequences that reinforce** the valued behaviours are equally important but work differently. Flow experiences typically produce what Csikszentmihalyi called *autotelic reward*—a sense of satisfaction, growth, and the desire to engage again. They build what Chapter 6 described as the VITAL orientation: intrinsic motivation, curiosity, and persistence. They also often produce tangible outcomes, such as a completed project, a deeper conversation, or a new skill, which create further opportunities for engagement. For instance, each time Peggy engaged in a valued work project, she felt a sense of competence, curiosity about what findings may emerge, a match between the challenge and her skills, and she felt like she was living more in line with her values. Questions to ask include: What happened after the flow experience? How did you feel? What did you do next?

Understanding the reinforcing consequences of flow is therapeutically powerful because it creates a counter-narrative to the reinforcement of avoidance. The client begins to see that there are two paths from emotional activation. First, there is *avoidance*, which provides short-term relief but long-term stagnation or worse mental health problems. Second, there is *approach*, which involves short-term discomfort but produces longer term engagement, growth, and the experiences that make life worth living. This is the dialectical dance between the basement and the attic, and the client can see it mapped out on two parallel chains.

Exposure in Both Directions

One of Swenson's most important insights is that *chain analysis itself functions as an exposure procedure.* When a therapist guides a client through a detailed recounting of the events surrounding a problem behaviour, the process inevitably brings the client's mind into contact with emotional material they have been avoiding, such as the shame of what they did, the fear that preceded it, or the vulnerability they tried to escape. Simply telling the story in detail, link by link, is an act of approach rather than avoidance. It is informal exposure, woven into the fabric of assessment.

The same is true—and perhaps even more powerfully so—for flow chain analysis. But here, the exposure runs in an unexpected direction.

Recall from Chapter 5 that beneath values lies vulnerability. Touching what you most yearn for in life carries enormous risk. In hoping for something more, you must accept that others may not approve, that you might not get it, or that you might lose it. Known suffering is less risky than facing the unknown. Many clients have learned to protect themselves from this vulnerability through fusion and avoidance, the very processes that block Values-Flow from occurring.

When a therapist guides a client through a detailed flow chain analysis, they are asking the client to approach not just the *mechanics* of the experience but the *emotional meaning* of it. Why did this activity matter to you? What value was being expressed? What did it feel like to care about something enough to lose yourself in it? These questions can be as emotionally activating as any problem chain analysis. Sometimes they can be even more emotionally activating, because they expose the longing and vulnerability that the client's protective patterns have been designed to conceal.

Importantly, a client who has spent years in the basement may find it genuinely frightening to acknowledge that they experienced something good. They are so used to experiencing bad things and often feel like they deserve punishment. The good experience carries implicit risk: *What if I can't have it again? What if it was a fluke? What if wanting more of this makes the absence more painful? What is life without my problem behaviour?* The therapist needs to approach these fears with the same skill and sensitivity they would bring to trauma-related exposure. Wilson's principle of "Slow is Fast" (Chapter 5) applies here. The therapist moves carefully, validating the vulnerability of caring about something, holding space for the ambivalence, and allowing the client to make contact with what matters to them at their own pace.

This means that flow chain analysis involves **exposure in two directions**. First, there is exposure to the difficult emotions that were present *during* the experience (the anxiety of challenge, the vulnerability of engagement, the discomfort of stretching beyond one's comfort zone, the boredom of an unstimulating environment). Second, there is the exposure to the difficult emotions that arise *from* the experience (the hope that it could happen again, the grief that it hasn't happened more often, the fear of wanting something you might not get to keep). Both are therapeutically important. Both require the clinician's full presence and skill.

Blocked Flow Chains: Understanding What Gets in the Way

Not every problem chain leads to crisis, and not every flow chain leads to flow experiences. There is a third type of chain that is particularly informative for therapists: the **blocked flow chain**. This is the chain where the readiness factors are adequate, the prompting event is present, the challenge–skill balance is approximately right, and yet flow does not emerge. Something in the links between the invitation and the experience got in the way.

Blocked flow chains are clinically valuable because they reveal the specific barriers to engagement for each individual client. Common barriers include:

- **Cognitive Fusion**: The client fuses with self-evaluative thoughts ("I'm not good enough for this," "I don't deserve to feel good," "What if I fail?") rather than with the task itself. Self-consciousness hijacks attention, preventing the merging of action and awareness that flow requires.
- **Emotional Escape**: The client encounters discomfort such as the anxiety of challenge, the vulnerability of caring, or the boredom of an unstimulating environment, and escapes before engagement can occur. They might check their phone, switch tasks, numb out, or retreat into a safer but less meaningful activity.
- **Dysregulation**: Emotional intensity exceeds the *window of tolerance*, tipping the client into *hyperarousal* (panic, overwhelm) or *hypoarousal* (shutdown, numbness). The REGULATE skills were insufficient for the level of challenge encountered.
- **Environmental Interference**: External factors, such as interruptions, noise, interpersonal conflict, and competing demands, disrupt the conditions for engagement. The RELATE skills (Chapter 9) may be relevant here, particularly around creating environments that support rather than undermine engagement.
- **Challenge–Skill Mismatch**: The challenge is too far above or below the person's skill level. Too high, and anxiety overwhelms engagement. Too low, and boredom extinguishes interest. The VITAL skills (Chapter 6) address this directly by adjusting challenge upwards or breaking tasks down until the balance point is found.

By comparing a successful flow chain with a blocked flow chain, the therapist and client can identify the exact point of divergence, the link where avoidance replaced approach or where dysregulation replaced engagement. This is the same process Swenson describes when comparing multiple problem behaviour chains across sessions to identify recurring patterns. The therapist looks across chains in the same way that a detective looks across crime scenes, searching for the common elements that make the pattern predictable and therefore changeable.

ARIA as the Therapist's Chain Analysis Process

In Chapter 5, we described the ARIA cycle. Importantly, the ARIA cycle maps directly onto the process of conducting a flow chain analysis in session. ARIA was designed as a cycle of engagement with life; chain analysis is a structured method of understanding engagement or its absence. When the therapist uses ARIA as the organising framework for flow chain analysis, the skills the client has been practising *between* sessions become the same skills they use *within* the session to understand their own experiences.

- **Attending**: The therapist slows the process down (Wilson's "Slow is Fast" principle) and helps the client mindfully attend to each element of the chain. Questions might include: What were you noticing in your body? What thoughts were passing through your mind? What was happening in the environment around you? The therapist and client attend to the details of the experience together, with curiosity rather than judgement.
- **Reflecting**: The therapist helps the client get granular (Wilson's "Small Is Big" principle). Rather than staying at the level of "I felt good," the therapist invites frame-by-frame reflection. For instance, "You said you felt absorbed. Can we slow that down? What was happening in the moment *just before* you felt absorbed? Was there a shift you can identify?" This is where the *Observing Self* (ACT) and *Wise Mind* (DBT) become therapeutic tools as the client learns to step back from the experience and examine its structure with its intimate details.
- **Informing**: The therapist and client gather feedback from the chain itself. What patterns emerge? Are the readiness factors for flow similar across different occasions? Do the same types of prompting events invite engagement? Are there recurring links—particular thoughts, emotions, or environmental conditions—that reliably appear in successful flow chains but are absent in blocked ones? This information becomes the basis for intentional action.
- **Acting**: Based on what the flow chain analysis has revealed, the therapist and client develop plans for values-based action. Perhaps the client needs to address a specific vulnerability factor (e.g., better sleep, reduced substance use) to increase flow readiness. Perhaps they need to create more opportunities for the types of prompting events that invite engagement. Perhaps they need to practise a specific ACCEPT skill at the point in the chain where avoidance has been replacing approach. Or perhaps they need to not do anything (Wilson's "Taking Action Off the Table" principle) to allow for rest and integration. The acting step connects the insights from chain analysis to the client's ongoing Values-Flow practice, tracked on the *Values-Flow Card* (Chapter 3).

A Step-by-Step Guide for Therapists

As summarised in Figure 11.3, here we provide a practical guide for conducting Values-Flow chain analysis in therapy sessions. It assumes familiarity with DBT behavioural chain analysis. If you're a therapist who hasn't trained in DBT, the core skills include the ability to ask detailed questions about a specific episode (rather than rushing through the episode or looking at it only from a distance), resist the urge to move too quickly to solutions (the process is particularly important), and stay curious about the link-by-link progression of events.

Step 1: Identify the Target Experience

Begin by identifying a specific episode to analyse. This might be a flow experience (a time when the client was genuinely absorbed in a meaningful activity), a blocked flow experience (a time when conditions seemed right for engagement but flow didn't happen), or both for comparison. The client might identify this from their Values-Flow Card or simply from reflecting on their week.

Ask the client to describe the experience in detail, just as you would with a problem behaviour. What were you doing? What did it feel like? What was happening in your body? What was the quality of your attention? Use present tense to bring the experience alive in the present moment: "Imagine that you're sitting at the piano now. What are you noticing?" Swenson emphasises that bringing the story to life in the session makes the details easier to recall, it activates the associated emotions, and it creates the conditions for informal exposure to emotional material the client might otherwise avoid.

Step 2: Locate the Prompting Event

Identify the moment that invited engagement. What happened that set things in motion towards the flow experience? This might be an external event (a work task, a conversation, an opportunity) or an internal one (a moment of curiosity, an urge to create, a feeling of readiness). Importantly, which prompting event you should focus on is somewhat arbitrary. Life is an endless chain, and different starting points will reveal different patterns. The key is to find a moment that is close enough to the flow experience to enable a meaningful link-by-link analysis within the session.

Step 3: Explore the Readiness Factors

Move to the left of the prompting event and explore what made the client ready for engagement on this particular day. Had they been practising their PLEASE skills? Had they resolved interpersonal tensions? Were they in an environment that supported concentration? Had they been engaging in the Values-Flow skills that built towards this moment? The readiness factors often

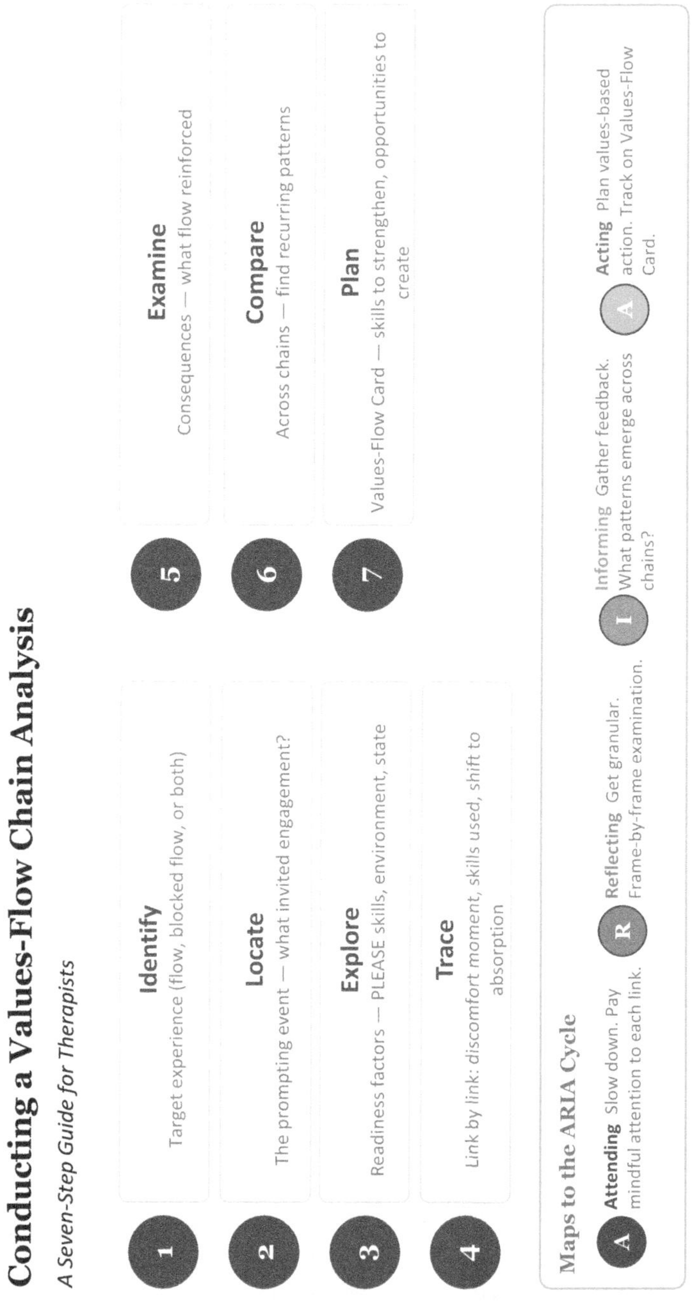

Figure 11.3 Seven Steps for Conducting Values-Flow Chain Analysis in Session.

reveal the cumulative impact of values-aligned living. The client's ongoing use of the Values-Flow skills may have been building the foundation for the experience without them realising it.

Step 4: Trace the Links

This is the heart of the analysis. Work through the chain link by link, from the prompting event to the flow experience, paying attention to thoughts, emotions, actions, physiological sensations, and environmental factors that occur at each step. Be particularly alert to three things:

1 **The Moment of Discomfort**: Almost every flow chain will contain a moment where the client encountered difficulty, such as anxiety about the challenge, uncertainty about their ability, the experience of boredom, or physical discomfort from effort. Identify this moment precisely. It is the fork in the road where avoidance and approach diverge, and understanding what the client did here is the most clinically valuable part of the analysis.
2 **The Skills That Enabled Approach**: When the client chose to stay with the discomfort rather than avoid, what skills did they use? Were they practising *mindfulness* (Attending)? Were they using *opposite action*, approaching when anxiety urged avoidance? Were they drawing on *willingness* (ACCEPT)? Were they using *emotion regulation* skills to keep arousal within their *window of tolerance* (REGULATE)? Naming these skills explicitly helps the client recognise that their flow experience was not luck, but rather it was the product of skills they have been deliberately developing.
3 **The Shift into Absorption**: At some point in the chain, there is typically a qualitative shift. This is the point where effort gives way to engagement, where self-consciousness recedes, and where the person becomes absorbed in the activity. This shift corresponds to what flow researchers describe as the merging of action and awareness. Locating this moment helps the client understand the conditions that preceded it, making future flow experiences more likely.

Step 5: Examine the Consequences

Trace what happened after the flow experience. How did the client feel? What did they think? What did they do next? Did the experience create any lasting effects on mood, motivation, or self-concept? Were there interpersonal consequences? The consequences of flow are important because they reveal the reinforcement structure that sustains values-aligned engagement. When a client sees clearly that flow experiences produce lasting feelings of satisfaction, growth, and meaningful engagement instead of the temporary relief of avoidance behaviours, the motivation to approach rather than avoid naturally strengthens.

Step 6: Compare Across Chains

When analysis of behavioural chains, including problem chains, flow chains, and blocked flow chains, is repeatedly done over time, the therapist and client build a library of chains. These chains can then be analysed and compared, revealing patterns that no single chain can show. Perhaps the client always needs a certain readiness factor in place (adequate sleep, reduced interpersonal stress) before flow becomes possible. Perhaps the same cognitive fusion ("I'm not good enough") appears both in problem chains and in blocked flow chains, revealing a core process that undermines functioning across contexts. Perhaps a specific ACCEPT skill (willingness to stay with discomfort) reliably predicts whether the client avoids or approaches at the critical moment.

These cross-chain patterns become the basis for targeted intervention. The therapist is no longer working with individual episodes in isolation but with the recurring patterns that shape the client's life across the floors of the House.

Step 7: Use the Values-Flow Card to Track and Plan

The use of the *Values-Flow Card* (Chapter 3) connects the insights from chain analysis to the client's ongoing Values-Flow practice. What skills need strengthening? What readiness factors need attention? What opportunities for values-aligned engagement can be deliberately created in the coming week? The Values-Flow Card provides the tracking structure that bridges session work with daily life, closing the loop of the ARIA cycle.

Two Chains, One House: The Dialectical Frame

We want to be clear about something important: we are not suggesting that flow chain analysis *replaces* problem behaviour chain analysis. We are suggesting that it *complements* it. The relationship between these two types of analysis is dialectical. They are opposing approaches that, when held together, create a more complete understanding of the client's life than either could provide alone.

Problem behaviour chain analysis looks down. It examines what went wrong, what skills were absent, and what vulnerability factors and reinforcement contingencies maintained destructive patterns. This is essential work, especially in the basement and on the lower floor. Clients who are burning in hell need therapists who can trace the chain of fire, as safety needs to be established.

Flow chain analysis looks up. It examines what went right, what skills were present, and what readiness factors and conditions produced engaged, values-aligned living. This is essential work for the upper floor and the attic. Clients who are ready to thrive need therapists who can trace the chain of engagement.

The dialectical synthesis is this: ***both chains operate on the same architecture, and many of the critical links are identical.*** The emotion regulation skills that prevent a crisis are the same skills that sustain engagement. The willingness that keeps a client from avoiding painful emotions is the same willingness that allows a client to approach a meaningful challenge. The mindfulness that grounds a client during distress is the same mindfulness that enables absorbed attention during creative work. The therapist who sees this, and who can help clients see it, transforms the therapeutic conversation from one about damage repair to one about life construction.

Swenson captures this beautifully in the House of Treatment metaphor. The purpose of building a solid lower floor (behavioural control, skills acquisition) was always to make the climb to the upper floors possible. The skills were never ends in themselves; they were stairs. Flow chain analysis is how the therapist helps the client look up the staircase and see where those stairs can lead.

Clinical Considerations

Several practical considerations are worth noting for therapists integrating flow chain analysis into their practice.

Timing Matters: Flow chain analysis is most appropriate for clients who have achieved sufficient stability that they have flow experiences to analyse. For clients in the basement, the priority remains safety and stabilisation. Problem behaviour chain analysis is an important tool for identifying what factors led to the problem behaviour. However, even in early treatment, the therapist can plant the seeds by asking about moments of engagement during the week and noting them for future analysis. Remember that glimpses of the attic are possible from any floor.

Both Chains Can Appear in the Same Session: A client might report both a crisis episode and a flow experience during the same week. The therapist can help the client analyse both, placing the two chains side by side. This comparison is often illuminating. The client can see, with concrete specificity, the divergence points where avoidance and approach led to radically different outcomes.

Validate the Difficulty of Looking Up: For clients with extensive histories of suffering, acknowledging positive experiences can feel dangerous. It can feel like tempting fate, like lowering one's guard, like caring about something that might be taken away. Intense positive feelings can be just as overwhelming as intense negative feelings. The therapist needs to validate this vulnerability. The ACCEPT skills (willingness, radical acceptance) apply as much to accepting positive experiences as to accepting painful ones.

Use the Client's Language: You do not need to use the terms "flow chain analysis" or "Values-Flow chain" with clients, though you can if it helps them. Some clients will want to map out their chain, seeing the factors that led to the problem behaviour or flow experience. For others, you are guiding them through the experience, with the structured analysis happening within your mind, while the client is simply being invited to describe their experience in detail. Just as Swenson notes that the most natural way to begin a problem chain is simply to say, "What happened?", the most natural way to begin a flow chain is to say, "That sounds like a really good experience. Tell me about it. I want to understand exactly how it happened."

The Therapist's Own Flow Matters: Swenson emphasises that the consultation team helps therapists undergo their own exposure to emotionally challenging material. Similarly, therapists who conduct flow chain analysis benefit from understanding flow in their own lives. When was the last time you, as a therapist, experienced genuine absorption in your work? What were the conditions? What blocked it? A therapist who has analysed their own flow chains will bring a richer, more embodied understanding to the process with their clients.

Flow Nudges

1. **Analyse a Flow Experience**: Have your client think about a recent time when they were genuinely absorbed in a meaningful activity. Using the five elements described in this chapter (readiness factors, prompting event, links, target experience, consequences), trace the chain of events that led to that experience. Pay particular attention to the moment of discomfort—the point where they encountered difficulty but chose to stay engaged rather than escape. What skills or qualities allowed them to approach rather than avoid?
2. **Analyse a Blocked Flow Experience**: Have your client think about a recent time when conditions seemed right for engagement but flow did not happen. Something got in the way. Using the same five elements, trace the chain and identify where it diverged. Was it cognitive fusion? Emotional escape? Dysregulation? Environmental interference? Challenge-Skill mismatch? Understanding the block is the first step towards removing it.
3. **Compare Two Chains**: Place a flow chain and a blocked flow chain or a problem behaviour chain side by side. What do they share? Where do they diverge? Can you identify the specific link where approach replaced avoidance, or vice versa? What skill or quality made the difference at that divergence point?
4. **The Fork-in-the-Road Journal**: Over the coming week, have your client notice moments when they encounter a challenge that invites skilful engagement. Have them note the moment of discomfort—the fork in the road. Did they approach or avoid? What happened next? Have them record these moments on their Values-Flow Card, and work together to identify the patterns that emerge over time.
5. **Flow Chains in Session**: In your next therapy session with a client on the ground or upper floor of the House, invite a detailed exploration of an

engaging experience from the past week. Use the step-by-step guide from this chapter. Resist the urge to move quickly—apply Wilson's "Slow is Fast" principle. Notice what emerges when you give the same detailed attention to what went right as you normally give to what went wrong.

Sound Bite Summary

1. **Chain Analysis Works in Both Directions**: The same structural framework (vulnerability factors, prompting event, links, target experience, consequences) that reveals how problem behaviours happen can reveal how flow experiences happen.
2. **Flow and Crisis Share the Same Starting Conditions**: Both begin with emotional activation in response to a challenge. The divergence point is whether the person avoids or approaches the difficult emotion.
3. **The Skills That Prevent Crisis Are the Same Skills That Enable Flow**: Emotion regulation, distress tolerance, mindfulness, and willingness serve both purposes.
4. **Blocked flow chains** reveal the specific barriers to engagement for each client, such as cognitive fusion, emotional escape, dysregulation, environmental interference, or challenge-skill mismatch.
5. **Flow chain analysis involves exposure in two directions**, to the difficult emotions present during engagement and to the vulnerability of acknowledging that something good happened and wanting more of it.
6. **The ARIA cycle** (Attending, Reflecting, Informing, Acting) maps directly onto the process of conducting flow chain analyses in session.
7. **Comparing chains across sessions** reveals recurring patterns, such as the readiness factors, prompting events, and critical links that reliably predict whether a client avoids or approaches at the fork in the road.

Final Word

Remember Anika, our therapist who had forgotten to look up? After she began conducting flow chain analyses alongside problem behaviour chain analyses, something shifted in her practice. She still traced the chains of crisis with rigour and care. That work remained essential for clients on the ground floor and in the basement. But now she also traced the chains of engagement with the same detailed attention. What she discovered surprised her.

The two types of chains were not as different as she had expected. The same emotions appeared in both, including anxiety, vulnerability, boredom, uncertainty, and the ache of caring about something that might not work out. The same skills appeared in both, such as mindfulness, willingness, emotion regulation, and the capacity to stay present when everything in you wants to flee. The difference was not in the landscape but in the direction of travel. Problem chains traced the path of avoidance. Flow chains traced the path of approach. The fork in the road—that critical moment where avoidance and approach diverge—was often a single link. A single thought. A single breath. A single choice to stay.

Anika began sharing this insight with her clients. She would place two chains on the whiteboard, one from a difficult week and one from a good one. She would ask: "What do you notice?" The clients would study the two chains, and almost invariably, they would see the same vulnerability factors. The same prompting events. The same initial emotions. And then the divergence, the moment where, in one chain, they avoided, and in the other, they stayed.

That moment of seeing was, for many clients, more powerful than any didactic teaching about skills or values. It was the lived recognition that they already possessed what they needed to move towards the upper floors. They didn't need to become different people. They needed to recognise when the fork in the road occurred, and then they needed to make a different choice at that fork. And if a client has a flow chain to analyse, then you've proven that they could make that approach choice.

This is the dialectical heart of Values-Flow in the therapy room. We are not building two separate skill sets, one for surviving and one for thriving. We are building one integrated capacity: the ability to stay present with difficult internal experiences and choose engagement over avoidance. When that capacity is directed downward towards crisis and suffering, it saves lives. When it is directed upward towards challenge and meaning, it creates the experiences that make lives worth living.

The House of Functioning is one house, after all. The stairs that lead out of the basement are the same stairs that lead to the attic. And chain analysis—in both directions—is how we help people find their way.

12 Values-Flow in the Classroom

Chapter Overview

This chapter applies Values-Flow to the classroom. Teachers are Flow-Helpers, with the potential to create a space where both they and their students experience flow. But this comes from creating both the right internal and external conditions. Teachers need to start with their own flow experiences before they can cultivate flow in their students. Kevin Rathunde's five Cs (Clarity, Centring, Choice, Commitment, and Challenge) provide a practical framework for creating classrooms where engagement is more likely to emerge. Values-Flow provides a map for understanding what makes learning genuinely absorbing, and it provides a daily practice for cultivating those conditions, one lesson at a time.

From Dread to Flow

Olga had been teaching Year 7 English for 11 years, and she was good at it. Her students performed well on standardised assessments. Her classroom management was tight. Her lesson plans were thorough. By any external measure, she was succeeding.

So why did Sunday evenings fill her with dread?

Olga could pinpoint the moment things shifted. It was a Thursday afternoon, third period, the worst slot in the timetable. She was teaching *To Kill a Mockingbird* to a class that had shown zero interest in anything since February. She had planned a structured comprehension activity including questions on the board, answers in the books, and a tick-the-box exercise. But something made her deviate. Instead of the worksheet, she asked a single genuine question: "Why do you think Atticus defends someone he knows he'll probably lose?"

What followed was 40 minutes of the most engaged discussion she had experienced in years. Students who never spoke were arguing passionately. A boy who usually spent the period drawing in the margins was leaning forward, challenging a classmate's interpretation. Olga lost track of time. She forgot to assign homework. She walked out of the room feeling something she hadn't felt in a long time: alive.

DOI: 10.4324/9781003771173-15

That night, she tried to work out what had happened. She'd experienced flow. But it wasn't just her. The whole room had shifted. And the harder question was: could she make it happen again?

She tried. She planned another discussion, this time with a carefully structured set of open-ended questions. She arranged the desks in a circle. She even wore the same cardigan. The lesson fell flat. The students gave polite, surface-level answers. Olga felt the familiar dread creeping back.

Olga had made the mistake that many of us make when we first encounter flow: she tried to reproduce the external conditions without understanding the internal ones. She was chasing the experience rather than cultivating the conditions from which it emerges. As we said in Chapter 2, flow is not the goal—values-aligned engagement is. Flow is what sometimes happens when conditions are right. Olga needed to understand what those conditions were, both for herself and for her students.

The Classroom as a House of Functioning

Throughout this book, we have incorporated the House of Functioning. While we have talked about this at the individual level, classrooms have their own version of the House. Classrooms have a climate that comprises students and teachers existing at different places within the House. Some students are in the basement. They are overwhelmed by what's happening at home, physiologically and psychologically dysregulated, disengaged with learning, or even engaging in self-harm behaviours, such as disordered eating, self-injury, and substance abuse. They often miss class or are completely checked out when in class. Others are on the ground floor. They show up each day, complete homework and classroom activities, and even participate in discussions, but they are simply going through the motions, disengaged from learning. Some students inhabit the upper floor. They are genuinely engaged, motivated, and connected to the work. They eagerly engage in discussions and carry their learning beyond the classroom into their daily life. They feel a sense of school belonging and thrive at school. And on rare occasions, when conditions align, some students visit the attic, so absorbed in what they're doing that they don't even hear the bell.

Teachers, too, occupy different floors at different times. Olga, despite her competence, had been living on the ground floor within her professional life. She was surviving but not thriving as a teacher. That Thursday afternoon discussion briefly took her to the attic, and the glimpse changed everything.

This chapter is about how teachers can use Values-Flow to help students—and themselves—spend more time on the upper floors of the House. This occurs not by forcing engagement or manufacturing flow, but by understanding and cultivating the conditions from which genuine engagement emerges.

The Prepared Teacher: Gardens Don't Grow by Accident

In Chapter 2, we introduced the garden metaphor for thriving. Different gardens look very different from one another yet still thrive. Gardens need care.

Thriving occurs across seasons, not only in spring and summer. And gardens exist within a community that either supports or undermines their growth.

This metaphor extends to classrooms. The classroom is a garden, and the teacher is the gardener. But here's the insight that Rathunde's research makes clear: the gardener's primary job isn't to make the plants grow. It's to prepare the soil, provide the right conditions, and then get out of the way. You can't force a seed to germinate. But you can create conditions where germination is likely.

The prepared environment requires a prepared teacher. A teacher who is fused with rigid beliefs about what "good teaching" looks like, who can't tolerate the uncertainty of an open-ended discussion, or who needs to control every moment of the lesson will struggle to create the conditions for flow, no matter how well they understand the theory. The teacher's own *psychological flexibility* is a prerequisite.

And just as we discussed seasons of practice in Chapter 3, classrooms have their own seasons. There will be spring lessons where curiosity blooms effortlessly, and engagement seems to come from everywhere. There will be winter lessons where everything feels flat and forced. The question isn't whether you'll have winter seasons; the question is whether you understand that beneath the frozen ground, seeds can still be germinating. That's the ACCEPT skill (Chapter 7) applied to teaching: willingness to stick with difficulty, trusting that the work is still happening even when you can't see it.

Start with Your Own House: The Teacher's Values-Flow

Values-Flow offers teachers a framework for understanding the absorbing feeling of flow, and for systematically cultivating it. But there's a prerequisite that many professional development programmes miss: teachers must understand and experience their own flow before they can help students find theirs. You cannot give what you don't have. A teacher who has never examined their own values, who doesn't practise the ARIA cycle in their own life, and who hasn't experienced the difference between drudgery and serious play will struggle to create these conditions for others. The work starts with you.

Remember from Chapter 4 that VIRTUE captures your why—the core values and character strengths that guide a life well lived. For teachers, this means regularly returning to the question: why did I become a teacher in the first place?

Teachers do not enter the profession to make money. Indeed, teaching is one of the most underpaid professions, compared to the amount of time, care, and effort that teachers give. Most teachers go into the profession because they care deeply about students. They might have had an influential teacher along the way, which makes them passionate about positively impacting other students. They might have a love of learning. Or they might feel a sense of calling. Whatever the reason, it is tied deeply to their core values.

For Olga, when she sat with this question honestly, she realised that she valued being part of the moment when a young person's understanding shifted, when something clicked. She had always been fascinated by how young people made sense of stories, and how to cultivate a love of literature in the students that she worked with.

When Olga mapped her Thursday afternoon experience through the Values-Flow skill domains, something revealing emerged. VIRTUE was high. She had asked a question connected to something she genuinely cared about, not just something the syllabus required. INVOLVE was high. She had been fully present, cycling through the ARIA steps without even realising it: Attending to what students were saying, Reflecting on what their responses meant, Informing her next question with what she'd observed, and Acting by following the conversation where it led rather than steering it back to the lesson plan. VITAL was high. She had approached the discussion with genuine curiosity rather than obligation, reflecting the autotelic orientation we described in Chapter 6. And ACCEPT was engaged. She had been willing to tolerate the uncertainty of not knowing where the discussion would go.

The failed attempts to reproduce the experience showed the opposite pattern. VIRTUE was low. The questions were manufactured rather than connected to genuine curiosity. INVOLVE was mechanical. She was following a plan rather than responding to what was actually happening. VITAL had collapsed into drudgery. It was the same content, but it was approached as an obligation rather than through serious play. And ACCEPT was absent. She was so busy trying to control the outcome that there was no space for the unexpected.

The insight here is crucial: flow didn't come from the lesson plan. It came from how Olga showed up. Her internal conditions—values alignment, genuine curiosity, willingness to tolerate uncertainty, and relational attunement—were the primary drivers. This is why replicating external arrangements without internal engagement often falls flat.

Before you can cultivate flow in your classroom, you need to understand your own flow experiences. Take a moment to recall the last time you were genuinely absorbed in teaching. Not just competent, but completely absorbed in the task. What were you doing? What made it matter to you? Which of the Values-Flow skills were active? What internal conditions were present?

If you haven't experienced genuine absorption in teaching, consider what might be missing. Did you go into the profession simply for a job to pay the bills or because you passionately care about learning? Does your classroom create an environment that allows both you and your students to thrive? How do you approach your teaching? Is it a task to complete or a learning journey to embark upon? Are you chained to the curriculum or are you willing to journey with the students as they discover what the content has to reveal? The skills provided in Chapters 4 through 9 are important to engage with to cultivate your own flow experiences. And when you experience flow, students are more likely to experience flow, connect with learning, feel good and function well in the classroom, and feel a sense of school belonging.

The Prepared Environment: Creating Autotelic Classrooms

Teachers are in a valuable position where they can create conditions for Values-Flow to occur. Many teachers are committed to creating the conditions where young people learn, grow, engage, and feel a sense of belonging. They enter and stay in the profession from a passion to positively impact the lives of the young people whom they work with. However, both teacher training and ongoing professional development often focus on curriculum delivery and classroom management—the ground-floor skills of the House. Very little attention goes to what makes teaching and learning genuinely interesting and absorbing.

Effective teachers are essentially creating autotelic contexts—environments that systematically support the development of serious playfulness and engaged learning. We described five characteristics of autotelic contexts in Chapter 6: Clarity, Centring, Choice, Commitment, and Challenge. These five Cs provide a practical framework for teachers who want to create classrooms where engaged learning is more likely to emerge.

- **Clarity**: Students know what they're working towards, what the goals are, and how their efforts connect to larger purposes. This doesn't mean spelling out every step in advance, which kills the exploratory quality that serious play requires. It means providing enough structure that students can direct their energy towards the work rather than wasting it on figuring out what's expected. Rather than obstructing learning, structure enables freedom to learn.
- **Centring**: Attention focuses on present, concrete experiences. This is the essence of *mindfulness*, as emphasised by both ACT and DBT (Chapter 2). In classrooms, centering means designing activities that draw students into the here-and-now rather than keeping them focused on abstract future events ("this will be on the exam"). When Olga asked "Why does Atticus defend someone he'll probably lose?", she was centring the class in a present, concrete experience, grappling with a real question in real time.
- **Choice**: Students feel they have genuine possibilities to choose from, and that their engagement is self-determined rather than imposed. This connects directly to the ACT understanding of values as freely chosen directions (Chapter 4). When choice is removed, engagement becomes compliance. When choice is present, even challenging activities can be experienced as self-directed. This doesn't mean abandoning the curriculum. It means offering choice within structure, including how to approach a task, which aspect to explore first, and how to demonstrate understanding.
- **Commitment**: Others in the environment provide genuine attention and engagement to what students say and do. This signals that the student's contribution matters, reinforcing the value of engagement. In Olga's Thursday discussion, her genuine curiosity about the students' answers communicated commitment. Students can tell the difference between authentic interest and merely checking for correct answers.

- **Challenge**: The environment provides appropriately calibrated opportunities for growth. This is the stretch zone, the space between the comfort zone where things feel safe but growth stalls, and the panic zone where overwhelm prevents learning. Creating appropriate challenges in a classroom of 30 students with 30 different skill levels is genuinely difficult. But it's one of the most important things that a teacher can do.

Rathunde's research suggests that these five conditions work together to create meaningful engagement in the classroom. You don't pick one and focus on it exclusively. You create a classroom where all five are present to some degree, and you notice which ones are missing when engagement drops.

The Challenge-Skill Dance in the Classroom

In Chapter 6, we described how autotelic individuals naturally calibrate the relationship between challenge and skill. When they notice boredom creeping in, they seek ways to increase challenge. When they notice anxiety rising, they find ways to build needed skills or break the task down into smaller, manageable chunks. This ongoing dance keeps them in the stretch zone where flow is possible.

Teachers do a version of this every day, often intuitively. The experienced teacher who notices glazed eyes and spontaneously raises the difficulty of a question or who sees panic and quickly provides scaffolding is performing the challenge-skill calibration that makes engagement possible. But most teachers do this spontaneously rather than systematically. Flow experiences are more likely if a teacher systematically creates the conditions for flow to arise.

The developmental psychologist Lev Vygotsky described a concept that maps beautifully onto the challenge–skill balance: the *Zone of Proximal Development*. This is the space between what a learner can do independently (their current skill level) and what they can do with appropriate support (their developing capacity). Learning, Vygotsky argued, is most likely to happen in this zone. It occurs when teachers stretch the learner just beyond what they can manage alone.

Notably, Vygotsky's Zone of Proximal Development and Csikszentmihalyi's challenge–skill balance are describing the same developmental sweet spot from different angles. One comes from developmental psychology, the other from the science of optimal experience, but both point to the same truth: growth happens when we're stretched just beyond our current capacity, with enough support to keep us engaged rather than overwhelmed.

Values-Flow adds something that neither Vygotsky nor Csikszentmihalyi fully addressed: the question of why it matters. A student can be in the zone of proximal development, working on a task that's appropriately challenging and well-scaffolded, and still feel no engagement because the task has no connection to anything they care about. The challenge–skill balance is necessary but not sufficient. As we've said throughout this book, values-aligned engagement is the goal. The challenge needs to connect to something meaningful.

This is where VIRTUE enters the classroom. When students understand what they value, and when they can see how a learning task connects to those values, the stretch zone becomes something they're willing to enter rather than something they must endure. The discomfort of learning still occurs, but it's purposeful discomfort. As we explored in Chapter 7, ACCEPT is the willingness to remain present even when things are difficult. Students who understand why the difficulty matters are more willing to stay in the stretch zone.

Serious Play in Learning

Classrooms often default to seriousness. Learning is framed as work, not play. Effort is praised, but enjoyment is treated with suspicion, especially in the higher grades where effort increasingly becomes focused on performing well on standardised tests. This is the drudgery trap, and it produces exactly the kind of disengagement that teachers spend their careers fighting.

However, the opposite trap of fooling is equally unproductive. Activities that are enjoyable but disconnected from genuine learning goals might produce short-term engagement, but they don't produce growth. The student who spends an entire lesson playing an "educational game" that teaches nothing has had fun, but they haven't learned.

Serious play integrates both. It means designing learning activities that are simultaneously genuinely interesting (playful) and genuinely challenging (serious). It means approaching a maths problem with the spirit of a puzzle rather than a chore. It means reading a novel with genuine curiosity about what happens next, not just dutiful attention to literary techniques. It means conducting a science experiment as an intriguing investigation of an unknown outcome, rather than as a ritual where you follow steps to confirm what the textbook already told you.

Olga's successful Thursday discussion was serious play in action. The question was serious, touching on genuine moral complexity. But the spirit was playful, such that there was no right answer, the discussion could go anywhere, and the quality of engagement mattered more than reaching a conclusion. The students were simultaneously enjoying the exchange and grappling with something that mattered.

ARIA in the Classroom

In Chapter 5, we introduced the ARIA cycle as the engine that transforms values into tangible engagement. We drew on Kelly Wilson's principles, which are as powerful in the classroom as they are in therapy or personal practice. Consider how each applies to teaching.

Attending: Slow Is Fast

Teachers often feel pressure to do more than is possible in the limited time that is available to them. Content must be covered, assessments must be prepared, timetables must be followed. There is ongoing pressure to keep the class moving, on track to hit performance goals. Wilson's principle reminds us that slowing down often produces faster results. A teacher who rushes through content might cover more material, but are students engaging with and learning the material? A teacher who pauses, genuinely attending to what students are experiencing in the moment, creates the conditions where deep learning becomes possible. Students are more likely to learn the content when they are fully engaging with it. Olga's Thursday discussion worked partly because she stopped rushing. She asked one question and then actually listened to the answers.

For students, Attending means being genuinely present with what's in front of them rather than operating on autopilot. The mindfulness practices we explored in Chapter 5 translate directly into classroom settings. Even 60 seconds of deliberate presence before beginning a task can shift the quality of engagement.

Reflecting: Small Is Big

The most transformative moments in learning are often small. A student who notices that they actually enjoyed solving a maths problem has made an observation worth more than a dozen motivational posters. Wilson's principle asks us to honour the small moments. In classrooms, this means creating space for reflection that goes beyond "What did we learn today?" to "What surprised you?" "What was hard in a way that felt good?" "When did you lose track of time?"

Reflecting also means accessing what we described in Chapter 5 as the *Observing Self* (from ACT) and *Wise Mind* (from DBT). Students can learn to notice their learning experience from a slight distance, through questions that allow them to reflect upon the learning experience itself. Taking a step back from the material supports *defusion* from overwhelming emotion, allowing them to observe that they're feeling frustrated without being consumed by that frustration. Notably, young people are often remarkably capable of this kind of noticing when they're given the language and space for it.

Informing: Meet Yourself in the Work

Wilson's principle of meeting yourself in the work means allowing activities to reveal something about who you are. In classrooms, this happens when learning tasks connect to students' own experiences and identity. A history lesson about civil rights becomes more engaging when students connect it to their own experiences of fairness and unfairness. A science experiment about ecosystems becomes more meaningful when students relate it to environments that they care about.

The Informing step involves gathering feedback. The power of feedback loops is well established in the learning sciences: the tighter the loop between action and feedback, the faster learning occurs. Teachers who build immediate, natural feedback into learning activities, rather than delaying all feedback until marking day, create the conditions where students can adjust their approach in real time.

Acting: Take Action off the Table

Wilson's paradox that sometimes taking action off the table is what allows genuine movement is often counterintuitive in educational settings. The emphasis is often on doing more, rather than doing less. Curricula are content-heavy, with more material to cover than is possible within the time available. This can cause teachers to keep pushing through the curriculum despite resistance by the students. They teach to the test, rather than focusing on learning for the sake of learning itself. But consider what happens when a teacher tells a struggling student: "You don't have to finish this. Just see what you notice about the first part." By removing the pressure of completion, you often release the anxiety that was blocking engagement in the first place. The student, freed from the demand to produce, might just produce their best work.

This connects to what we discussed in Chapter 7 about the difference between *willingness* and *wilfulness*. Willingness is an active opening to experience. Wilfulness is insisting that things be a certain way. When students feel forced to act, they become wilful—resistant, protective, shut down. When the demand is removed and they're invited instead to participate as they are able, willingness can emerge.

Learning by Doing: Experiential Practice in the Classroom

Consider a music teacher who spent two years reading about piano—scales, chord progressions, music theory, the biographies of great pianists—without ever sitting down to play. He could describe the difference between major and minor keys, explain what made jazz improvisation distinctive, and discuss the technical challenges of various classical pieces. But when he finally placed his hands on the keys, he froze. He had learned *about* piano. He had never learned *how* to play piano. Knowing about something is not the same as knowing how to do it.

Psychologists distinguish between two fundamentally different types of knowledge that map directly onto classroom practice.

- **Declarative knowledge** is factual information. For instance, you might know that Australia's capital is Canberra, that water boils at 100 degrees Celsius, or that values are freely chosen principles that guide meaningful living. This is the kind of knowledge you can state, write down, or explain to someone else. You can learn it through reading, listening, or watching.

- **Procedural knowledge** is knowing how to do something, such as how to ride a bicycle, play a musical instrument, or stay present during a difficult conversation. Procedural knowledge lives in your body and your automatic responses. It begins with effortful and repeated action, but over time becomes semi-automatic and increasingly fluid through repeated practice.

Consider learning to drive. At first, you consciously think about every action: check the mirrors, release the handbrake, shift into drive. Each step requires deliberate attention. But as you practise more and more, these actions become automatic. Your procedural knowledge takes over, freeing your conscious mind to navigate, hold a conversation, or plan your day while driving. The transition from laboured declarative processing to smooth procedural execution is what is called *skill acquisition*, and it applies as much to the psychological skills of engagement as it does to any physical competency.

The same distinction applies to learning in classrooms. Teachers and students might learn about flow and the importance of meaningful engagement in learning, but it's not until they experience flow that they understand what it really means. Learning to engage is procedural. It develops through lived experience, repeated practice, and immediate feedback. At first, it is effortful, but over time it becomes semi-automatic.

David Kolb's *experiential learning cycle* provides a useful framework for classroom practice. The cycle moves through concrete experience (doing something), reflective observation (stepping back to consider what happened), abstract conceptualisation (drawing conclusions), and active experimentation (trying again with a new understanding). This is repeated over time, moving concepts from declarative knowledge to procedural knowledge. Teachers who design learning around this cycle are creating the conditions described by both Kolb and Values-Flow. The cycle itself has the structure of flow: clear goals at each stage, immediate feedback from the experience, progressive challenge as skills deepen, and the kind of active engagement that makes absorption possible.

Neuroscience shows that when we repeatedly perform an action over time, new connections are made in the brain. Research on expertise shows that practice leads to automaticity—the ability to perform skilled actions with minimal conscious attention. The more we practise, the stronger those connections become. This is why consistent practice matters more than intensity. Regular daily engagement, even for just a few minutes, builds automaticity more effectively than occasional marathon sessions. The brain needs repetition over time to strengthen neural pathways and consolidate procedural learning.

For teachers, this means that brief, frequent engagement with the Values-Flow skills, such as a daily two-minute reflection or a weekly check-in with the *Values-Flow Card*, will produce more durable change than an intensive professional development workshop followed by nothing. The same principle applies to students: short, regular opportunities to practise presence, reflection, and values awareness build the neural architecture of engagement more effectively than sporadic deep dives.

There is a beautiful connection between this kind of deliberate practice and the flow states we explored earlier. Flow requires a balance between challenge and skill. When students are first learning Values-Flow techniques, their skill level is low, so even simple exercises may feel challenging. As their skills develop through practice, they need greater challenges to reach the flow zone. That challenge may arise from going deeper with the skills, or practising them across different contexts, as the more varied the contexts in which students practise, the more flexible and transferable their skills become.

Helping Students Find Their Own Values-Flow

The ultimate goal of practising Values-Flow skills is not to become good at the exercises but to transform how students engage with everyday learning, supporting their wellbeing in the process. Thus, we encourage using Values-Flow skills across the school day, not just during dedicated sessions. Begin with focused lessons on the skills. Then encourage the students to apply the skills through the different parts of their day, including in the classroom, on the playground, during lunch break, and before and after school.

Notably, one of the most powerful things a teacher can do is help students understand their own patterns of engagement. This isn't something you do to students. It's something you do with them.

Begin with flow itself. Ask students to recall a time when they were so absorbed in something that they lost track of time. This can be any activity, such as gaming, sports, art, music, cooking, building, reading, or arguing with a friend about something they care about.

Then explore it together, using Values-Flow language. What were you doing? What made it challenging? What skills were you using? Why did it matter to you? What were you feeling? How did you know you were doing well or poorly? These questions map directly onto the Values-Flow skill domains: VIRTUE (why it mattered), INVOLVE (what you were paying attention to), VITAL (how you showed up for it), ACCEPT (what discomfort you were willing to tolerate), REGULATE (how your emotions were working), and RELATE (what the interpersonal and environmental conditions were).

This exercise transforms the student's relationship to their own engagement. "I was having fun" becomes "I was doing something that challenged me in a way that connected to what I care about, and I was willing to stick with the difficulty because the feedback was immediate and the task was interesting." That's not just self-awareness. That's the beginning of being able to deliberately create those conditions.

Putting It into Practice: Seven Steps for the Classroom

How do you apply Values-Flow in the classroom? There's no rigid protocol. Values-Flow is not a one-size-fits-all solution. Rather, the invitation is to explore the different parts of Values-Flow, first in your own life, and then with your students. Consider what works for your students and what doesn't work.

Step 1: Map Your Own Flow

Before you do anything with students, spend a week noticing your own engagement. When during the school day are you genuinely absorbed? When are you going through the motions? Use the *Values-Flow Card* from Chapter 3 to track your daily experience across the six skill domains. Look for patterns. What conditions support your engagement, and what conditions undermine it?

Step 2: Assess Your Classroom's Five Cs

Use Rathunde's five characteristics of autotelic contexts—Clarity, Centring, Choice, Commitment, and Challenge—to audit your classroom. Where are you strong? Where is there room to develop? Be honest. Many classrooms are reasonably strong on Clarity (students know what's expected) and weak on Choice (students have little genuine autonomy) and Challenge (tasks are calibrated for the middle of the class, leaving some students bored and others overwhelmed).

Step 3: Introduce Flow Language to Students

You don't need to teach the entire Values-Flow framework. Start simple. Help students identify their own flow experiences. Talk about the challenge–skill balance in accessible language: too easy is boring, too hard is stressful, but there's a sweet spot where things are hard in a good way. This language gives students a framework for understanding their own engagement that they can carry across other subjects.

Step 4: Design Learning for the Stretch Zone

The stretch zone is where learning happens. It's uncomfortable, but it's productive discomfort. Design tasks that push students just beyond what they can do independently (the upper edge of Vygotsky's zone), with scaffolding that prevents them from tipping into overwhelm. Then gradually withdraw the scaffolding as competence develops.

Step 5: Build Feedback Loops into Every Lesson

The tighter the loop between action and feedback, the faster learning occurs. In many classrooms, the feedback loop is measured in weeks. Students do work, submit it, and receive marks at a later time. Design activities where feedback is immediate and natural. Peer discussion, self-checking procedures, or tasks where the work itself provides feedback all tighten the feedback loop.

Step 6: Cultivate Serious Play

Deliberately shift the spirit of at least one activity per week from obligation to exploration. This might mean asking a genuine question (one you don't know the answer to), introducing an element of choice, framing a task as a challenge or puzzle rather than as an assignment, or simply approaching the content with visible curiosity yourself. As we said in Chapter 6, the ***autotelic orientation*** is contagious. When a teacher is genuinely interested, students notice.

Step 7: Track, Reflect, Adjust

Use the *Values-Flow Card* to create the ongoing feedback loop that transforms random attempts into genuine development. The tracking and reflection components are not busywork. They are essential parts of the learning cycle. For your own practice, rate your teaching engagement at the end of each day. Notice patterns over the week. Adjust. This is the ARIA cycle applied to your professional practice. Attend to what's happening, Reflect on what it means, Inform your approach with what you've learned, and Act differently tomorrow. For students, you can use a simplified version of the Card, as described below. Take time each week or month to reflect upon their experiences or lack of experiences with meaningful engagement in learning. Then adjust your practice accordingly.

A Few Important Caveats

The Values-Flow approach does not mean every lesson needs to produce flow. Flow is often found in the attic of the House, a place to visit, not to live permanently. Much valuable teaching and learning occurs on the lower and upper floors. This includes mastering foundational skills, building knowledge structures, practising procedures, and developing the competencies that enable future flow. Not every maths lesson needs to be a transcendent experience. Sometimes students need to practise long division, and that's fine.

It does not mean abandoning structure. Rathunde's Montessori research showed that flow-promoting environments have more structure, not less. But it's a different kind of structure. Clarity and Challenge, two of the five Cs, require clear expectations and well-designed tasks.

It does not mean ignoring institutional constraints. Many schools operate within rigid timetables, standardised curricula, assessment frameworks, and accountability pressures. These are real and dismissing them with platitudes about "flow-based learning" helps no one. The approach we describe here works within existing constraints. Even small experiments with engagement, such as one genuine question per lesson, one moment of choice, one feedback loop tightened, can shift the quality of a classroom.

And it does not mean that engagement equals entertainment. Flow is not about feeling good. It often involves real effort, frustration, and difficulty. The difference is that the effort is connected to something that matters. Students who are genuinely engaged are not necessarily smiling. They might be frowning with concentration, arguing with passion, or struggling with determination. The visible sign of engagement is absorption, not happiness.

Why Some Students Can't Engage

While the framework that we've presented in this chapter points to ways to apply Values-Flow in the classroom, even with cultivation of the right conditions, some students cannot engage. In Chapter 8, we introduced the *window of tolerance*. Above the window lies *hyperarousal*: anxiety, panic, racing thoughts. Below lies *hypoarousal*: shutdown, numbness, emotional flatness. We described the window of tolerance as your personal flow zone—the emotional range within which challenge can meet skill in productive engagement.

This concept is essential for teachers because many students who appear disengaged or oppositional are outside their window of tolerance. A student who has experienced trauma at home may arrive at school with a window so narrow that even the ordinary demands of classroom interaction push them into hyperarousal. A student who is chronically sleep-deprived or hungry may have slipped below the window into the flat, disconnected state of hypoarousal. These students cannot engage with learning because their nervous system is in survival mode. They are in the basement of the House, and as we said in Chapter 1, when you're in the basement, stabilisation and safety are the goals that matter.

Before you can help these students experience flow, you need to help them widen their window of tolerance—or at least help them get back inside it. Some of the REGULATE skills from Chapter 8 translate directly into classroom settings. Brief grounding exercises (e.g., five things you can see, four things you can hear), paced breathing before a test, or simply acknowledging that a student is having a hard day without demanding they "get over it" can help bring students back within their window where engagement becomes possible.

This also means accepting that not every student will be ready for flow-promoting activities on any given day. All exercises are voluntary. Willingness cannot be forced. Coerced acceptance is a contradiction. A teacher who respects where a student is today—even if that means the student sits quietly and does minimal work while they regulate—is practising the ACCEPT skill we described in Chapter 7. Sometimes the most flow-promoting thing a teacher can do is create safety.

Using the Values-Flow Card in the Classroom

The Values-Flow Card from Chapter 3 can be adapted for classroom use in two ways. First, for teachers, the Card can act as a reflective practice tool. At the end of each day, rate your teaching engagement across the six skill domains:

- **VIRTUE**: Did I connect today's lessons to something I genuinely value?
- **INVOLVE**: Did I cycle through the ARIA steps—attending to students, reflecting on what I observed, informing my approach with feedback, and acting flexibly?

- **VITAL**: Did I bring genuine curiosity and serious playfulness to at least one activity?
- **ACCEPT**: Was I willing to tolerate uncertainty, unexpected directions, or difficult moments?
- **REGULATE**: Did I stay within my own window of tolerance when things got stressful?
- **RELATE**: Did I create interpersonal and environmental conditions that supported engagement?

If you experienced high engagement in one or more areas, what factors contributed? If you struggled to engage, what hindered your Values-Flow practice? Track without attachment. The numbers are data, not judgement. A daily check-in like this only takes a few minutes, but provides invaluable data about your own Values-Flow practice. The act of noticing, rating, and adjusting mirrors the Attending–Reflecting–Informing–Acting loop. The Values-Flow Card keeps the learning cycle turning throughout the week.

Second, for older students, you can use a simplified version of the Card that captures the core of Values-Flow, as illustrated in Figure 12.1. First, on the front of the Card (Figure 12.1), students are asked to write a goal for the week. Then, each day, have them select where they are in the House. Third, on the back (Figure 12.1), students are asked to write: What mattered to me today? (VIRTUE), When did I feel engaged? (VITAL/INVOLVE), What helped me engage? (ACCEPT/RELATE), and What stopped me from feeling engaged? (REGULATE). At the end of the week, on the front of the Card (Figure 12.1), the students can reflect upon what they noticed, what worked, and what they struggled with. Over time, patterns emerge that help both students and teachers understand what conditions support genuine engagement.

Flow Nudges: Values-Flow in the Classroom

1. **The One Genuine Question**: Every lesson, ask at least one question to which you genuinely don't know the answer. Notice the difference in your own engagement when the question is real versus rhetorical. Students pick up on this difference instantly. Genuine curiosity is contagious; performed curiosity is not.
2. **The Three-Minute Flow Recall**: At the start of a lesson, invite students to spend 60 seconds recalling a recent moment of absorption in any context, in or out of school. Let the sensory memory of that engagement settle. Then begin the lesson. This brief grounding in the experience of engagement can shift the quality of attention for the entire period.
3. **The Challenge Calibration Check**: Midway through a lesson, pause and ask students: "Is this too easy, too hard, or in the stretch zone?" Use their responses to adjust in real time. This takes 30 seconds and gives you immediate data about the challenge–skill balance across the room. It also teaches

students to notice their own engagement patterns—a skill they can carry into other areas of their lives.

4 **The Serious Play Shift**: Take one activity per week that you normally frame as work and reframe it as a challenge, puzzle, or experiment. Notice what changes in the students and in yourself. As Boris discovered in Chapter 6, the shift from drudgery to serious play doesn't require changing the content. It requires changing the spirit with which you meet it.

5 **The Five-Cs Audit**: Once a month, spend ten minutes reviewing your classroom through the lens of Rathunde's five Cs: Clarity, Centring, Choice, Commitment, and Challenge. Which are strong this month? Which need attention? Use this audit to inform your planning for the weeks ahead.

6 **The Evening Reflection**: At the end of each teaching day, take two minutes with your Values-Flow Card. Where were you in the House today? Rate your Values-Flow practice. Note one moment of genuine connection

Values-Flow Practices for Students

At the beginning of the week, write what your goal for the week is

At the end of the week, reflect upon the following questions:

- What mattered to me this week?
- What helped me feel engaged?
- What stopped me from feeling enaged?

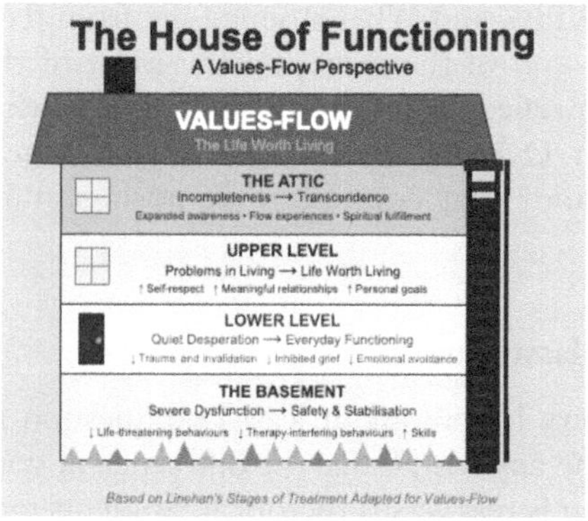

Daily Reflection: Where am I in the house today?

Monday
Tuesday
Wednesday
Thursday
Friday
Saturday
Sunday

Figure 12.1 A Modified Values-Flow Card for Students (Back, Left, Front, Right).

(*Continued*)

Values-Flow Skills for Students

MON	TUE	WED	THU	FRI
What mattered to me today? (VIRTUE)				
When did I feel engaged? (VITAL/INVOLVE)				
What helped me to engage? (ACCEPT/RELATE)				
What stopped me from feeling engaged? (REGULATE)				

Figure 12.1 (Continued)

with the work. As we said in Chapter 3, a day of low scores isn't failure—it's information. What conditions made engagement difficult? What might help tomorrow?

Sound Bite Summary

Key points to remember from this chapter:

1 **Teachers must understand their own flow** before they can cultivate it in students. Start by mapping your own engagement using the Values-Flow Card.
2 **Rathunde's five Cs** (Clarity, Centring, Choice, Commitment, and Challenge) provide a practical framework for creating classrooms where engagement is more likely to emerge.

3 Vygotsky's Zone of Proximal Development and Csikszentmihalyi's challenge–skill balance describe the same **developmental sweet spot** from different angles. Values-Flow adds the crucial question: why does this challenge matter?
4 The **ARIA cycle** (Attending, Reflecting, Informing, Acting) and **Wilson's principles** apply directly to classroom practice for teachers and students alike.
5 **Students who understand their own flow patterns**, who can identify what conditions support their engagement, carry that understanding into every classroom and every area of life.
6 **Not every lesson needs flow**. Flow is the attic, which is a wonderful place to visit. But most learning happens on the lower and upper floors.
7 **Serious play**, the integration of genuine enjoyment and genuine purpose, is what distinguishes absorbing classrooms from drudgery or fooling.
8 **Knowing About Is Not Knowing How**: Engagement skills are procedural. They live in the body and develop through repeated practice, not intellectual understanding alone.
9 **Consistent Practice Matters More Than Intensity**: Regular brief engagement builds neural pathways and automaticity more effectively than occasional marathon sessions for teachers and students alike.
10 **Transfer Requires Varied Practice**: Skills learned in one context do not automatically carry over to others. Practising Values-Flow across different classroom situations and school-day moments builds the flexible, transferable skills that genuinely change how students engage with learning.

Final Word

Olga stopped asking "Did you enjoy that?"

It wasn't that enjoyment didn't matter. It was that she'd learned it was a by-product of something deeper, something she couldn't manufacture but could cultivate.

She started asking better questions. Before lessons, she asked herself: What am I genuinely curious about in today's content? Where is the stretch zone for these students? Which of the five Cs needs attention today? After lessons, she asked students: "When were you most absorbed? What was hard in a good way? What surprised you?"

Her classroom didn't transform overnight. She still had flat lessons, disengaged students, and difficult days. She still taught to the test sometimes, because the test still matters. But she had something she'd lacked before: a framework for understanding engagement rather than just hoping for it. She understood the conditions from which absorbed learning emerges, and she could systematically cultivate those conditions, even within the constraints of a timetable and a structured curriculum.

On the best days, when a genuine question sparked a discussion that went places she hadn't predicted, when a student who usually sat silent leaned forward and said something that changed the room, or when nobody wanted to leave when the bell rang, she remembered why she became a teacher. She remembered because she was living it. She wasn't just teaching content and managing behaviour. She started living in alignment with her values, through her strengths, with willingness and genuine curiosity. She found herself inhabiting the upper floor, with occasional visits to the attic.

That's what Values-Flow offers teachers. Not a guarantee of flow. Not a formula for engagement. But a map for understanding what makes learning genuinely absorbing. And it provides a daily practice for cultivating those conditions, one lesson at a time.

Tomorrow, when you walk into your classroom, remember: you are a Flow Helper. The seeds are in the ground. Your job is to prepare the soil.

13 Values-Flow in Coaching and Managing

Chapter Overview

This chapter applies Values-Flow to coaches and managers in the workplace. Central to good coaching and managing is holding the dialectical tension of acceptance and change. Effective coaching and managing is fundamentally an exposure-based activity, as you help people face what they'd rather avoid, tolerate the discomfort that comes with growth, and discover through experience that they are more capable than they believe. DBT and ACT skills are practical tools for coaches and managers that help the people they lead stay in the stretch zone long enough for new learning and growth to occur. The coach or manager is a flow architect, designing conditions that make flow possible in the people that they lead.

The Coach Who Couldn't Let Go

Meet Arianna. She's 42 years old, a senior operations manager at a logistics company, and she's stuck in a pattern she can't seem to break. Her team of 12 is talented but underperforming, and Arianna knows why. Every time a team member faces a difficult client, an ambiguous decision, or a task that stretches beyond their current skill set, Arianna swoops in. She rewrites the emails. She takes over the calls. She stays late redoing the reports. Her team calls her "the safety net," and they mean it as a compliment, but Arianna's coach sees the problem clearly. By rescuing her team from every uncomfortable moment, Arianna has inadvertently taught them that discomfort is something to be avoided rather than navigated.

"I know I should let them struggle," Arianna told her coach during their third session. "But when I see them floundering, I can't just sit there. It feels wrong. It feels like I'm failing them."

Arianna's coach asked a simple question: "What are you afraid will happen if you don't step in?"

Arianna paused. "They'll make mistakes. The client will be unhappy. My manager will think I'm not doing my job. And honestly… they'll think I don't care about them."

DOI: 10.4324/9781003771173-16

Beneath the rescuing behaviour lay a tangle of predictions about catastrophic outcomes, others' judgements, and what it means to be a good leader. Arianna wasn't just managing a team. She was managing her own anxiety by ensuring that neither she nor her people ever had to sit with discomfort long enough to learn from it. From an ACT perspective, Arianna's rescuing was her version of the *control agenda* (see Chapter 2). She believed that discomfort needed to be eliminated before anyone could perform well. The belief that her team needed to feel comfortable before they could be effective is the same belief that keeps individuals stuck on the lower floors of the House. ACT's insight applies to coaching and managing as much as to individual application. You do not need to feel ready before you can act. Growth happens through willingness to move towards what matters with whatever feelings are present.

Arianna's situation illustrates that effective coaching and managing is, at its heart, an **exposure-based activity**. It involves helping people face what they'd rather avoid, tolerate the discomfort that comes with growth, and discover through direct experience that they are more capable than they believe. Importantly, it requires the coach or manager themselves to tolerate their *own* discomfort in the process, including the anxiety of watching someone struggle, the vulnerability of stepping back, and the uncertainty of not knowing whether things will work out.

In this chapter, we turn to coaching and managing—contexts where one person's role is to facilitate another person's growth, performance, and engagement. Whether you are a workplace manager, an executive coach, a freelance coach, a sports coach, a mentor, or a similar role, the principles are the same. You are helping other human beings move towards the upper floors of the House of Functioning. The pathway involves navigating discomfort rather than eliminating it. For simplicity, we use the words "coach" and "manager" interchangeably, but we encourage you to apply whichever term is relevant to your context.

Coaching as Exposure: The Principle That Changes Everything

Exposure therapy is a robustly supported intervention in clinical psychology. At its simplest, exposure involves systematically and gradually approaching feared or avoided situations, locations, or experiences until the person develops an alternative relationship with the discomfort those situations produce.

For instance, if you have a fear of public speaking, exposure might involve small, gradual steps towards speaking publicly. You might first think about giving the speech, which raises your heart rate and makes your palms sweat. You sit with the discomfort until it passes. Then you might write out your speech. Then read it to a friend, then a small group of friends, then a small group of strangers, then a larger group of strangers, and ultimately in front of a larger audience, using notes to guide you rather than reading verbatim. At each step, you learn through direct experience that the catastrophe your mind predicted either didn't happen or was survivable. That builds confidence that you can try the next step without the world ending.

For decades, the dominant model assumed that exposure worked through a process called *habituation*. This suggests that repeated contact with a feared stimulus gradually reduces the anxiety response, making something that was intolerable tolerable. Alternatively, Michelle Craske and her colleagues introduced the *inhibitory learning model*. In this model, the original fear association is not erased during exposure. Instead, a new, competing association is formed that says that you can withstand the stressor. This occurs through *expectancy violation*—the mismatch between what a person feared would happen and what actually occurs.

This distinction matters for coaches and managers. The goal of developmental experiences is not simply to reduce an employee's discomfort with challenging tasks. The goal is to help them discover, through their own experience, that they can handle more than they thought they could.

When Arianna's coach helped her step back and let a team member navigate a difficult client call, the point wasn't that the team member would stop feeling nervous about client calls. The point was that the team member would learn, through direct experience, "I predicted I would freeze and lose the client, but what actually happened was that I stumbled through it, recovered, and the client appreciated my honesty." That's an expectancy violation. That's where growth happens.

Effective coaches and managers regularly assign stretch projects or tasks that push people beyond their current capabilities. They create opportunities for employees to present to senior leadership when the employee would rather let someone else do it. They provide honest feedback that the recipient would rather not hear. They hold people accountable for commitments they'd rather quietly abandon. They resist the urge to rescue when someone is struggling. In each case, the coach or manager is facilitating an encounter with something the other person wants to avoid. In doing so, they create the conditions for new learning, increased self-efficacy, and ultimately, greater engagement.

Albert Bandura's research on self-efficacy, a person's belief in their capability to succeed in spite of challenges, explains why this works. One of the most powerful sources of self-efficacy is *mastery experiences*: doing the thing that you feared and discovering that you can do it. The mastery doesn't come from being told you can do it or watching someone else do it. It comes from doing it. This is what happens in gradual exposure. A person is gradually stretched beyond their comfort zone, finds they can do it, and learns that more is possible than they first thought.

In House of Functioning terms, exposure-based coaching helps people furnish their upper floor. The employee who successfully navigates a challenging presentation doesn't just add a skill. They have a tangible experience of competence they can return to when the next challenge arrives. Over time, these accumulated mastery experiences transform the upper floor from an aspirational idea into a place they can inhabit.

The DBT Coaching Model: Where Clinical Wisdom Meets Real-World Practice

One of the most underappreciated contributions of DBT is that it includes a coaching component. When most people think of DBT, they think of individual therapy sessions and group skills training. But Marsha Linehan designed a comprehensive DBT with four modes of treatment, and one of those modes is *telephone coaching*—brief, focused, in-the-moment support designed to help clients apply their skills in real-life situations. This is not therapy on the phone. It is coaching in the truest sense: helping someone use what they've learned when it matters most.

DBT phone coaching serves a specific function that Linehan considered essential: *generalising skills to the natural environment.* It's one thing to practise a distress tolerance skill like *TIPP* or *STOP* in the safety of a therapy room or a skills group. It's another thing to use that skill at 2 a.m. when you're overwhelmed, and every fibre of your being is screaming at you to engage in self-destructive behaviours. Phone coaching bridges that gap. The therapist doesn't process the client's emotions or explore their childhood. Instead, they help the client identify what's happening right now, determine which skill applies, and guide them in using that skill. Calls typically last 5–15 minutes. The goal is competence in context, not insight in isolation.

This model is important for coaching and managing because the gap between knowing and doing is the place where most people get stuck. An employee might understand intellectually that they should use assertive communication with a difficult colleague. They might have practised it in a coaching session or a training workshop. But when they're face-to-face with the colleague and their heart is racing and their mind is generating all sorts of catastrophic predictions, the skill evaporates. What they need in that moment is brief, focused support that helps them access the skill in the moment that it matters.

A good manager doesn't wait until a weekly one-on-one to address performance challenges. They provide brief, targeted coaching in the moment. A quick conversation before a difficult meeting ("Remember, lead with curiosity rather than judgement"). A check-in immediately after a challenging presentation ("What did you notice? What would you do differently?"). Or a text of encouragement when they know an employee is facing something hard. This real-time, skills-focused support mirrors DBT phone coaching. The manager is helping the employee generalise their capabilities to the environment where those capabilities are needed.

DBT phone coaching also teaches us something crucial about what coaching is *not.* It is not extended emotional processing. It is not an opportunity for the employee to vent at length about how unfair the situation is. It is not the coach or manager solving the problem for the person. The structure of DBT coaching—brief, focused, and skills-oriented—is itself therapeutic. It communicates: "I believe you have the skills to handle this. I'm here to help you find them, not to do the work for you."

DBT Skills for Every Coach and Manager

Beyond the coaching model, DBT's four skill modules (*mindfulness*, *distress tolerance*, *emotion regulation*, and *interpersonal effectiveness*) offer practical tools for managers and coaches to both use in their own lives to improve their effectiveness as a coach or manager, as well as encourage employees to function effectively in the workplace. As we've seen in Chapters 8 and 9, the DBT skills are not just for therapy. They are practical skills that make it possible to effectively navigate the inevitable challenges that arise in life. Applied within the workplace, they become skills that add value whenever people work together.

Mindfulness skills help people to stay present in the moment, rather than being swept away by ruminations about the past or worries about the future. This does not mean ignoring problems from the past or plans for the future. Workplaces need to be forward-looking to be prepared for what is to come, and they need to learn from past mistakes. But mindfulness allows managers to stay grounded in the here and now, giving full energy and attention to the current circumstance, even while keeping the past and future in mind. Mindful presence also allows managers and coaches to be fully present in a conversation, actively listening and responding to employees, which contributes to the sense that employees are seen and heard and provides a sense of psychological safety.

Distress tolerance skills equip professionals to manage high-pressure situations to respond effectively rather than impulsively react. For instance, the *STOP skill* (Stop, Take a step back, Observe, Proceed mindfully) can be useful in a heated meeting. Rather than reacting with anger or frustration, the STOP skill allows both managers and employees to separate themselves from the emotion triggered by the meeting and instead respond in a manner that not only does not make the situation worse, but can even improve the moment. *Radical acceptance* (accepting reality as it is without trying to fight it) helps managers to navigate organisational changes they can't control, budget cuts they didn't ask for, and team dynamics that resist easy solutions. As we explored in Chapter 7, acceptance is not approval; it is the foundation from which effective response becomes possible.

Emotion regulation skills make it possible for managers and coaches to maintain a calm presence through the day-to-day happenings of the workplace. For instance, *opposite action* offers coaches a direct strategy for helping people break patterns that keep them stuck. The employee who avoids giving feedback because they're anxious about conflict is coached to *approach* the conversation. The manager who wants to micromanage because they're anxious about a project is coached to *delegate and trust*. The employee who withdraws when they feel criticised is coached to *stay engaged and ask clarifying questions.*

Interpersonal effectiveness skills make it possible to communicate with and relate to others while achieving the goals that you have, be those meeting your objective, maintaining the relationship, or sustaining self-respect. *DEAR WOMAN* (Describe, Express, Assert, Reinforce, Willingness, Openness, stay Mindful, Appear confident, Negotiate) equips people to make requests and navigate negotiations effectively. *GIVE* (be Gentle, act Interested, Validate, use an Easy manner) helps maintain relationships even during difficult conversations. *FAST* (be Fair, don't over-Apologise, Stick to your values, be Truthful) helps preserve self-respect. A manager who teaches their team these skills and then encourages them to use them in real-time application is doing exactly what Linehan envisioned: helping people generalise skills to the environments where they're needed most.

It's important to note that coaching and managing styles vary across cultures. In some organisational cultures, direct feedback is expected and valued. In others, indirect communication and saving face are essential. The DEAR WOMAN framework assumes a degree of directness that may need adaptation in cultures where hierarchy, deference, and relational harmony take precedence over individual assertiveness. Similarly, the exposure-based approach to coaching works differently across cultures. In some contexts, stretching a team member publicly may be motivating. In others, it may be humiliating. The underlying principles remain valid across cultures. People grow through facing challenges that matter to them. But how those challenges are presented, supported, and debriefed must honour the cultural expectations of the people involved.

The Dialectic at the Heart of Coaching

DBT's central dialectic—embracing both acceptance *and* change—is central to effective coaching and managing. Consider the tension every coach faces. You must accept where the person currently is while simultaneously expecting them and helping them to grow. You must validate their struggle while pushing them towards discomfort. You must communicate "You're doing your best" and "You can do better" in the same breath. If you lean too far towards acceptance, you become permissive, being the coach who is nice but never challenges them to grow. If you lean too far towards change, you become demanding, being the coach who pushes relentlessly without acknowledging the human cost. The dialectical stance holds both simultaneously, and it is in this tension that genuine development occurs.

Linehan herself modelled this dialectic with her clients. She would validate a client's suffering ("Of course you're struggling—anyone would be, given what you're going through") and then pivot seamlessly to change ("And you still need to use your skills, because the alternative is worse").

The simultaneous use of acceptance and change is a stance to be inhabited. The manager who says to a struggling employee, "I understand this project is overwhelming, and I'm not going to take it off your plate, because I know you can handle it and I'm here to support you through it," is embodying this dialectic. They are simultaneously validating the struggle, communicating confidence in the person's capacity, and offering support. This is *Wise Mind* applied to coaching. *Emotion Mind* might tell you to rescue the struggling employee because their distress activates your own. *Reasonable Mind* might tell you to push harder because the deadline is approaching. Wise Mind holds both realities and finds the response that is simultaneously compassionate and effective. For coaches and managers, learning to pause and access Wise Mind before responding to a team member's struggle is perhaps the single most important skill to develop.

Values-Guided Exposure: Where ACT Transforms Coaching

In traditional exposure therapy, the motivation for facing feared situations is often framed in terms of symptom reduction: "If you keep confronting your fear, the anxiety will eventually decrease." But ACT reframes exposure. The question is not "How do I get rid of this anxiety?" but "What do I value enough to be willing to feel anxious for?" Research by Hebert, Wilson, and Kellum demonstrates that people are significantly more likely to approach aversive situations when that approach is connected to a personal value than when it is connected to an arbitrary reward or no consequence at all. Values don't make the discomfort disappear. They make it meaningful.

Wilson illustrated this with a vivid clinical example. A woman with severe agoraphobia and panic disorder had made limited progress with traditional exposure therapy. But when Wilson connected the exposure to what she truly valued, everything shifted. She wasn't doing exposure to reduce panic. She was doing it because her daughter's graduation mattered more to her than the panic. The panic didn't go away. Her willingness to experience that panic did.

This principle has important implications for coaching. Rather than offering arbitrary rewards, words of encouragement, or harsh criticism, the effective coach connects the behaviour to the employee's values. When Arianna's coach helped her step back from rescuing her team, the coach didn't frame it as "Stop helicopter managing." The coach connected it to Arianna's values.

Through VIRTUE work (Chapter 4), Arianna identified that she deeply valued contributing to the development of others. She wanted to be the kind of manager who builds people up rather than making them dependent. When the coach reframed her stepping back not as negligence but as *an expression of her deepest values as a leader*, the willingness to tolerate the discomfort shifted. She wasn't abandoning her team. She was investing in their growth. The anxiety of watching them struggle didn't vanish. But the values gave her a reason to sit with the discomfort.

A number of researchers and practitioners have explored ACT-based principles and practices in the workplace, which add further nuance. Frank Bond has found that *psychological flexibility* (the ability to be present, open to experiences, and willing to persist in behaviour when doing so serves valued ends) predicts good mental health, better job performance, reduced burnout, and increased resilience for employees.

Taking this a step further, Kevin Polk's ACT Matrix offers an accessible tool to bring psychological flexibility to life. The Matrix simplifies ACT's six core processes into a two-dimensional visual (see Figure 13.1). The vertical axis distinguishes direct sensory experience from mental chatter. The horizontal axis sorts behaviour into "towards values" and "away from discomfort." When an employee is stuck, the Matrix helps them see: "What am I moving towards? What am I moving away from? Is my current behaviour serving my values or managing my anxiety?" This mirrors the ARIA cycle. Sorting a present experience on the Matrix walks the same loop as ARIA: you Attend to what is showing up, Reflect on whether the behaviour is a towards or away move, let the observation Inform your next step, and then Act in the values direction.

Creating Flow Conditions: The Coach as a Flow Architect

Values provide the motivation for approaching challenges, and DBT and ACT provide the skills for managing the discomfort that arises. Flow Theory describes the optimal state that can emerge when everything comes together. The coach or manager is, in essence, a **flow architect**—someone who designs conditions that make flow experiences possible for the people they lead.

First, **clear goals** involve ensuring that people know what success looks like at any given time. Keith Sawyer's research found that the biggest barrier to team flow was unclear objectives. A manager who communicates "I need this report by Friday" has set a deadline but not a flow-conducive goal. In contrast, the manager who says "The purpose of this report is to help the executive team understand our third quarter customer retention patterns so they can make informed decisions about next quarter's strategy" has given the work meaning, direction, and a standard against which progress can be measured. The clearer the goal, the more completely attention can be invested in the task rather than wasted on uncertainty about what's expected.

Second, **immediate feedback** involves creating systems where people can see the impact of their actions without having to wait for a formal review. Arnold Bakker's research consistently shows that job resources like supervisory coaching, autonomy, and performance feedback facilitate the translation of challenges into flow experiences. A coach who debriefs immediately after a challenging conversation, or a manager who provides real-time data dashboards so employees can track their own performance, is building feedback infrastructure that supports flow experiences. This mirrors the ARIA cycle: the feedback enables the *Reflecting* and *Informing* phases that keep engagement dynamic rather than stagnant.

Third, **challenge–skill balance** involves calibrating challenges to be in the employee's stretch zone, where demands are high enough to require full engagement but not so overwhelming that the person shuts down.

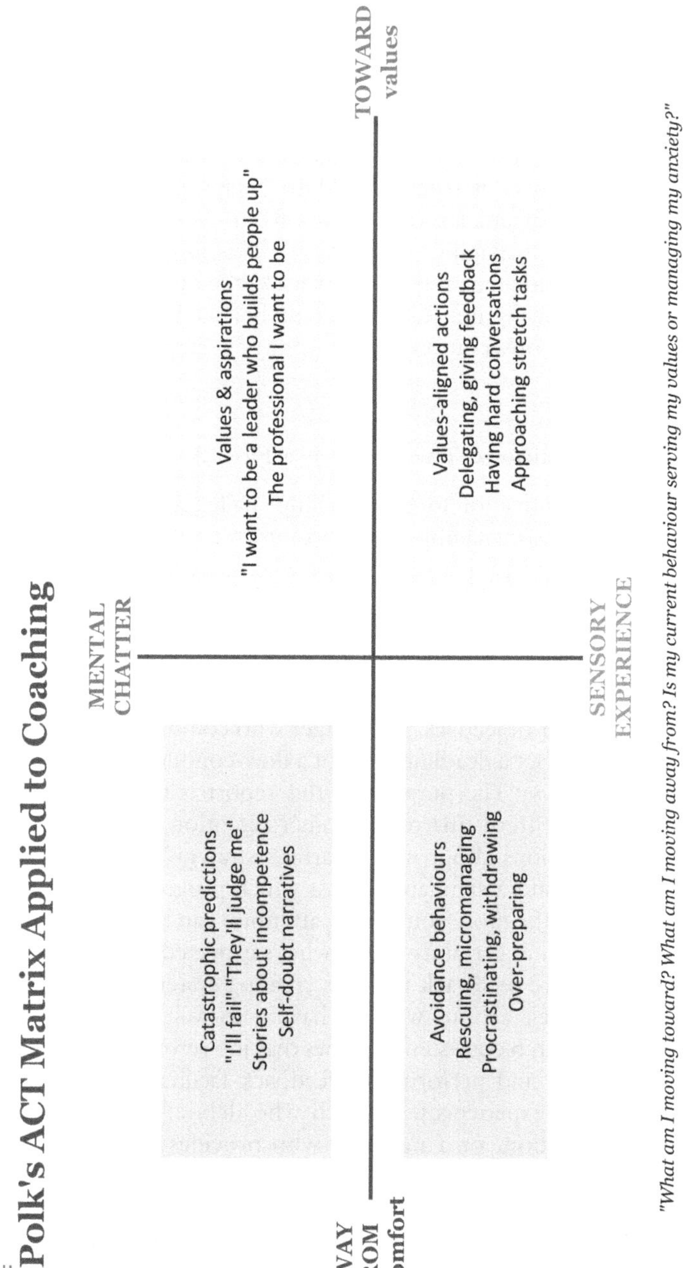

Figure 13.1 The ACT Matrix.

Here's where the Values-Flow framework adds something that neither exposure therapy nor Flow Theory provides on its own. Exposure therapy tells us *why* approaching challenges produces growth (inhibitory learning, expectancy violation, mastery experiences). Flow Theory tells us *what* optimal engagement looks like (absorbed, intrinsically motivated, balanced between challenge and skill). But neither tells the coach what to do when the person is *in the stretch zone and wants to quit*. That's where DBT and ACT skills come in. *Distress tolerance skills* (such as *STOP* and *radical acceptance* described in Chapter 8) help the person to stay in the stretch zone long enough for new learning to occur. *Emotion regulation skills* help them manage the anxiety, frustration, or self-doubt that arise during challenging tasks. And *values* provide the reason to persist when every instinct says retreat.

Consider how this played out for Arianna's team member, Amir. When Arianna finally stepped back and let Amir handle a difficult client negotiation on his own, the first five minutes were excruciating for both of them. Amir's palms were sweating. His mind was generating catastrophic predictions ("The client will walk. I'll lose the account. Arianna will lose faith in me"). Arianna, watching from her office, felt the gravitational pull to intervene. But Amir was prepared. The negotiation was important to him, as he valued being a contributing employee. Using the ARIA cycle, he Attended to what was happening, noticing the anxiety in his chest and observing the client's body language. He Reflected, thinking that the client seemed frustrated but not hostile. He Informed himself. This was a DEAR WOMAN moment, where he needed to describe the situation clearly, express the company's position, and negotiate. And then he Acted.

The conversation wasn't perfect. Amir stumbled in places. But he recovered, the client agreed to a revised timeline, and something shifted. Amir's prediction—that he would fail catastrophically without Arianna's intervention—didn't happen. New learning was formed. Over the following weeks, as Arianna continued to create these exposure opportunities while coaching Amir through the ARIA process, something else began to emerge: Amir started experiencing flow during client interactions. The challenge matched his growing skills. The goals were clear. The feedback was immediate. The engagement became intrinsically rewarding.

The nine flow dimensions from Chapter 2 provide a practical diagnostic tool that can be applied here. When a team member reports a good experience, the coach can listen for which dimensions were present. Was concentration total? Did action and awareness merge? Did self-consciousness recede? When a team member reports a flat or frustrating experience, the coach can ask which dimensions were missing. Was the challenge too low (no engagement of skill)? Were goals unclear (no direction for attention)? Was feedback delayed (no sense of progress)? Listening for the conditions that make flow possible turns vague conversations about engagement into specific, actionable coaching interventions.

The Values-Flow Sequence in Coaching

Values-Flow offers a specific sequence that coaches and managers can follow to facilitate growth, resilience, and engagement in the people they lead.

The sequence begins with **values clarification**. Before you can ask someone to face discomfort, you need to help them connect with why the discomfort is worth facing. This is the VIRTUE work from Chapter 4. A coach helps the employee identify what kind of professional, leader, or team member they want to be. What do they value in their work? What matters enough to be willing to feel anxious, uncertain, or inadequate for? Without this foundation, exposure feels punitive. It is something being done to them. With values clarity, exposure becomes purposeful. It is something they are choosing to do in service of what matters most to them.

Second, values provide the **motivation for exposure**. When a coach helps an employee connect a stretch assignment to their values, they are harnessing the same mechanism that makes values-guided exposure more effective than arbitrary exposure. For instance, the coach might say, "You said you value creative problem-solving. This project will stretch your ability to solve problems in real time, with real stakes." The willingness to approach discomfort increases because the discomfort is no longer pointless. It is the price of admission to a values-aligned life. This is Wilson's insight applied to the workplace. You don't do hard things to make the hardness go away. You do hard things because it matters to you.

Third, when the person enters the stretch zone, they need **skills for managing the arising discomfort**. This is where DBT and ACT contribute. The employee facing a high-stakes presentation needs to know how to use the *STOP skill* when panic surges. The manager navigating a conflict needs to be able to deploy *opposite action* when their urge is to withdraw or attack. The manager facing organisational upheaval needs *radical acceptance* before they can respond effectively. *Distress tolerance skills* keep the person in the stretch zone long enough for new learnings to occur. Without them, the person either avoids the challenge entirely or enters it and becomes overwhelmed, reinforcing the fear that keeps them stuck.

As the person develops skills through repeated exposure, the **challenge–skill balance shifts**. What was once overwhelming becomes manageable. What was once anxiety-provoking becomes engaging. The person's *window of tolerance* (the range within which they can function effectively) widens. And when perceived challenges match perceived skills, with clear goals and immediate feedback in place, **flow becomes possible**. The employee who once dreaded client negotiations begins to find them absorbing. The manager who once avoided difficult conversations begins to experience them as opportunities for genuine connection. The coach who once felt anxious every time a team member struggled begins to find satisfaction in watching growth unfold.

Coaching the Coach: The Manager's Own Exposure Journey

Importantly, the Values-Flow coaching process is just as much an exposure exercise for the coach as it is for the person being coached.

When Arianna began stepping back from rescuing her team, her own anxiety skyrocketed. Her mind generated a relentless stream of catastrophic predictions: "They're going to fail. It's going to be my fault. My manager will think I've checked out. The team will resent me." Sitting with those thoughts without acting on them was its own form of exposure, requiring its own set of skills. Wilson's principle to assume magnificence is possible (Chapter 5) applies here. When you assume magnificence, you are choosing to see the person in front of you as capable of more than their current behaviour suggests. It's not a belief about what the person will achieve, but reflects a choice about how you hold them. That assumption changes how you coach. It changes how you wait. It changes how you respond when they stumble. It changes the entire quality of the coaching relationship, because people tend to rise to the expectations that are genuinely held for them.

Arianna's coach taught her to use the ARIA cycle on her own internal experiences. *Attend*: notice the anxiety rising when a team member struggles. *Reflect*: recognise that the urge to rescue is driven by her anxiety, not by the team member's actual inability. *Inform*: this is a moment for opposite action. My urge says intervene, but the effective behaviour is to stay back and let them grow. *Act*: remain present, offer validation ("I can see this is challenging, and I believe you can handle it"), and resist the rescue.

Over time, Arianna's negative predictions didn't come true. Her team didn't collapse. Her manager noticed that the team was becoming more autonomous and gave Arianna positive feedback. Team members didn't resent her stepping back. They felt trusted and empowered. Arianna discovered that the discomfort of watching her team struggle was the price of the leadership she most valued: leadership that builds independence rather than dependence.

This dual exposure—the coach facing their own discomfort while facilitating the coachee's growth—is the dialectical heart of the coaching relationship. Both parties are doing hard things in service of what matters. Both are practising *willingness* (see Chapter 7) as the gateway to engagement. And both are discovering, through direct experience, that they are more capable than they believed.

The VITAL Spirit in Coaching: Serious Play at Work

Effective coaching and managing is not only about facing hard things. It is also about cultivating the spirit of engagement. This is the VITAL quality we explored in Chapter 6 that transforms work from obligation into opportunity. The *autotelic personality* develops through bringing playful curiosity, intrinsic motivation, and creative experimentation to everyday challenges.

A coach who embodies the VITAL spirit approaches each coaching conversation with genuine curiosity about what might emerge. They don't arrive with a script. They arrive with interest in the person, in the situation, and in the creative possibilities that might unfold during the conversation. Like Linehan's jazz musician metaphor from Chapter 1, they improvise in response to what's happening. They bring an attitude of *serious playfulness* to the work.

Managers can cultivate this same quality in their teams. A manager who helps employees craft their roles to emphasise tasks that leverage their strengths and values is creating flow conditions. A manager who encourages creative experimentation is fostering the serious play orientation that makes intrinsic motivation possible. A manager who celebrates effort and learning as much as outcomes is building the autotelic culture that sustains engagement long after any single coaching conversation ends.

Supporting the Values-Flow skills in those you lead helps them move from the lower floors of the House to the upper floor. Helping them recognise and live according to their values helps them stay on the upper floor. But the VITAL spirit is what takes people to the attic—that space of transcendence, flow, and genuine engagement. It's the difference between a manager who competently runs a meeting and a manager who creates the kind of meeting where people lose track of time because they're so engaged in what they're building together.

Flow Nudges

1 **Identify Your Coaching Dialectic**: Think about someone you coach or manage. What is your natural tendency? Do you lean too far towards acceptance, being supportive but never challenging? Or do you lean too far towards change, pushing hard but not acknowledging the struggle? This week, practise holding both simultaneously in one conversation. Validate the person's experience and ask them to be willing to stretch.
2 **Map the Exposure**: Choose one person you work with who is avoiding something important. Ask that person: What are you afraid will happen? What value would approaching this serve? What skill would help you manage the discomfort? Facilitate a conversation that connects all three.
3 **Practise Real-Time Coaching**: This week, rather than saving feedback for formal meetings, offer brief, focused coaching in the moment, such as a quick word before a challenge and a debrief immediately after. Keep it short (five minutes or less) and skills-focused: "What did you notice? What worked? What skill might help next time?"
4 **Coach Yourself Through Your Own Exposure**: Identify one situation where your own anxiety drives you to intervene, rescue, or control. Use the ARIA cycle on your own internal experience: Attend to the anxiety, Reflect on what's driving it, Inform yourself about what opposite action looks like, and Act in alignment with your leadership values rather than your anxiety.

5 **Design for Flow**: Take one task or project you're overseeing and audit it against the three flow conditions: Are the goals clear enough that the people always know what they're working towards? Is feedback immediate enough that they can see the impact of their actions? Is the challenge calibrated, high enough to engage but not so high as to overwhelm? Then adjust one element this week and notice what shifts.

Sound Bite Summary

1 **Effective Coaching and Managing Is Fundamentally an Exposure-Based Activity**: You are helping people face what they'd rather avoid, tolerate the discomfort that comes with growth, and discover through experience that they are more capable than they believe.
2 **DBT's phone coaching model** provides a blueprint for real-time, skills-focused support that helps people generalise their capabilities to the moments when those capabilities are most needed. Brief, targeted coaching in the moment is more powerful than extended processing after the fact.
3 **Values Provide the Motivation for Facing Discomfort**: When stretch experiences are connected to what people truly value, willingness to approach challenge increases. Values don't eliminate discomfort; they make it meaningful.
4 **DBT and ACT skills are practical tools** for coaches and managers that help the people they lead stay in the stretch zone long enough for new learning and growth to occur.
5 **The Coach's or Manager's Own Journey Is an Exposure Exercise Too**: Stepping back, tolerating the discomfort of watching others struggle, and resisting the urge to rescue requires the same willingness, skills, and values alignment that you ask of those you lead.
6 **Coaches and Managers Are Flow Architects**: By providing clear goals, immediate feedback, and challenge–skill balance, they create the conditions in which flow becomes possible.

Final Word

Coaching and managing effectively involves having faith in another person's capabilities. They require you to believe that the person in front of you can handle more than they think they can. That the discomfort of growth is temporary but the capability it builds is lasting. And that your role is not to smooth every path but to walk alongside others as they navigate the rough paths.

The Values-Flow framework provides the map for this journey. Values tell you *why* to move forward. Exposure principles explain *how* growth happens. DBT and ACT skills provide the *tools* for managing distress that arises along the way. And Flow theory describes the *destination*—the state of absorbed, meaningful engagement that makes the whole journey worthwhile.

Arianna is a different manager now. Not because she learned to stop caring about her team, but because she learned that the deepest form of care is trust. She learned to trust others enough to let them struggle, supporting them with skills rather than rescuing them, and believing in their capability to find their own way to the upper floors of the House. Her team is more autonomous, more engaged, and more capable than they've ever been. And Arianna herself, freed from the exhausting burden of being everyone's safety net, has found something she hadn't experienced in years: flow in her own leadership. She is, at last, inhabiting the upper floor with regular visits to the attic.

Whether you coach one person or manage a hundred, the invitation is the same: trust the process, tolerate the discomfort, stay connected to your values, and watch what becomes possible when people are supported in facing life's challenges rather than shielded from them.

14 The Life Well Lived

Chapter Overview

This chapter brings together key learnings from the book, which is designed with layered attention. At its surface, the book provides practical skills for living a richer, more engaged life. Beneath that, it provides strategies to support others, be they clients, students, employees, or other individuals. And at its deepest layer, it holds the tensions amongst ACT, DBT, and Flow Theory together, not skirting around the tensions, but wrestling with them. Importantly, the skills in this book are not intended to be a 12-week programme that you read about and then move on; they are capabilities that develop, deepen, and evolve over the course of a lifetime through regularly practising the Values-Flow skills.

Coming Home

Let's return to where we began. It's been one of those days. The kind where every email demands urgency, every conversation requires effort, and by the time you close your laptop, you're running on fumes. You stand in the kitchen with a choice on how to unwind from the day. Ice cream? Wine? An hour of scrolling through your phone?

Or perhaps there is something else. A quiet reflection on the wins of the day. A satisfaction with a positive conversation with a colleague or family member. A sense of a day well lived, despite the challenges you faced. Something that is harder to name but more sustaining when you find it.

As you reflect on your journey through this book, has anything shifted? We are not expecting a dramatic transformation. But perhaps something simpler has occurred. Perhaps you've climbed up a floor in the House of Functioning. Perhaps you've even had glimpses of the attic.

If so, that noticing is itself a kind of homecoming. It means you've been practising, even if imperfectly, even if inconsistently, the skills that this book has been building towards. And if nothing feels particularly different yet, that's okay too. Seeds germinate underground before anything visible appears. The winter garden, as we said in Chapter 2, can still be thriving.

DOI: 10.4324/9781003771173-17

The Layers of This Book

Have you ever watched a Pixar movie, like *Inside Out* or *Up*? On the surface, a Pixar film is a children's story with colourful characters and a satisfying storyline. But underneath, there are layers that adults recognise, including deep emotional truths, philosophical questions, and moments of genuine insight. A child watches *Inside Out* and learns that it's okay to feel sad. An adult watches the same film and confronts the bittersweet reality that growing up means losing the simplicity of childhood joy, and that this loss is itself a form of love.

We have designed this book with the same layered intention. If you picked up this book because you want to live a richer, more engaged life, we hope the practical skills, the Values-Flow Card, the flow nudges, and the stories of Vecky, Boris, Marcus, Tatiana, Vienna, Olga, Arianna, and Peggy have given you concrete tools for that journey. That is the surface layer, and it is genuinely important. The everyday adventurer who wants to spend more time on the upper floor of the House and make occasional visits to the attic has everything they need in these pages to begin that practice and move towards a life well lived.

If you are a therapist, a counsellor, a coach, a manager, or a teacher, there is a second layer. You will have noticed that the applied chapters (Chapters 11–13) don't merely apply the earlier skills to professional contexts. They reframe the therapeutic relationship itself. Flow chain analysis in Chapter 11 doesn't replace DBT's problem behaviour chain analysis. It complements it. The coaching-as-exposure framework in Chapter 13 draws on one of clinical psychology's most robustly supported interventions and shows that every coach and manager is already doing exposure work, whether they know it or not. If you work with people, these chapters offer you a framework for understanding why your clients, students, or team members get stuck and what it looks like when they move forward into the brave unknown.

And there is a third layer, one for readers who care about theory and who will have noticed the creative tensions running beneath the surface of every chapter. This layer is about the dialogue amongst ACT, DBT, and Flow Theory, a dialogue that is not always comfortable, not always resolved, but all the richer for it.

The House Revisited

We have returned to the House of Functioning repeatedly throughout this book. Importantly, the House is not a ladder you climb once, moving from the basement through the middle floors and up to the attic. It is a place you inhabit. Where you are in the House can change from day to day, sometimes from hour to hour. Different parts of you might be on different floors. For instance, Peggy was flying high on the upper floor in terms of academic achievements, but floundered in the basement with her mental health (Chapter 10). You might wake up on the upper floor and then encounter a crisis at work that drops you to the lower floor. You use your REGULATE skills to stabilise and find a moment of genuine engagement with a colleague that lifts you back towards the upper floor. You end the day with a brief, unexpected visit to the attic while playing with your children. That is not an inconsistency. That is the rhythm of a life lived with skill and awareness.

The goal was never to reach the attic and stay there. Marsha Linehan herself understood this. The attic is not a permanent address. It is a place you visit when conditions converge, engagement deepens, and self-consciousness falls away. Something larger than your ordinary experience opens up. You cannot live in the attic any more than you can live in a state of permanent ecstasy. But you can live your everyday life in such a way that visits to the attic become a part of the texture of your life, woven in amongst the ordinary moments that make up most of your waking hours.

What the skills in this book provide is the capacity to navigate the House with increasing fluency. VIRTUE orients you towards what matters. INVOLVE gives you the ARIA cycle for engaging with life's challenges through attending, reflecting, informing, and acting. VITAL cultivates the autotelic spirit of serious play that transforms obligation into genuine engagement. ACCEPT develops the willingness to be present with whatever arises, including the absence of flow. REGULATE builds the emotional stability from which engagement can emerge. RELATE extends your practice outward into the relationships and environments where much of life's meaning is found.

Together, these six skills create a practice – not a perfect life, but a practised life. And over time, you just might find that life gets better. When these skills are working together, the nine flow dimensions (Chapter 2) become more accessible. Your concentration deepens. Your actions and awareness begin to merge. Self-consciousness recedes. Time transforms. The activity feels intrinsically rewarding. You do not need to chase these experiences. They emerge naturally when you tend to the conditions. The six skills are how you tend the conditions. The nine dimensions are how you recognise that something is working.

A Practice for the Long Haul

Importantly, the skills in this book are not intended to be a 12-week programme that you read about and then move on. They are capabilities that develop, deepen, and evolve over the course of a lifetime through regularly practising the Values-Flow skills. Just as a musician never finishes learning their instrument, you will never finish practising Values-Flow.

Why? Because it means that wherever you are right now, there is always more to discover. The seasons of practice that we described in Chapter 3 will cycle many times over the decades ahead. You will have spring seasons of fresh curiosity, summer seasons of abundant flow, autumn seasons of necessary transition, and winter seasons of apparent dormancy. Each cycle teaches you something the previous one could not, because you bring the accumulated wisdom of prior seasons to each new beginning.

Research on optimal experience across the lifespan supports this view. Antonella Delle Fave and her colleagues have documented how flow experiences shape personal development at different life stages, from adolescence through old age. The specific activities that produce flow change as life circumstances change, but the capacity for optimal engagement does not diminish with age when it is cultivated. Older adults who have spent decades investing in meaningful, challenging activities report flow experiences that are every bit as rich as those of younger people. Indeed, sometimes their experiences are even richer, because decades of skill development allow for engagement at higher levels of complexity. Importantly, Delle Fave's research spans dozens of countries and cultural contexts. The life well lived looks different in different places. The activities that produce flow, the values that guide engagement, and the relational contexts in which meaning is found are all culturally shaped. But the underlying capacity for optimal experience is universal. Whatever your background, whatever your circumstances, the capacity for engaged, values-aligned living is there.

Csikszentmihalyi and his colleague Fausto Massimini described a process they called **psychological selection**, the tendency for human beings within their cultural contexts to prioritise activities that are more likely to produce optimal experiences. When you find flow in an activity, you are drawn back to it. You develop greater skill. You seek out higher challenges. The challenge–skill balance recalibrates upwards, and the potential for deeper, more frequent flow experiences increases.

Over months and years, this process shapes your life trajectory. The activities you select, the skills you cultivate, and the values you express through engaged action become progressively more central to who you are. Psychological selection is not something you do once; it is the ongoing process through which you become yourself through the quality of your engagement with life.

This is why aspiring to a life well lived is not naive optimism. It is grounded in the observable reality that people who consistently create conditions for engaged, values-aligned living experience more flow over time, compared to those who do not create such conditions. Remember the garden metaphor (Chapter 2). You cannot force a flower to bloom, but you can prepare the soil, water regularly, ensure adequate sunlight, and protect against frost. Over a growing season, the garden that receives consistent care will produce more blooms than the one that is neglected. Not every day. Not on command. But over the course of a life, the difference is unmistakable.

This is psychological selection in action. The ongoing, lifelong process of investing in what produces optimal experiences and meaning. Each flow experience you have this week plants a seed for the experiences you will have next month, next year, and in the decades to come. The person you are becoming through your engagement with life is shaped by the quality of that engagement.

Creative Tensions

We want to be honest with you. Writing this book required us to sit with genuine intellectual discomfort. ACT and DBT are not the same therapy. Although they share common ancestry in the behavioural tradition and common commitments to acceptance and mindfulness, they disagree, sometimes sharply, on questions that matter. Rather than glossing over these differences, we wrestled with their intersections and divergences. What are some of these tensions?

Can emotions be directly changed? ACT says that the struggle to control internal experiences typically makes things worse. It encourages *changing your relationship* to emotions rather than changing the emotions themselves. If you're feeling anxious, ACT doesn't ask you to stop feeling anxious. It asks whether you can carry that anxiety with you while moving towards what matters. DBT, by contrast, explicitly teaches that some emotions can and should be changed, and provides specific skills to make those changes.

Is optimal engagement a legitimate target? ACT is cautious about making any particular emotional state a goal, because the pursuit of pleasant experiences can become its own form of experiential avoidance. This is a subtle version of the *control agenda* that ACT works to undermine. If you are chasing happiness, you might be running from discomfort, and it's quite possible that you will create misery in the process. DBT, on the other hand, explicitly includes "building positive experiences" as a therapeutic target and sees nothing wrong with deliberately cultivating states that feel good. Our position throughout this book has been dialectical: flow is not the goal, *and* creating conditions for engaged, absorbed living is legitimate and skilful. Both truths can coexist.

What is the self? ACT's *Observing Self* is a perspective, a vantage point from which you witness your thoughts, feelings, and experiences without being defined by them. It is the "you" that has watched your entire life unfold. In contrast, DBT's *Wise Mind* is an integration of *Emotion Mind* and *Reasonable Mind* that accesses a deeper knowing. Wise Mind has an experiential quality that overlaps with flow, an intuitive sense of rightness, of knowing what to do in the moment. Throughout this book, we have drawn on both constructs because both are needed. Sometimes you need the spacious witness of the Observing Self. Sometimes you need the integrated knowing of Wise Mind. Wisdom is in discerning which one to use at what time.

These tensions are not problems to be solved. They are the engine of Values-Flow. Just as DBT teaches that acceptance and change are both necessary and that the synthesis of apparent opposites creates something richer than either alone, the tensions amongst ACT, DBT, and Flow Theory are what make this integration more than the sum of its parts. We have not resolved these tensions, and we do not think they should be resolved. We think they should be inhabited, the way a jazz musician inhabits the tension between structure and improvisation, finding something alive in the space in between.

Why Flow Belongs at the Table

We argue that Flow Theory has a legitimate and necessary place within both ACT and DBT. This is not a claim we make lightly. Both ACT and DBT are rigorous, evidence-based therapies with their own theoretical and empirical foundations, and we are not suggesting that either is incomplete without flow. We are suggesting that flow enriches both, and that both enrich Flow Theory in return.

ACT provides a sophisticated understanding of why people get stuck, how the "word machine" of language creates suffering, how experiential avoidance keeps people living small, and how values can orient action even in the presence of pain. What ACT provides less of is a detailed account of what optimal engagement looks and feels like when it happens. ACT tells you to take committed action in the direction of your values. Flow Theory tells you what that committed action looks like at its best: the merging of action and awareness, the dissolution of self-consciousness, and the total absorption in something that matters. Flow gives ACT a vocabulary for the experience that values-aligned living can produce. It's not a guaranteed outcome, but it is a possibility that makes the hard work of acceptance and commitment worthwhile.

DBT provides concrete, teachable skills for managing the emotional intensity that blocks engagement. *Distress tolerance skills* keep you in the game when frustration peaks. *Emotion regulation skills* maintain the stability from which flow can emerge. *Mindfulness skills* sharpen the present-moment attention that flow requires. *Interpersonal effectiveness skills* allow for the *interpersonal flow* that emerges when two people genuinely meet in conversation. But DBT lacks a framework for what all that skill-building is ultimately for. The *House of Functioning* tells us we are climbing towards the upper floor and the attic, but Swenson himself acknowledged that the attic remains largely unfurnished. Flow Theory helps furnish that attic. It describes the quality of experience that becomes possible when skills are in place, when emotions are regulated, when relationships are effective, and when the person is fully engaged with what matters to them.

Flow is also enhanced by ACT and DBT. Csikszentmihalyi's research described the conditions for flow: challenge–skill balance, clear goals, immediate feedback. But Flow Theory on its own says relatively little about what to do when those conditions aren't met, when you're too anxious to concentrate, when your emotions are flooding your senses, when your relationships are in crisis, or when the challenges of life have overwhelmed your skills. ACT provides the acceptance and defusion skills that allow you to show up for challenges even when your mind is screaming that you can't. DBT provides the regulation and distress tolerance skills that bring you back within your ***window of tolerance*** where flow becomes possible.

What We Cannot Control, and What We Can

Although we have talked about flow as an optimal state that can arise when the conditions are right, it's very important to understand that you cannot make flow happen on demand. You cannot force yourself into absorption. You cannot force the merging of action and awareness. You cannot schedule transcendence for Tuesday at 3 p.m. Flow is, by its nature, an emergent experience. It arises when conditions are right, when challenge meets skill, when attention is fully absorbed, when self-consciousness recedes. But even if you create these conditions, flow may or may not show up.

If you have been practising the skills in this book and yet have not had any flow experiences, that is not failure. It is life. And here is where the ACT perspective becomes essential. The willingness to continue engaging with what matters, with or without the reward of flow, is itself a form of thriving. You can act on your values right now, with whatever feelings are present. You do not need to feel absorbed first. You do not need to be in the zone. You need only to show up for what matters, one step at a time, one moment at a time. That showing up reflects living on the upper floor of the House.

It's equally important to emphasise that while you cannot control whether flow occurs in any given moment, you can dramatically increase the frequency of flow over the course of your life. This is the core premise of Values-Flow, and it is grounded in decades of research on optimal experience, psychological selection, and the cultivation of the autotelic personality.

The Journey of Creation

Through the course of this book, we have shared with you what we have come to know about living well despite the challenges that life presents. We have drawn from decades of clinical practice, wellbeing research, personal experience, and accumulated wisdom about what it means to thrive as a human being. We have been honest about what we know and what we don't, about where the science is clear and where genuine uncertainty remains, and about the tensions between the theoretical traditions and the richness that comes from holding those tensions rather than collapsing them.

We have also tried to practise what we preach. The writing of this book has been its own Values-Flow experience, complete with spring seasons of creative energy and winter seasons where the words would not come. As Peggy described in Chapter 10, the Values-Flow skills were crucial for moving her from burning in the basement to living on the upper floor of the House. Both individually and together, we have had genuine flow experiences, being fully absorbed in the process of creation. We used the skills we describe in these pages. We attended to what was present. We reflected on what was emerging.

We informed our next steps with feedback. We acted in alignment with our values, which include a commitment to creating something that we genuinely hope is useful and authentic.

The book you are holding is the product of that process. It is imperfect, as all things created by human beings are imperfect. But it is honest, practical, and grounded in the best evidence we could find about what helps people thrive. We hope that you benefit from its words as much as we benefited from the writing.

Flow Nudges: Continuing the Journey

1 **The Intention-Set Week**: At the beginning of the week, spend ten minutes with your Values-Flow Card. Where in the House are you sitting, across different domains of life (physical, emotional, mental, social, spiritual)? Identify specific goals for the week.
2 **The Weekly Review**: At the end of the week, spend ten minutes with your Values-Flow Card, identifying the patterns that appear. When did engagement come most easily? When did it feel blocked? What conditions supported your practice, and what conditions undermined it? Over months, these weekly reviews become a map of your own engagement. You will begin to see that the conditions for your flow are consistent, and knowing them gives you the power to create them more often.
3 **The Annual Values Check**: Once a year, revisit your values. Have they shifted? Has the garden of your life changed in ways that require different tending? The values you clarified in Chapter 4 are not fixed forever. They evolve as you evolve. An annual values check ensures that your practice remains connected to what matters to you now, not to who you were when you first picked up this book.
4 **The Lifespan Perspective**: When you are having a difficult season, zoom out. Instead of asking yourself, "Is my life good today?", change the focus to, "Am I building a life that, over the years, will have been well lived?" Even when a period of difficult days occurs, through practising the Values-Flow skills, you are creating the conditions for improvement. With a longer-term perspective, you can see that you are moving towards the life well lived, despite the ups and downs that inevitably occur. The winter garden, viewed from the perspective of a whole year, is not dying. It is preparing.
5 **The Dialectical Reminder**: When you find yourself stuck in one side of any dialectic, whether acceptance or change, process or outcome, ACT or DBT, gently remind yourself: both can be true. Write on a card and carry it with you: "I am doing the best I can with what I have right now, AND I can build towards more engagement and deeper living."
6 **Teach Someone Else**: One of the most powerful ways to deepen your own practice is to share it with others. You do not need to be an expert. You need only to say to someone you care about: "I've been learning about this thing called Values-Flow, and it's been helpful for me. Can I share it with

you?" Teaching strengthens your own understanding, creates accountability, and contributes to the relational garden in which your individual thriving is embedded.

Sound Bite Summary

1 **This book is intended to operate on multiple layers**. For the everyday adventurer, it offers practical skills for living well. For the therapist, coach, manager, or teacher, it offers a framework for understanding engagement and facilitating growth. For the theoretically minded, it offers a creative synthesis that honours the tensions amongst ACT, DBT, and Flow Theory.
2 **The House of Functioning** is not a ladder you climb once. It is a place you inhabit, and where you are can change from day to day. The goal is not to reach the attic and stay there but to live with the skills and awareness that make regular visits possible.
3 **You cannot control whether flow occurs in any given moment**. Flow is emergent, arising when conditions converge. The willingness to continue engaging with what matters, with or without the reward of flow, is itself a form of thriving.
4 You can increase the frequency of flow over the course of your life through the process of **psychological selection**, the ongoing investment in activities, skills, and values that produce optimal experiences. This is why aspiring to the life well lived is not naive but grounded in how optimal human development works.
5 The **tensions between ACT and DBT**, whether emotions can be directly changed, whether flow is a legitimate therapeutic target, and what the self is, are not problems to be resolved but creative dialectics that make Values-Flow richer than any single approach.
6 **Flow Theory has a legitimate place within both ACT and DBT**. Flow gives ACT a vocabulary for what values-aligned living can feel like at its best. Flow gives DBT a description of what the unfurnished attic might contain. ACT and DBT give Flow Theory the tools for what to do when conditions for engagement do not exist.
7 **Values-Flow is a lifespan practice**. The capacity for optimal engagement does not diminish with age when it is cultivated. Each season of practice teaches something that the previous one could not.

Final Word

Throughout this book, we have taken you on a journey towards creating a life well lived. Each chapter is an invitation to be curious and see what is possible, within the constraints of your everyday life. Values-Flow offers a capacity for noticing what you previously took for granted or ignored. This has included a willingness to sit with discomfort. A set of skills for navigating the emotional weather of your life. A connection to what matters. And a lived experience, however intermittent, of what it feels like when all of these come together and you lose yourself in something meaningful.

That experience, that moment of absorption and aliveness, is not something that you can summon at will. But it is something you can cultivate across a lifetime. Every time you attend to the present moment rather than ruminating about the past or worrying about the future, you are preparing the soil. Every time you reflect on what matters rather than going through the motions, you are planting seeds. Every time you engage with a challenge that stretches your skills, you are tending the garden. Every time you accept what is rather than fighting reality, you are removing the weeds that choke growth. Every time you regulate your emotions rather than being capsized by them, you are strengthening the roots. Every time you show up in your relationships with genuine presence, you are nurturing the ecosystem in which your garden grows.

The life well lived is not a destination. It is a practice. You will never get it perfectly right. You will have days on the upper floor and days in the basement. You will have seasons of abundant flow and seasons of dormancy. What matters is not perfection but direction: the slow, cumulative movement towards a life of greater engagement, deeper meaning, and more frequent moments of that absorption.

You are a human being, living in a complex world, doing the best you can with what you have. And you are capable of more than you know. Not because you are extraordinary, though you very well may be, but because the capacity for flow, for meaning, and for engaged values-aligned living is built into the architecture of human experience. The extraordinary is available to you in the ordinary moments of an ordinary day.

And here is ACT's final gift to this journey. You do not need to feel ready. You do not need to have your emotions under control, your values perfectly clarified, your skills fully developed, or your environment optimally arranged. The *control agenda*, the belief that everything needs to be right before you can begin, is the last obstacle to clear. You can begin right now, with whatever you have, wherever you are. The feelings can come along for the ride. The doubts can sit in the passenger seat. The uncertainty can tag along. What matters is that you are moving in the direction of what matters to you. That movement, however imperfect, is the life well lived in action.

The seeds are planted. The garden is yours to tend.

Go gently. Be curious. Invite willingness towards whatever arises. And know that every step you take in the direction of your values, whether or not flow comes along for the ride, is a step towards a life well lived.

Bibliography

Bakker, A. B. (2008). The work-related flow inventory: Construction and initial validation of the WOLF. *Journal of Vocational Behavior*, *72*(3), 400–414. https://doi.org/10.1016/j.jvb.2007.11.007

Bandura, A. (1997). *Self-Efficacy: The Exercise of Control*. W. H. Freeman.

Barnes-Holmes, Y., & McEnteggart, C. (2025). Creative hopelessness and why it is so central in ACT. In L. Bruyninx, Y. Barnes-Holmes, C. McEnteggart, M. Vleugel, & R. Thewissen (Eds.), *Practicing Acceptance and Commitment Therapy with Head and Heart: Understanding the Why Behind Each Intervention* (pp. 60–80). Routledge. https://doi.org/10.4324/9781032699691-5

Baumann, N. (2012). Autotelic personality. In S. Engeser (Ed.), *Advances in Flow Research* (pp. 165–186). Springer. https://doi.org/10.1007/978-1-4614-2359-1_9

Baumann, N. (2021). Autotelic personality. In C. Peifer & S. Engeser (Eds.), *Advances in Flow Research* (2nd ed., pp. 231–261). Springer. https://doi.org/10.1007/978-3-030-53468-4_9

Bennett, R., & Oliver, J. (2019). *Acceptance and Commitment Therapy: 100 Key Points and Techniques*. Routledge. https://doi.org/10.4324/9781351056144

Beresford, K., Kern, M. L., & Jarden, A. (2025). The creative-being model: The role of negative emotion in creative flourishing and the impact on positive education. *The Journal of Positive Psychology*, *20*(1), 59–71. https://doi.org/10.1080/17439760.2024.2322467

Biglan, A. (2015). *The Nurture Effect: How the Science of Human Behavior Can Improve Our Lives and Our World*. New Harbinger Publications.

Biswas-Diener, R. (2010). *Practicing Positive Psychology Coaching: Assessment, Activities, and Strategies for Success*. Wiley. https://doi.org/10.1002/9781118269633

Bond, F. W., Hayes, S. C., Baer, R. A., Carpenter, K. M., Guenole, N., Orcutt, H. K., Waltz, T., & Zettle, R. D. (2011). Preliminary psychometric properties of the Acceptance and Action Questionnaire–II: A revised measure of psychological inflexibility and experiential avoidance. *Behavior Therapy*, *42*(4), 676–688. https://doi.org/10.1016/j.beth.2011.03.007

Brickman, P., Coates, D., & Janoff-Bulman, R. (1978). Lottery winners and accident victims: Is happiness relative? *Journal of Personality and Social Psychology*, 36(8), 917–927. https://doi.org/10.1037/0022-3514.36.8.917

Butler, J., & Kern, M. L. (2016). The PERMA-Profiler: A brief multidimensional measure of flourishing. *International Journal of Wellbeing*, *6*(3), 1–48. https://doi.org/10.5502/ijw.v6i3.526

Carr, A., Finneran, L., Boyd, C., Shirey, C., Canning, C., Stafford, O., Lyons, J., Cullen, K., Prendergast, C., Corbett, C., Drumm, C., & Burke, T. (2024). The evidence-base for positive psychology interventions: A mega-analysis of meta-analyses.

The Journal of Positive Psychology, *19*(2), 191–205. https://doi.org/10.1080/17439760.2023.2168564

Ciarrochi, J., Hayes, S. C., Oades, L. G., & Hofmann, S. G. (2022). Toward a unified framework for positive psychology interventions: Evidence-based processes of change in coaching, prevention, and training. *Frontiers in Psychology*, *12*, 809362. https://doi.org/10.3389/fpsyg.2021.809362

Ciarrochi, J., Parker, P., Kashdan, T. B., Heaven, P. C. L., & Barkus, E. (2015). Hope and emotional well-being: A six-year study to distinguish antecedents, correlates, and consequences. *The Journal of Positive Psychology*, *10*(6), 520–532. https://doi.org/10.1080/17439760.2015.1015154

Colla, R., Williams, P., Oades, L. G., & Camacho-Morles, J. (2022). "A new hope" for positive psychology: A dynamic systems reconceptualization of hope theory. *Frontiers in Psychology*, *13*, 809053. https://doi.org/10.3389/fpsyg.2022.809053

Craske, M. G., Treanor, M., Conway, C. C., Zbozinek, T., & Vervliet, B. (2014). Maximizing exposure therapy: An inhibitory learning approach. *Behaviour Research and Therapy*, 58, 10–23. https://doi.org/10.1016/j.brat.2014.04.006

Crowell, S. E., Beauchaine, T. P., & Linehan, M. M. (2009). A biosocial developmental model of borderline personality: Elaborating and extending Linehan's theory. *Psychological Bulletin*, *135*(3), 495–510. https://doi.org/10.1037/a0015616

Csikszentmihalyi, M. (1988). The flow experience and its significance for human psychology. In M. Csikszentmihalyi & I. S. Csikszentmihalyi (Eds.), *Optimal Experience: Psychological Studies of Flow in Consciousness* (pp. 15–35). Cambridge University Press. https://doi.org/10.1017/cbo9780511621956.002

Csikszentmihalyi, M. (1990). *Flow: The Psychology of Optimal Experience*. Harper & Row.

Csikszentmihalyi, M. (1996). *Creativity: Flow and the Psychology of Discovery and Invention*. HarperCollins.

Csikszentmihalyi, M. (1997). *Finding Flow: The Psychology of Engagement with Everyday Life*. Basic Books.

Csikszentmihalyi, M. (2014). *Flow and the Foundations of Positive Psychology: The Collected Works of Mihaly Csikszentmihalyi*. Springer. https://doi.org/10.1007/978-94-017-9088-8

Csikszentmihalyi, M., & Larson, R. (1987). Validity and reliability of the experience-sampling method. *The Journal of Nervous and Mental Disease*, *175*(9), 526–536. https://doi.org/10.1097/00005053-198709000-00004

Csikszentmihalyi, M., & LeFevre, J. (1989). Optimal experience in work and leisure. *Journal of Personality and Social Psychology*, *56*(5), 815–822. https://doi.org/10.1037/0022-3514.56.5.815

Csikszentmihalyi, M., & Massimini, F. (1985). On the psychological selection of bio-cultural information. *New Ideas in Psychology*, *3*(2), 115–138. https://doi.org/10.1016/0732-118x(85)90002-9

Csikszentmihalyi, M., Rathunde, K., & Whalen, S. (1993). *Talented Teenagers: The Roots of Success and Failure*. Cambridge University Press.

Deci, E. L., & Ryan, R. M. (1985). *Intrinsic Motivation and Self-Determination in Human Behavior*. Plenum Press. https://doi.org/10.1007/978-1-4899-2271-7

Delle Fave, A., & Massimini, F. (2005). The investigation of optimal experience and apathy: Developmental and psychosocial implications. *European Psychologist*, *10*(4), 264–274. https://doi.org/10.1027/1016-9040.10.4.264

Delle Fave, A., Massimini, F., & Bassi, M. (2011). *Psychological Selection and Optimal Experience Across Cultures: Social Empowerment Through Personal Growth*. Springer. https://doi.org/10.1007/978-90-481-9876-4

Diener, E. (1984). Subjective well-being. *Psychological Bulletin*, *95*(3), 542–575. https://doi.org/10.1037/0033-2909.95.3.542

Dindo, L., Van Liew, J. R., & Arch, J. J. (2017). Acceptance and commitment therapy: A transdiagnostic behavioral intervention for mental health and medical conditions. *Neurotherapeutics*, *14*(3), 546–553. https://doi.org/10.1007/s13311-017-0521-3

Flückiger, C., Munder, T., Del Re, A. C., & Solomonov, N. (2023). Strength-based methods—A narrative review and comparative multilevel meta-analysis of positive interventions in clinical settings. *Psychotherapy Research*, *33*(7), 856–872. https://doi.org/10.1080/10503307.2023.2181718

Fredrickson, B. L. (2001). The role of positive emotions in positive psychology: The broaden-and-build theory of positive emotions. *American Psychologist*, *56*(3), 218–226. https://doi.org/10.1037/0003-066X.56.3.218

Fredrickson, B. L. (2009). *Positivity: Groundbreaking Research Reveals How to Embrace the Hidden Strength of Positive Emotions, Overcome Negativity, and Thrive*. Crown.

Gloster, A. T., Walder, N., Levin, M. E., Twohig, M. P., & Karekla, M. (2020). The empirical status of acceptance and commitment therapy: A review of meta-analyses. *Journal of Contextual Behavioral Science*, *18*, 181–192. https://doi.org/10.1016/j.jcbs.2020.09.009

Harris, R. (2008). *The Happiness Trap: How to Stop Struggling and Start Living*. Trumpeter.

Harris, R. (2010). A quick look at your values. *ACT Mindfully*. www.actmindfully.com.au https://www.actmindfully.com.au/wp-content/uploads/2019/07/Values_Checklist_-_Russ_Harris.pdf

Harris, R. (2019). *ACT Made Simple: An Easy-to-Read Primer on Acceptance and Commitment Therapy* (2nd ed.). New Harbinger.

Hayes, S. C. (2004). Acceptance and commitment therapy, relational frame theory, and the third wave of behavioral and cognitive therapies. *Behavior Therapy*, *35*(4), 639–665. https://doi.org/10.1016/S0005-7894(04)80013-3

Hayes, S. C. (2013). The genuine conversation: What kind of dialogue should we have about the nature of "positive psychology"? In T. B. Kashdan & J. Ciarrochi (Eds.), *Mindfulness, Acceptance, and Positive Psychology: The Seven Foundations of Well-Being* (pp. 303–319). New Harbinger.

Hayes, S. C. (2019). *A Liberated Mind: How to Pivot Toward What Matters*. Avery.

Hayes, S. C., Barnes-Holmes, D., & Roche, B. (Eds.). (2001). *Relational Frame Theory: A Post-Skinnerian Account of Human Language and Cognition*. Kluwer Academic/Plenum.

Hayes, S. C., Hofmann, S. G., Stanton, C. E., Carpenter, J. K., Sanford, B. T., Curtiss, J. E., & Ciarrochi, J. (2019). The role of the individual in the coming era of process-based therapy. *Behaviour Research and Therapy*, *117*, 40–53. https://doi.org/10.1016/j.brat.2018.10.005

Hayes, S. C., & King, G. A. (2024). Acceptance and commitment therapy: What the history of ACT and the first 1,000 randomized controlled trials reveal. *Journal of Contextual Behavioral Science*, *33*, 100809. https://doi.org/10.1016/j.jcbs.2024.100809

Hayes, S. C., Luoma, J. B., Bond, F. W., Masuda, A., & Lillis, J. (2006). Acceptance and commitment therapy: Model, processes and outcomes. *Behaviour Research and Therapy*, *44*(1), 1–25. https://doi.org/10.1016/j.brat.2005.06.006

Hayes, S. C., Strosahl, K. D., & Wilson, K. G. (1999). *Acceptance and Commitment Therapy: An Experiential Approach to Behavior Change*. Guilford Press.

Hayes, S. C., Strosahl, K. D., & Wilson, K. G. (2012). *Acceptance and Commitment Therapy: The Process and Practice of Mindful Change* (2nd ed.). Guilford Press.

Hayes, S. C., Wilson, K. G., Gifford, E. V., Follette, V. M., & Strosahl, K. (1996). Experiential avoidance and behavioral disorders: A functional dimensional approach to diagnosis and treatment. *Journal of Consulting and Clinical Psychology*, *64*(6), 1152–1168. https://doi.org/10.1037/0022-006X.64.6.1152

Hebert, E. R., Flynn, M. K., Wilson, K. G., & Kellum, K. K. (2021). Values intervention as an establishing operation for approach in the presence of aversive stimuli. *Journal of Contextual Behavioral Science*, *20*, 144–154. https://doi.org/10.1016/j.jcbs.2021.04.001

Hofmann, S. G., Hayes, S. C., & Lorscheid, D. N. (2021). *Learning Process-Based Therapy: A Skills Training Manual for Targeting the Core Processes of Psychological Change in Clinical Practice*. New Harbinger.

Ignjatovic, C. (2020). *Investigating flow at work and vital engagement of working adults across three years* [Doctoral dissertation, University of Melbourne]. Minerva Access. https://hdl.handle.net/11343/234388

Ignjatovic, C., Beresford, K., & Kern, M. L. (2025a). Reviving the creative academic: Integrating the creative being and values-flow models to promote wellbeing in higher education. In N. Lemon, S. McDonough, & M. Selkrig (Eds.), *Creating Wellbeing: The Role of Making Practices in Academic Contexts* (pp. 16–25). Routledge. https://doi.org/10.4324/9781003664123-3

Ignjatovic, C., Kern, M. L., Allen, M. K., & Delle Fave, A. (2025b). Does positive climate moderate the relationship of strengths use and knowledge with flow at work? A three-year study. *The Journal of Positive Psychology*, *21*(1), 125–134. https://doi.org/10.1080/17439760.2024.2431698

Ignjatovic, C., Kern, M. L., Delle Fave, A., & Allen, M. K. (2026). Finding hope in creative hopelessness: Hope and flow as mechanisms leading to wellbeing. *Psychotherapy and Counselling Journal of Australia*, *14*(1). https://doi.org/10.59158/001c.156091

Ignjatovic, C., Kern, M. L., & Oades, L. G. (2022a). Flow support at work: Examining the relationship between strengths use and flow at work among school staff over a three-year period. *Journal of Happiness Studies*, *23*(2), 455–475. https://doi.org/10.1007/s10902-021-00409-x

Ignjatovic, C., Kern, M. L., & Oades, L. G. (2022b). The VIVA sustainable work engagement model: A conceptual introduction and preliminary test over three years. *International Journal of Applied Positive Psychology*, *7*, 337–356. https://doi.org/10.1007/s41042-022-00064-4

Ignjatovic, C., Kern, M. L., & Oades, L. G. (2022c). Values-flow in contextual psychotherapy: The 'what', 'why', and 'how' of sustainable values-based behaviour. In F. Irtelli & F. Gabrielli (Eds.), *Happiness and Wellness: Biopsychosocial and Anthropological Perspectives*. IntechOpen. https://doi.org/10.5772/intechopen.106594

Kabat-Zinn, J. (1994). *Wherever You Go, There You Are: Mindfulness Meditation in Everyday Life*. Hyperion.

Kabat-Zinn, J. (2013). *Full Catastrophe Living: Using the Wisdom of Your Body and Mind to Face Stress, Pain, and Illness* (Rev. ed.). Bantam Books.

Kashdan, T. B. (2009). *Curious? Discover the Missing Ingredient to a Fulfilling Life*. William Morrow.

Kashdan, T. B., & Biswas-Diener, R. (2014). *The Upside of Your Dark Side: Why Being Your Whole Self, Not Just Your "Good" Self, Drives Success and Fulfillment*. Hudson Street Press.

Kashdan, T. B., & Ciarrochi, J. (Eds.). (2013). *Mindfulness, Acceptance, and Positive Psychology: The Seven Foundations of Well-Being*. New Harbinger.

Kashdan, T. B., & Rottenberg, J. (2010). Psychological flexibility as a fundamental aspect of health. *Clinical Psychology Review*, *30*(7), 865–878. https://doi.org/10.1016/j.cpr.2010.03.001

Kaufman, S. B. (2020). *Transcend: The New Science of Self-Actualization*. TarcherPerigee.

Kern, M. L., Benson, L., Steinberg, E. A., & Steinberg, L. (2016). The EPOCH measure of adolescent well-being. *Psychological Assessment*, *28*(5), 586–597. https://doi.org/10.1037/pas0000201

Kern, M. L., Waters, L. E., Adler, A., & White, M. A. (2015). A multidimensional approach to measuring well-being in students: Application of the PERMA framework. *The Journal of Positive Psychology*, *10*(3), 262–271. https://doi.org/10.1080/17439760.2014.936962

Kern, M. L., & Wehmeyer, M. L. (Eds.). (2021). *The Palgrave Handbook of Positive Education*. Palgrave Macmillan. https://doi.org/10.1007/978-3-030-64537-3

Kern, M. L., Williams, P., Spong, C., Colla, R., Sharma, K., Downie, A., Taylor, J. A., Sharp, S., Siokou, C., & Oades, L. G. (2020). Systems informed positive psychology. *The Journal of Positive Psychology*, *15*(6), 705–715. https://doi.org/10.1080/17439760.2019.1639799

Keyes, C. L. M. (2002). The mental health continuum: From languishing to flourishing in life. *Journal of Health and Social Behavior*, *43*(2), 207–222. https://doi.org/10.2307/3090197

Keyes, C. L. M. (2005). Mental illness and/or mental health? Investigating axioms of the complete state model of health. *Journal of Consulting and Clinical Psychology*, *73*(3), 539–548. https://doi.org/10.1037/0022-006X.73.3.539

Koerner, K. (2012). *Doing Dialectical Behavior Therapy: A Practical Guide*. Guilford Press.

Kolb, D. A. (1984). *Experiential Learning: Experience as the Source of Learning and Development*. Prentice-Hall.

Lee, H. (1960). *To Kill a Mockingbird*. J. B. Lippincott.

Linehan, M. M. (1993a). *Cognitive-Behavioral Treatment of Borderline Personality Disorder*. Guilford Press.

Linehan, M. M. (1993b). *Skills Training Manual for Treating Borderline Personality Disorder*. Guilford Press.

Linehan, M. M. (2015). *DBT Skills Training Manual* (2nd ed.). Guilford Press.

Linehan, M. M. (2020). *Building a Life Worth Living: A Memoir*. Random House.

Linehan, M. M. (2025). *DBT Skills Training Manual* (Rev, 3rd ed.). Guilford Press.

Linehan, M. M., Armstrong, H. E., Suarez, A., Allmon, D., & Heard, H. L. (1991). Cognitive-behavioral treatment of chronically parasuicidal borderline patients. *Archives of General Psychiatry*, *48*(12), 1060–1064. https://doi.org/10.1001/archpsyc.1991.01810360024003

Maslow, A. H. (1968). *Toward a Psychology of Being* (2nd ed.). Van Nostrand Reinhold.

Massimini, F., & Delle Fave, A. (2000). Individual development in a bio-cultural perspective. *American Psychologist*, *55*(1), 24–33. https://doi.org/10.1037/0003-066X.55.1.24

May, G. G. (1982). *Will and Spirit: A Contemplative Psychology*. Harper & Row.

McKay, M., Wood, J. C., & Brantley, J. (2019). *The Dialectical Behavior Therapy Skills Workbook: Practical DBT Exercises for Learning Mindfulness, Interpersonal Effectiveness, Emotion Regulation, and Distress Tolerance* (2nd ed.). New Harbinger.

Nakamura, J., & Csikszentmihalyi, M. (2002). The concept of flow. In C. R. Snyder & S. J. Lopez (Eds.), *Handbook of Positive Psychology* (pp. 89–105). Oxford University Press.

Nakamura, J., & Csikszentmihalyi, M. (2009). Flow theory and research. In S. J. Lopez & C. R. Snyder (Eds.), *The Oxford Handbook of Positive Psychology* (2nd ed., pp. 195–206). Oxford University Press.

Nakamura, J., & Csikszentmihalyi, M. (2014). The concept of flow. In M. Csikszentmihalyi (Ed.), *Flow and the Foundations of Positive Psychology: The Collected Works of Mihaly Csikszentmihalyi* (pp. 239–263). Springer. https://doi.org/10.1007/978-94-017-9088-8_16

Neacsiu, A. D., Rizvi, S. L., & Linehan, M. M. (2010). Dialectical behavior therapy skills use as a mediator and outcome of treatment for borderline personality disorder. *Behaviour Research and Therapy*, *48*(9), 832–839. https://doi.org/10.1016/j.brat.2010.05.017

Neff, K. D. (2003). Self-compassion: An alternative conceptualization of a healthy attitude toward oneself. *Self and Identity*, *2*(2), 85–101. https://doi.org/10.1080/15298860309032

Niemiec, R. M., & Pearce, R. (2021). The practice of character strengths: Unifying definitions, principles, and exploration of what's soaring, emerging, and ripe with potential. *Frontiers in Psychology*, *11*, 590220. https://doi.org/10.3389/fpsyg.2020.590220

Norrish, J. M. (2015). *Positive Education: The Geelong Grammar School Journey*. Oxford University Press.

Ong, C. W., Barthel, A. L., & Hofmann, S. G. (2024). The relationship between psychological inflexibility and well-being in adults: A meta-analysis of the acceptance and action questionnaire. *Behavior Therapy*, *55*(1), 26–41. https://doi.org/10.1016/j.beth.2023.05.007

Peterson, C., & Seligman, M. E. P. (2004). *Character Strengths and Virtues: A Handbook and Classification*. Oxford University Press.

Polk, K. L., & Schoendorff, B. (Eds.). (2014). *The ACT Matrix: A New Approach to Building Psychological Flexibility Across Settings and Populations*. New Harbinger Publications.

Rathunde, K. (1988). Optimal experience and the family context. In M. Csikszentmihalyi & I. S. Csikszentmihalyi (Eds.), *Optimal Experience: Psychological Studies of Flow in Consciousness* (pp. 342–363). Cambridge University Press. https://doi.org/10.1017/cbo9780511621956.021

Rathunde, K., & Csikszentmihalyi, M. (2005). Middle school students' motivation and quality of experience: A comparison of Montessori and traditional school environments. *American Journal of Education*, *111*(3), 341–371. https://doi.org/10.1086/428885

Ryan, R. M., & Deci, E. L. (2000). Self-determination theory and the facilitation of intrinsic motivation, social development, and well-being. *American Psychologist*, *55*(1), 68–78. https://doi.org/10.1037/0003-066X.55.1.68

Ryan, R. M., & Deci, E. L. (2001). On happiness and human potentials: A review of research on hedonic and eudaimonic well-being. *Annual Review of Psychology*, *52*, 141–166. https://doi.org/10.1146/annurev.psych.52.1.141

Ryff, C. D. (1989). Happiness is everything, or is it? Explorations on the meaning of psychological well-being. *Journal of Personality and Social Psychology*, *57*(6), 1069–1081. https://doi.org/10.1037/0022-3514.57.6.1069

Ryff, C. D., & Keyes, C. L. M. (1995). The structure of psychological well-being revisited. *Journal of Personality and Social Psychology*, *69*(4), 719–727. https://doi.org/10.1037/0022-3514.69.4.719

Sawyer, R. K. (2007). *Group Genius: The Creative Power of Collaboration*. Basic Books.

Schaufeli, W. B., & Bakker, A. B. (2004). Job demands, job resources, and their relationship with burnout and engagement: A multi-sample study. *Journal of Organizational Behavior*, *25*(3), 293–315. https://doi.org/10.1002/job.248

Schwartz, S. H., & Cieciuch, J. (2022). Measuring the refined theory of individual values in 49 cultural groups. Psychometrics of the revised portrait value questionnaire. *Assessment*, *29*, 1005–1019.

Schwartz, S. H., Cieciuch, J., Vecchione, M., Davidov, E., Fischer, R., Beierlein, C., et al. (2012). Refining the theory of basic individual values. *Journal of Personality and Social Psychology*, *103*(4), 663–688. https://doi.org/10.1037/a0029393

Seligman, M. E. P. (2011). *Flourish: A Visionary New Understanding of Happiness and Well-Being*. Free Press.

Seligman, M. E. P., Steen, T. A., Park, N., & Peterson, C. (2005). Positive psychology progress: Empirical validation of interventions. *American Psychologist*, *60*(5), 410–421. https://doi.org/10.1037/0003-066X.60.5.410

Siegel, D. J. (1999). *The Developing Mind: Toward a Neurobiology of Interpersonal Experience*. Guilford Press

Siegel, D. J., & Bryson, T. P. (2012). *The Whole-brain Child: 12 Revolutionary Strategies to Nurture Your Child's Developing Mind*. Scribe Publications.

Snyder, C. R. (1994). *The Psychology of Hope: You Can Get There from Here*. Free Press.

Snyder, C. R., Harris, C., Anderson, J. R., Holleran, S. A., Irving, L. M., Sigmon, S. T., Yoshinobu, L., Gibb, J., Langelle, C., & Harney, P. (1991). The will and the ways: Development and validation of an individual-differences measure of hope. *Journal of Personality and Social Psychology*, *60*(4), 570–585. https://doi.org/10.1037/0022-3514.60.4.570

Snyder, C. R., Rand, K. L., & Sigmon, D. R. (2002). Hope theory: A member of the positive psychology family. In C. R. Snyder & S. Lopez (Eds.), *Handbook of Positive Psychology* (pp. 257–276). Oxford University Press. https://doi.org/10.1093/oso/9780195135336.003.0019

Swenson, C. R. (2016). *DBT Principles in Action: Acceptance, Change, and Dialectics*. Guilford Press.

Tedeschi, R. G., & Calhoun, L. G. (2004). Posttraumatic growth: Conceptual foundations and empirical evidence. *Psychological Inquiry*, 15(1), 1–18. https://doi.org/10.1207/s15327965pli1501_01

Tse, D. C. K., Lau, V. W., Perlman, R., & McLaughlin, M. (2020). The development and validation of the autotelic personality questionnaire. *Journal of Personality Assessment*, *102*(1), 88–101. https://doi.org/10.1080/00223891.2018.1491855

Ullén, F., de Manzano, Ö., Almeida, R., Magnusson, P. K. E., Pedersen, N. L., Nakamura, J., Csikszentmihalyi, M., & Madison, G. (2012). Proneness for psychological flow in everyday life: Associations with personality and intelligence. *Personality and Individual Differences*, *52*(2), 167–172. https://doi.org/10.1016/j.paid.2011.10.003

Vygotsky, L. S. (1978). *Mind in Society: The Development of Higher Psychological Processes* (M. Cole, V. John-Steiner, S. Scribner, & E. Souberman, Eds.). Harvard University Press.

Wilson, K. G. (n.d.). *Exploring Values in ACT* [Online course]. Praxis Continuing Education and Training. https://www.praxiscet.com/exploring-values-in-act-evergreen-signup/

Wilson, K. G., & DuFrene, T. (2009). *Mindfulness for Two: An Acceptance and Commitment Therapy Approach to Mindfulness in Psychotherapy*. New Harbinger.

Wilson, K. G., & Murrell, A. R. (2004). Values work in acceptance and commitment therapy: Setting a course for behavioral treatment. In S. C. Hayes, V. M. Follette, & M. M. Linehan (Eds.), *Mindfulness and Acceptance: Expanding the Cognitive-Behavioral Tradition* (pp. 120–151). Guilford Press.

Wilson, K. G., Sandoz, E. K., Kitchens, J., & Roberts, M. (2010). The valued living questionnaire: Defining and measuring valued action within a behavioral framework. *The Psychological Record*, *60*(2), 249–272. https://doi.org/10.1007/BF03395706

Index

Pages in *italics* refer to figures and pages in **bold** refer to tables.